Native Waters

T0294667

Native Waters

Contemporary Indian Water Settlements and
the Second Treaty Era

Daniel McCool

The University of Arizona Press
Tucson

The University of Arizona Press
© 2002 The Arizona Board of Regents

Library of Congress Cataloging-In-Publication Data
McCool, Daniel, 1950–
Native waters : contemporary Indian water settlements and the second treaty era /
Daniel McCool.
p. cm.
Includes bibliographical references and index.
ISBN-13: 978-0-8165-2227-9 (cloth : alk. paper)—ISBN-10: 0-8165-2227-8
ISBN-13: 978-0-8165-2615-4 (pbk: alk. paper)—ISBN-10: 0-8165-2615-x
1. Indians of North America—Legal status, laws, etc. 2. Water rights—West (U.S.).
3. Indians of North America—Claims. I. Title.
KF8210.N37 .M38   2002
346.7304'32—dc21
2002001766

Manufactured in the United States of America on acid-free, archival-quality paper
containing a minimum of 50% post-consumer waste and processed chlorine free.

11 10 09 08 07 06   7 6 5 4 3 2

This book is dedicated to

the greatest son in the world,

Weston Craig McCool

Contents

Tables

Preface

Before I began doing interviews for this book, I asked an elderly Navajo woman, whom I had known for a number of years, what kind of reception I might expect from Indian people when I interviewed them about water settlements.

"You want something from them?" she asked, already knowing the answer.

"I guess you could put it that way," I responded defensively.

"Yep, just like all the other white people," she said, chuckling.

It is my hope that this book does more than that. I hope it gives something back to the native people who for so long have been the object of the acquisitive desires of Anglos.[1] But to be a success, it will need to do more than that. Any book on water settlements should, like the settlements themselves, offer something for everyone. Thus the objective of this book is to enhance our understanding of the settlements in the belief that increased understanding will lead to better settlements for all parties.

Indian water rights and the settlements regarding them have been the focus of decades of debate, conflict, and misunderstanding. A great deal has been written, often in anger and occasionally in ignorance, about Indian water. Much of the literature consists of legal analyses, and a few studies focus on history and politics. Much of this research is quite technical in nature, dealing with case law, acre-feet, or costs and benefits. One cannot understand contemporary Indian water settlements without discussing these technical issues. But I have striven to move beyond that in order to explore what is, essentially, a very human subject and to demonstrate how water settlements actually affect the lives of individual people.

I began this project with a grant from the U.S. Geological Survey's water resources research program.[2] The original grant proposal was couched in the terms and methodology of formal policy assessment: establish a performance baseline and then empirically assess the extent to which policy objectives have been realized. My research proposal included a travel budget that allowed me to travel to various Indian reservations and discuss water with the people most directly affected by settlements. But as I met with individual tribal members and non-Indians who live near reservations, I began to see the inadequacy of my original research design. There is of course a great deal of arcane information, but reams of data tend to sanitize; real people become abstractions, and the true richness of water and its connection to life gets lost in the numbers. At the most basic level, the politics of water is a human interest story, a personal narrative that is best told by those who have experienced it. Thus this book uses a combination of methodologies, approaches, and styles designed to capture the richness, complexity, and human texture of the water rights conflict. The reader will encounter everything from dialogue, descriptive narrative, and personal testimony to traditional social science methodology.

This book also relies on history as a context. Everything from Columbus to Custer to Clinton is relevant to the present Indian water dilemma. It is not possible to understand the settlement era without looking at antecedent conditions and events. In Anglo culture, history is often pedantic, the subject of academic discourse. But Indian people do not relegate their past to history. It is an integral part of their contemporary lives, as though the past is standing there looking over their collective shoulder. When asked to explain their water situation, many Indian people begin their explanation with events that happened centuries ago. Typical is the Navajo who, when asked to explain the current stalemate over the Little Colorado River negotiations, said, "Well, it all started with the Spanish." In addition, many Indian people have a compensatory notion of the water settlements. They view them as an opportunity to redress past injustices and want to know how a settlement fits into the long-term pattern of Anglo-Indian relations. Joe Ely, past chairman of the Pyramid Lake tribe, used a historical metaphor to describe how some Indian people feel about the settlement process: "It's like your neighbor has been stealing your horses for many years, and now we have to sit down and decide how many of those horses they get to keep."

There are innumerable perspectives on this issue, and it is quite easy to slip into simple categorization; this is the "Indian view," or that is the "state position." But water is too central to our existence, too complex, to lend itself to such simplicity. True, there are significant trends in thought and action, but there is no rote-step to fighting over water. The only truly common thread is that it is worth fighting for.

To a certain extent this book is a follow-up to my previous book on Indian water, *Command of the Waters: Iron Triangles, Federal Water Development, and Indian Water*.[3] That volume compared the history and politics of both Indian and non-Indian water resource programs, and the role played by reserved water rights. I completed that manuscript just as the settlement policy was beginning to bear fruit, so this book is a logical extension of that line of research. However, the approach used in this book is quite different.

Over my years of research on Indian policy I have sometimes been asked why a white man would select this research topic; is not research on Indian policy best left to Indian scholars? There are two parts to the answer to that question. First, "Indian policy" is a gratuitous misnomer; nearly all Indian policy is made by white people, not Indian people. A more accurate term would be "Anglo policy imposed on Indians." There are a few exceptions, such as the tradition in the twentieth century of selecting an Indian to be the commissioner of the Bureau of Indian Affairs (BIA) and the current "638 process," which allows tribes more control over their own destiny. But for the most part, historically significant decisions involving land, water, culture, and other policy issues have been unilaterally applied to Indians by the white-controlled government. In addition, policy making has taken place well within the context of western European decision-making—a process that is completely alien to traditional forms of indigenous government.[4] As a Zuni leader put it, "The whole decision-making process is imposed upon us, without us having a choice. We're a square peg pushed into a round hole."[5] Thus, as a white man and a political scientist, I am quite familiar with the way "Indian policy" is made.

The second part of the answer concerns the problem of Anglos speaking for Indians. Throughout our history well-meaning but naive whites have often voiced the "Indian" point of view. Their interpretation of that point of view was often tainted by assumptions of cultural superiority and basic ignorance. I have worked hard to avoid that pitfall by interviewing many Indian people and quoting extensively from Indian writing, speeches, and testimony. Nearly all of the interviews I conducted for this book with Indian people were done in person on Indian reservations. I felt I should meet them on their home ground in Indian country in order to maximize my understanding of their situation and to make it more comfortable for them to talk with a stranger so full of questions. I also conducted dozens of interviews with Anglos, primarily over the phone; I am already familiar with their cultural context.

In my travels to Indian reservations, water offices, and the seats of power, I met hundreds of people. I visited capitals from Washington to Window Rock. Some of the people I interviewed hold high elective office or have prestigious titles in the bureaucracy. Others are simply people whose lives have changed—or have failed to change—as a result of water settlements. I was repeatedly amazed at the diversity of opinion and experience. Some people, both Indian and non-Indian, believe water settlements are the best thing to happen in Indian country in the twentieth century; others regard the settlements as a sellout, another great theft of Indian resources similar to nineteenth-century land losses. But the jury is still out on water settlements. The earliest settlements are barely twenty years old, and the water settlement era is still in full swing. When I asked Ernie Robinson, Northern Cheyenne, if his tribe's settlement was a good one, he replied, "I won't be around any longer by the time we know the answer to that question." He is quite right, and thus this study can be considered only a preliminary assessment of a policy that will have a pervasive impact for centuries to come.

A book project that spans nearly a decade involves travel from coast to coast, entails hundreds of interviews, and generates a lot of thank-yous. I should first thank all of the people whom I interviewed. Some of them spent several hours with me; many revealed information that could possibly make their lives a bit tougher, but they wanted to tell me the full story. Many of them asked for anonymity and thus are not identified in the book.

In my travels I was assisted by many people, but a few went far beyond the customary, and I would like to recognize their generosity. Gail Martin of the Shoshone-Bannock tribes; Jason Whiteman of the Northern Cheyenne tribe; Stan Pollack, water attorney for the Navajo Nation; Joe Ely, former chairman of the Pyramid Lake Paiutes; Curtis Ccsspooch of the Northern Ute tribe; and Daniel Preston and Renee Reddog of the San Xavier District of the Tohono O'odham Nation were enormously helpful when I was doing interviews on reservations. I also owe a debt of gratitude to numerous congressional staffers and many people in state and federal agencies, with special thanks to Betsy Rieke, Mike Jackson, Debby Saint, Cathy Wilson, Frank Lane, Patricia Zell, Owen Dolan, Joe Miller, Hank Meshorer, and Norm Starler. I also received considerable assistance from a number of private organizations, including the Native American Rights Fund, the Western States Water Council, Taxpayers for the Animas River, and the Western Governors' Association. Several individuals provided valuable feedback and comments: Reid Chambers, Dan Decker, Craig Bell, Peter Sly, and Joe Ely.

Closer to home, the Canyon family, Terry Whitehat, and Laura Kirwan provided invaluable assistance. I also want to thank four individuals at the University of Utah: Donna Gelfand, former dean of the College of Social and Behavioral Science; Floyd O'Neil, former director of the American West Center; Don Hanson, former chair of the political science department (who helped me figure out the nightmare of a "matching" federal grant); and Susan Olson, another former chair of the political science department. And I would be remiss if I did not thank two people who, years ago, first taught me about water, bureaucrats, and Indians: Jeanne Nienaber Clarke of the University of Arizona and Vine Deloria Jr. of the University of Colorado. Thanks also goes to Yvonne Reineke and Stacey Shropshire of the University of Arizona Press; their assistance and encouragement are much appreciated.

And finally, I thank my son, Weston, for putting up with my absences and the many times I was lost in this manuscript when I should have been rough-housing with him.

—Daniel McCool
Salt Lake City

Native Waters

1

Rivers of Ink

The Parable of Navajo Mountain

It is hard to believe there is still a place like this in the rapidly developing American Southwest. A vast area that is still largely pristine, the word "remote" does not quite do justice to Navajo Mountain. From the vantage point of a rock outcrop on the flank of the mountain, I can see a vast forest of juniper and pinyon pine, split by an occasional cliff of red- or buff-colored rock. Higher up the side of the mountain, the trees turn to pine. A series of canyons emanates in all directions. To the north, across the canyon of the Colorado River, are the Henry Mountains—the last range in the West to be mapped.

There is a single dirt road into this area—twenty miles of axle-bending washboard that discourages the occasional tourist and helps isolate the tiny communities of Rainbow City and Navajo Mountain. The widely scattered homes in the area were electrified quite some time ago, but there is no water delivery system. At night one can see only a few lights; the absence of outdoor lighting creates a darkness at night that is, for a city dweller, overwhelming in its intensity. There are so many stars it is difficult to pick out the constellations.

But there is one aspect of this place that is incongruous with the natural state of the countryside. In the distance is a man-made reservoir with a shoreline longer than that of California; a body of water so vast that more water evaporates from it than the giant Central Arizona Project delivers. Amidst this vast natural landscape, Lake Powell spreads out like a torn blue blanket across the canyons and in between the mesas.

In this land of canyons and escarpments, the geographic features seem to compete for dramatic effect. The colors are bold, the landforms surreal. At the downstream end of each remote canyon, the "lake" has found its way. It fits in like a sullen giant at the dinner table, trying to dominate a land that can be described only in superlatives.

By visually surveying this area of Navajo Mountain, one can discern three basic geographic truths that can be applied to nearly all of the intermountain West. First, the horizontal scale is awe-inspiring. The natural features are expansive; it seems the creator had plenty of space and material when this land was formed. Indeed, immensity is a hallmark of the western landscape. Second, the vertical scale is also overwhelming; there are great mountains that lie in rows and folds across the landscape, and between them are innumerable canyons—deep fissures that cut giant grooves into the earth. The difference in vertical relief between the damp, sandy canyon bottoms and the rocky heights of the tallest mountains gives the land a physical boldness—a kind of geographic courage—that cannot be found in the flatlands. The third element of the physical profile is water; it can be found, but only in measured amounts, concentrated in specific locations at certain times.

I have come to Navajo Mountain with one of my students, Terry Whitehat, who is finishing a Master of Public Administration degree at the University of Utah.[1] Terry came home for spring break, and I tagged along. The Whitehat family lives in the shadow of Navajo Mountain. Some of the families in this area carry names that reflect geographic features: Smallcanyon and Greymountain. Some names have been borrowed from distant cultures: Folgheraiter and Tomasiyo. There is even a family name "Navajo," and one family is called simply "Chief."

Terry and I decide to go for a hike. He wants to show me the family's traditional grazing area in Jack Rabbit Canyon where, as a small boy, Terry herded sheep. As we prepare to leave we listen to KTNN radio news, delivered by Selena Manychildren. Her newscast is in Navajo, occasionally punctuated by an English phrase: "supplemental appropriation," "historic site," "McKinley Mine."

As we walk down into the canyon we pass Anasazi ruins; they blend in with the cliff so well that Terry has to point them out to me. Near the bottom of the canyon we come upon the remains of a small hogan, the traditional dwelling of the Navajo people.

"My grandfather grazed this whole area," Terry explains, waving his arm in a long, horizontal arc. "He had sheep, cows, and horses. He was a medicine man, and people often paid him in livestock for his services, so he was pretty wealthy in livestock."

"Did he live here by himself in this little hogan?" I point to the hogan and the remains of a corral behind it. I couldn't comprehend the isolation of such a lifestyle.

"Just part of the time," Terry says, smiling. "This is a female hogan. You can tell by the way the logs are laid and the shape of the door."

"Does your family run livestock here now?" I ask.

"We have a few cattle but no horses or sheep." Terry points across the canyon to some cattle that he can see but I cannot, no matter how hard I search.

"Why does your family graze so few animals now? Are they still permitted to use this area?" I keep asking questions, knowing the answers are obvious to Terry, but I still hadn't figured it out.

"This whole canyon is still our traditional use area. We can still keep our animals here. But today we have real jobs."

"Real jobs?" I ask. "Isn't raising livestock a real job?"

"You know what I mean—work in town. My sister, her husband, and my dad all work at the power plant. They're building the new smokestacks and scrubbers. My mom works in a restaurant in Page."

A connection began to form in my head. The people of Navajo Mountain used to make a living off the land; now they make a living off the water, or more precisely, off the dam, the town of Page, and the power plant, none of which would exist without the water. There is a complex and important relationship between what has been done to the land and what has been done to the water.

To understand what has happened to the land, we need a little history. For three hundred years the measure of Navajo wealth was livestock. After the Spanish introduced sheep, cattle, and horses, the Navajos proved to be excellent at animal husbandry. Their herds grew to massive proportions, and the tribe became one of the wealthiest in America. When an area began to show the wear of too many animals, the family moved on to, literally, greener pastures. But after the Navajos were restricted to a reservation, beginning in 1868, this movement was no longer possible. The reservation was expanded several times, but it still did not keep up with the burgeoning population and the even larger increases in livestock. In time, the land became overgrazed, which caused a score of problems. The soil eroded, the washes cut deep into the earth, and exotic species of plants replaced the natural ground cover. In the 1930s, after several expansions of the reservation, the government unilaterally decided it would "solve" the overgrazing problem. The result was a disastrous program called the Navajo livestock reduction program. Great herds were killed by government officials and left to rot in the sun. The Navajos were not compensated for their losses, nor were they provided with an alternative means of existence. It was a setback from which neither the people nor the land has recovered.

Despite the stock reduction program, grazing remained the primary economic activity for most Navajos at Navajo Mountain for many decades. However, other changes have occurred, and one of the biggest is Glen Canyon Dam. The project was so huge the government carved a new town site out of the reservation, gave the Navajos some land in Utah in trade, and built a town from scratch—Page. The dam had a devastating impact on the river ecosystem, but ironically it may have saved the land around Navajo Mountain. The former sheepherders now work in Page, at the dam, or at the power plant. Overgrazing is not a concern now. All of this was made possible by one of the nation's first formal Indian water agreements, signed by the Navajo Nation and the federal government.

There is an important lesson in this brief history: the building of the dam had many unforeseen impacts on land, culture, and people. The dam did not simply alter the flow of a river; it altered the entire region. Navajos who once herded sheep are now building smokestacks at the power plant. Navajo women who once wove rugs now serve tourists in Page. And young men who might have once studied to be medicine men now work the night shift at the dam. And a few, like Terry, go to graduate school to learn how the white man's bureaucracy works (or doesn't work). As a result, the land is finally recovering from years of overgrazing. Clearly there is a direct relationship between the use of water and the use of the land. The dam changed both in profound ways.

The impact of the dam on Navajo culture is more difficult to ascertain. The newfound wealth derived from "real" jobs has helped many Navajos improve their standard of living. Some of them have moved from traditionally based subsistence to the comforts of middle-class living. Their once-remote homes and traditional lifestyle are now much more subject to the dominating presence of non-Indian America. Today many of the people of Navajo Mountain can purchase modern pick-ups that are much more adept at negotiating the road to town. The old stone building that housed the trading post is boarded up; people can go to Page for their necessities. And some homes now possess that great cement mixer of cultures, the satellite dish TV. Perhaps Chuck Norris will replace Manuelito, a traditional nineteenth-century chief, as a cultural hero.

On the other hand, life is more comfortable. Anglos often have an image of Indians living "quaint" lives, which is another word for poverty. Like all peoples, Indians enjoy the ease and comfort of modern living. To decry their shift from traditional subsistence to middle-class life is to rob them of a choice available to the rest of us. As one Navajo put it, "We aren't museum Indians anymore." It was the development of their water resources that helped the people of Navajo Mountain achieve this new status. Thus, when we speak of water development, we are really talking about much more than water; the water affects the land, and both mold the people and their culture. The same is true for water settlements; they broadly affect the relationship between Indian and non-Indian people and their shared physical environment.

The Second Treaty Era

The conflict between American Indians and Europeans is one of history's longest wars. It is the story of a murderous struggle for land and identity. In this unrelenting conflict between fundamentally different worldviews, the only commonality between the protagonists was their desire to live on the land in their own fashion. The costs of such a prolonged conflict are incalculable, and it is only recently that the leaders of both sides have begun to see the possibilities of a more constructive approach to resolving differences.

In regard to water, this approach has taken the form of negotiated settlements, reached through an open process of good-faith bargaining, that one hopes will bring a resolution to water conflicts that is acceptable to all parties. The current effort to settle Indian water claims has the potential to reshape the entire water regime of the American West.

— Seventeen settlements have been signed thus far:

> Ak-Chin, Arizona, 1978, PL 95-328 (renegotiated in 1984, PL 98-530; amended in 1992, PL 102-497)
>
> Tohono O'odham (Papago), Arizona, 1982, PL 97-293 (amended in 1992, PL 102-497)
>
> Fort Peck–Montana Compact, May 15, 1985
>
> San Luis Rey (Mission tribes), California, 1988, PL 100-675
>
> Colorado Ute (Animas–La Plata) Settlement, 1988, PL 100-585
>
> Salt River Pima-Maricopa, Arizona, 1988, PL 100-512
>
> Fort Hall, Idaho, 1990, PL 101-602
>
> Fort McDowell, Arizona, 1990 (part of the Clark Fork Wild and Scenic River Designation Act), PL 101-628
>
> Fallon Paiute-Shoshone/Truckee-Carson–Pyramid Lake, Nevada, 1990, PL 101-618
>
> Jicarilla Apache Water Settlement Act, 1992, PL 102-441
>
> Northern Cheyenne Reserved Water Rights Settlement Act, 1992, PL 102-374
>
> Ute Indian Rights Settlement Act, 1992, PL 102-575
>
> San Carlos Apache Tribe Water Rights Settlement Act, 1992, PL 102-575 (amended 1994, PL 103-435)
>
> Yavapai-Prescott Indian Tribe Water Rights Settlement, 1994, PL 103-434
>
> The Las Vegas Paiute settlement (negotiated with the state of Nevada)
>
> Chippewa Cree Tribe of the Rocky Boys Reservation Indian Reserved

Water Rights Settlement and Water Supply Enhancement Act, 1999, PL 106-163

Shivwits Band of the Paiute Indian Tribe of Utah Water Rights Settlement Act, 2000, PL 106-263.[2]

— A partial settlement for the Gila River Reservation has also been introduced.[3] In addition, several amendments or modifications to existing settlements have been introduced.

— Eighteen settlements, involving twenty-five Indian reservations in eight western states, are currently in negotiations.[4]

— Still other tribes await negotiation teams.

These settlements and negotiations involve nearly every significant watershed in the West and offer the possibility of changing Indian country forever.

In many respects, the current policy of negotiating Indian water rights is similar to the nineteenth century policy of signing treaties with Indians. In the nineteenth century the federal government grudgingly recognized that Indian tribes were separate political entities that had to be dealt with through treaties. As a result, the government signed nearly four hundred treaties with tribes, often using language that promised permanency, couched in the metaphoric tongue of the Indian.[5] The objective was to settle claims to land by specifically delineating which lands would remain Indian and which were to pass to the pressing masses of white settlers. In other words, land ownership was quantified and uses were stipulated, often accompanied by a monetary settlement. This is exactly what settlements are doing today with water; the government is signing government-to-government agreements with tribes in order to quantify Indian water, stipulate uses, and make monetary awards. We have, quite simply, entered the second treaty era, only this time it is water rather than land that is the object of these agreements. In Indian Country, water was to the twentieth century what land was to the nineteenth. One hopes the process will be more benign this time around.

Perhaps we can learn from the mistakes of the first treaty era. In one sense that era was tragic for American Indians; it signaled the end of their traditional way of life, transferred enormous tracts of land to their enemies, and imposed a use regime that was utterly alien to them. On the other hand, it is the treaties that now stand between tribes and the omnipresent dominant society. Without these written guarantees of separateness, officially sanctioned by Anglo law, Indian tribes would have been swallowed up by the dominant society long ago. The reservations that resulted from the first treaty era are now the last vestiges of indigenous culture and political autonomy.

The arguments for water settlements are essentially the same as those in the first treaty era. Although water settlements put an end to tribal dreams of an ever-expanding reserved water right, they provide the legal and political recognition that will protect Indian water the way treaties protect Indian land. Settlements offer a combination of legally recognized and quantified water rights, funding, and a certain level of tribal control and administration. On the other hand, the entire framework of the settlements takes place wholly within the confines of Anglo political and social institutions, and it all depends on the integrity of the U.S. government to honor its commitments. Indian people can only hope that the treaties of the second era are not routinely breached, which would be a sorry sequel to the first treaty era.

There is an age-old paradox at work here: to survive as a separate culture, Indian people have once again had to delve deeper into the Anglo way. In the case of settlements, the Anglo way emphasizes politics, and that means compromise. Can this strategy of political compromise, via an alien system of values, truly protect the long-term best interests of Indian tribes? It certainly means a considerable amount of sacrifice; negotiation is, by definition, a give-and-take process. Is the "give" in the equation another example of white hegemony that will eventually spell doom for American Indians? Or is the "take" the best way to compensate tribes for past injustices and ensure that their future is guaranteed, at least in reference to water? Of course, in purely practical terms, the only real question is whether settlements provide a solution that is better than the alternatives. There is no room for absolute justice when it comes to western water; too many promises have already been broken, too much water has already been allocated. Can settlements provide an approximation of justice in an imperfect world? This question cannot be answered without first looking at the history of Indian water because, in a very real sense, the settlement era is the scion of many frustrations and failures from the past.

Winters vs. the New Eden

Henry Winter was one of those intrepid settlers who thought a whole new agricultural paradise could be created by plowing the Great Plains. The upturned soil would draw the precious rain, and seemingly endless work would do the rest. To them, manifest destiny meant more than just taking land from Indians; it meant bringing the Jeffersonian ideal to the West—and then having the creator oblige them with a munificent change in weather patterns. It was this "blaze of mystical fervor," as Wallace Stegner called it,[6] that drew thousands of settlers to the arid West, which, according to its promoters, was to become the "New Eden."

The expected increase in precipitation did not materialize. But if rain did not follow the plow, politics did. Western farmers and their representatives began pushing for government assistance to help them overcome aridity with irrigation. In the absence of a divine blessing of increased rainfall, a government-sponsored project was an acceptable substitute.

As the deluge of hopeful settlers descended upon the arid region, some of them were drawn to lands in northern Montana that had been formerly set aside as a huge Indian reservation. Most of the reservation had been thrown open to settlement, with just a few remnants remaining in the hands of indigenous tribes. Henry Winter moved to that area and claimed a piece of land near the Fort Belknap Indian Reservation, the home of the Assiniboine and Gros Ventre Indian tribes.

By the turn of the twentieth century, Mr. Winter and a few other hardy souls had settled in isolated farming communities along the Milk River. Town names reflected ethnic origins: Malta, Saco, Hinsdale, Zurich, Glasgow, and Harlem. Winter and another farmer, Mose Anderson, shared a ditch and irrigated 440 acres along the river. Up and down the valley there was talk that the new Reclamation Service (forerunner of the Bureau of Reclamation) was going to help farmers irrigate their lands. These farmers had been fighting among themselves over the waters of the Milk. Canada and other upstream appropriators had not left them much water, and in late summer the river often dried up entirely. The Reclamation Service began investigating the possibility of building a project for them called the St. Mary–Milk River Project.

Northern Montana is big, open, rolling country, a tough place to farm. Blistering summers, arctic winters, violent rainsqualls followed by weeks of parching sun — these were the threats that made every planting something of an act of faith. But in 1905, the biggest threat did not come from nature. Carl Rasch, the strong-willed Justice Department attorney for Montana, had filed a lawsuit on behalf of the Fort Belknap Indian Reservation claiming sufficient water for the Indians' planned irrigation project. Winter's partner, Mose Anderson, was named the lead defendant. This was a threat that would shake the farmers' faith in both their government and the promise of a New Eden.

The apoplectic settlers could not believe that the federal government, which had made such efforts to lure them out west to break sod, would undercut their water supply for a mere Indian reservation. The policy of the government had always been to give priority to the needs of "civilized" white men. Suddenly the water rights to the Milk River were unclear, their farms threatened.

The Reclamation Service immediately halted its construction planning until a clear water right could be established.

Attorney Rasch was committed to securing a source of water for the Fort Belknap project, but he fully realized the precariousness of his claim. All the major forces were arrayed against him. The prevailing water doctrine in the West, the Prior Appropriation Doctrine, was developed as a response to the unique needs of western water users. It holds that the first water user to file a water claim with the state has priority over all subsequent water users. In an arid region where rivers and streams might dwindle to nothing in the summer heat, having the right of first appropriation often means the difference between bringing in a crop and watching it burn in the sun. This establishes a very rigid hierarchy based on time; the first to file a water claim is permitted to use his or her entire allocation, and only then can subsequent water users open their headgates. It is a water right almost regal in effect; one individual is wholly superior to another in terms of access to the one element that is most often in short supply.

But Rasch persevered, arguing that the Fort Belknap Reservation held riparian rights. This claim was based on the traditional water law of the eastern United States, where the use of water has always been tied to the land. The Riparian Doctrine focuses on the community rather than the individual; everyone who lives along the river shares its bounty. But bringing the Riparian Doctrine west was a strategy full of pitfalls, and Rasch knew it. So he also claimed that the Indians' treaty with the United States created a water right, and then for good measure he argued that, in any event, no state could abrogate the federal government's rights as a landowner and as the trustee for the Indians. Surely one of these arguments would connect with a judge, Rasch thought.

He was right. To the utter astonishment of nearly everyone, a federal district court upheld the Indians' right to water, even though it would force upstream non-Indians to reduce their diversions. Judge Hunt's decision in *United States v. Mose Anderson et al.* began with a statement of history and treaty rights: "Prior to 1888 nearly the whole of northern Montana north of the Missouri River, and eastward from the main chain of the Rocky Mountains was recognized as Indian country, occupied in part by the tribes of Indians now living upon the Fort Belknap Reservation. By treaty of May 1, 1888, the Indians 'ceded and relinquished to the United States' their title and rights to lands not embraced within the reservation then established as their permanent homes. The purposes of the treaty were that means might be had to enable the Indians to become 'self-supporting as a pastoral and agricultural people, and to educate their children in the paths of civilization.' "[7]

Judge Hunt then developed a rationale for a wholly new water doctrine based on the promises inherent in Indian treaties: "In my judgment, when the Indians made the treaty granting rights to the United States, they reserved the right to the use of the waters of Milk River, at least to an extent reasonably necessary to irrigate their lands. The right so reserved continues to exist against the United States and its grantees as well as against the state and its grantees."[8]

The 1,209 Assiniboines and Gros Ventres of the Fort Belknap Indian Reservation had picked a fight with the entire western establishment and, with a little help from a tenacious attorney, had won. It was a heroic deed or dastardly treason, depending upon which side of the argument one supported. The stunned settlers of the upper Milk River Valley became "very much excited" about their loss.[9] The Indian agent quickly applied his new leverage: "Some of the private canals have been enjoined by the Indian Agent, and some have not. He is holding a threat over the heads of these people to bring contempt proceedings against the enjoined ones, and injunctions against the others, if the reduced supply of water, 2,500 inches, does not come down regularly to him as long as it is in the river."[10]

The Anglo farmers, with the support and encouragement of the Reclamation Service, immediately appealed. Mose Anderson, apparently disgusted with Judge Hunt's decision, dropped out of the case. His partner, Henry Winter, became the lead appellant and in so doing lent his name to one of the most dramatic court decisions in history. An errant bureaucrat added an "s" to Winter's last name when the appeal was filed, titling the case *Winters v. United States*.

The settlers argued that they had filed for their water rights according to the laws of Montana, the laws of the United States, and "the customs of the country," while the Indian tribes had offered "no proof" that they had abided by these laws.[11] In essence, they were arguing that, while the treaty of 1888 reserved land, it did not explicitly reserve water. It requires a certain kind of boldness to make such an argument, much like saying, "I sold you some land, but not the air above it." The farmers, emboldened by the smugness of conquest, had every reason to believe their appeal would be successful. It was they, not the Indians, who had national policy on their side. More than a hundred years of oppressive Indian policy made it possible for the settlers to argue with a considerable degree of credibility that it was indeed the intent of Congress to set aside land for Indians but not water; to allow them to keep the ground where they pitched their tepees, but not allow them access to the life-giving creeks and rivers nearby. On its face it seems an absurd argument, but such was the nature of Indian policy that Anglos could be quite confident such an argument would prevail in the courts.

It did not. Henry Winter and his stalwart colleagues were shocked again as the Ninth Circuit Court of Appeals upheld in full the district court's decision, quoting verbatim the language cited above regarding reserved waters. Panic spread as farmers, reclamation officials, and western politicians began talking about the possible precedential value of the decision. In a remarkably prescient analysis, H. N. Savage, the supervising engineer for the Reclamation Service in Montana, speculated about the impact of the Winters decision:

> In case this decision holds, I see no reason why the Fort Peck Indian Reservation, which has for a portion of its western boundary the Milk River, should not also be similarly entitled to a decree giving it prior right to the Milk River water in parallel time and quantity to the Fort Belknap Reservation. . . .
>
> And continuing, I do not see why the Blackfeet Indians might not make a claim to the waters of St. Mary River, with equal propriety.
>
> And going a step further, I don't see why the Wind River or Shoshone Indians in central western Wyoming might not claim prior rights to the waters of Muddy Creek, Big Wind River, Little Wind River and Popo Agie. . . . This matter . . . seems to me entitled to careful consideration at this time.[12]

The nascent Reclamation Service, which would later become the powerful Bureau of Reclamation, heeded Savage's warning and began a coordinated resistance to the Winters Doctrine that lasted nearly a century.

The settlers appealed again to the Ninth Circuit, were again rejected, and then appealed to the U.S. Supreme Court. In this struggle, both sides made claims regarding "good faith."[13] The settlers argued that irrevocable harm would come to them if the decision was upheld, contending that "the controversy is between the Government and the Indians on one side, and the settlers on the other; settlers who, in good faith, accepted the grant of the Government, settled upon and reclaimed these lands, at a great expense, and established their homes and civilized communities in that country. The Courts should not . . . deprive these pioneer citizens of the fruits of their labor, destroy their homes and make their farms barren wastes."[14] The government attorneys chose to emphasize the obvious injustice of providing a reservation homeland devoid of water, quoting the 1888 act that established the Fort Belknap Reservation: "Article V [provides] that in the distribution of materials advanced by the United States preference shall be given especially to the Indians who "in good faith undertake the cultivation of the soil or engage in pastoral pursuits as a means of obtaining a livelihood." It is inconceivable that the Indians, by the agreement of 1888, intended to cede away a large portion of their lands, and at the same time surrender the right to the use of the waters of Milk River for the small fraction of the original reservation which they retained.[15] In short, both sides could claim moral high ground; the government had indeed solicited good faith and encouraged farming along the Milk River—whites on the north bank, Indians on the south. But there simply was not enough water to make all this "good faith" effort bear fruit. Both sides had a claim based on government promises; this was not to be a clear choice between thieves in the night and righteous victims.

When the U.S. Supreme Court entertained oral arguments in October of 1907, it is doubtful that they were aware of the legacy of conflict they were about to commence. At that time it was thought that American Indians would be gradually absorbed into the dominant society—"the vanishing race" they were called. The assimilation was to be accomplished through the gradual reduction of Indian land and government assistance, and an aggressive policy of discouraging Indian culture in favor of the "paths of civilization." Indeed, the Indian Service argued that the true value of the Indian irrigation project was in "converting the Fort Belknap Reservation into a community of prosperous Indian farmers who will be independent of future Government support."[16] In other words, the government wanted water so they could make the Indians just like their Anglo neighbors across the river.

In the first month of 1908 the Supreme Court announced its decision; it was an unqualified victory for the government attorneys representing the Fort Belknap Reservation. The court reasoned that, if the Indians had agreed to give up all their water rights in the treaty of 1888, then they were either "awed by the power of the government or deceived by its negotiators."[17] Neither was the case; "it would be extreme to believe that within a year [of passing the 1888 Act] Congress destroyed the reservation and took from the Indians the consideration of their grant, leaving them a barren waste—took from them the means of continuing their old habits, yet did not leave them the power to change to new ones." The Court concluded that the "government did reserve" the waters of the Milk River "for a use which would be necessarily continued through the years."[18]

Eight years after the Winters decision, the local irrigation superintendent for the Indian Service wrote that there was still "considerable hard feeling" among the upper Milk River water users over the case.[19] It is a feeling that continues to this day and has borne a legacy of nearly continual litigation, confrontation, and frustration. The Winters case was the first in a long series of court cases that have come to be known as federal reserved water rights, or simply the Winters Doctrine.[20]

The legal action over reserved water began while Winters was being appealed to the Supreme Court. True to the prediction made by reclamation engineer Savage, a reserved rights claim was filed for the Blackfeet Reservation, with the Ninth Circuit concluding that the Indians held reserved rights for both present and future uses.[21] Then a succession of rulings applied the reserved rights doctrine to all Indian reservations (not just those created by treaty),[22] and permitted reserved water to be transferred to lessees[23] and allottees.[24] The Ninth Circuit forcefully reaffirmed its commitment to the Winters doctrine in a 1956 case.[25]

The biggest boost to reserved water rights came in *Arizona v. California*, an epic water case that dragged on for ten years and produced forty-three volumes of testimony. In *Arizona*, the U.S. Supreme Court applied the doctrine of federal reserved water rights to all federal reservations, not just Indian reservations. Thus, national parks and forests, federal wildlife sanctuaries, and military bases could all claim reserved rights. In addition, the court in *Arizona* established the first definitive standard by which reserved water could be quantified, ruling that five Indian reservations along the Colorado River were entitled to sufficient water to irrigate all their "practicable irrigable acreage" (PIA). This standard remains in effect today.[26] A subsequent case before the Supreme Court applied the reserved rights doctrine to groundwater.[27]

These cases and many others firmly established the legal concept of reserved water rights.[28] In the words of former Secretary of the Interior Bruce Babbitt, these court victories have given "real meaning to reserved water rights."[29] But the high court's attitude toward reserved water rights began to change in the late seventies. In *United States v. New Mexico*, the court ruled that reserved water rights for a national forest could not be claimed for "secondary uses."[30] Another blow came when the high court agreed to allow state courts, which have a long history of hostility to Indian claims, to adjudicate federal reserved water rights.[31]

Then, in 1983, the Supreme Court issued a series of decisions that signaled a significant shift in attitude. In two cases, one involving the Pyramid Lake Paiutes and the other a rehearing of *Arizona v. California*, the court indicated it was quite willing to accept a level of legal representation for Indian tribes that was clearly inferior. In the Pyramid Lake case the court let stand an unfair 1944 decree, even though the government had provided inadequate counsel with a clear conflict of interest in that case. The court admitted that the tribe had been served poorly by the Bureau of Indian Affairs (BIA) and Justice Department lawyers, but "the Government cannot follow the fastidious standards of a private fiduciary."[32] In the *Arizona* rehearing, the court refused to reconsider the size of the Indian tribes' claim in the original 1963 case, even though it was clear that errors were made in calculating the tribes' water rights.[33] In short, professional activity that would land a private attorney in jail was deemed acceptable when it came to representing Indians. In a third case, the high court again decided that protecting the status quo—known as res judicata in legalese—was more important than correcting past errors in determining water rights for Indian tribes.[34] The Western States Water Council, long an opponent of reserved rights, gloated that the 1983 opinions "signify a flat rejection of the theory that Indian water rights were open-ended and susceptible to expansion at any time."[35]

The high court, the only national institution charged with protecting the rights of minorities, suddenly appeared callous to the unique status of American Indians. It had become risky to take a reserved water rights case to court. This risk was clearly illustrated in the long and bitter saga of the Big Horn adjudication in Wyoming.

On a Plateau All by Itself

The Bighorn River basin today is home to two tribes, the Eastern Shoshone and the Northern Arapaho, who had been enemies for many generations. After both were brought under federal control, the government, in an act of marked insensitivity to history and culture, placed them together on the same Wind River Reservation in Wyoming. The reservation takes its name from a river that flows out of the mountains—also named after the river—and then directly across the reservation to its confluence with the Pop Agie to form the Bighorn River. Much of the reservation is sagebrush country—high, dry, and sparse; access to the few rivers and streams in the area means the difference between modest prosperity and perennial destitution. The land looks barren but comes alive with the touch of water.

The BIA started irrigation work here just after the turn of the twentieth century, but so much of the land ended up in the hands of whites that one entire project was converted to a non-Indian project and transferred to the Bureau of Reclamation. The BIA then sold reservation lands to incoming settlers for $1.50 an acre. The sale occurred despite language in the second Fort Bridger treaty that guaranteed the Shoshone the "absolute and undisturbed use and occupation" of the reservation as a "permanent home." Destitute Arapahos were later forced on to the reservation.[36] The tribes were then forced to sell 1.5 million acres to generate funds for their remaining irrigation project.

In 1977, the year after the U.S. Supreme Court decided that Indian water rights could be adjudicated in state courts, the state of Wyoming filed suit to determine all water rights to the Bighorn basin, which includes all of the Wind

River Reservation. Thus began a legal odyssey that gave us the litany of Big Horn I, Big Horn II, and Big Horn III; consumed an estimated $20 million in legal fees;[37] and resulted in much confusion, inconsistency, and inconclusive legal action. Twenty-three years later the conflict over the Bighorn "is not anywhere near settlement."[38] These cases starkly demonstrate the pitfalls of contemporary Indian water litigation.[39]

In the first month of 1977 the state of Wyoming initiated the legal proceedings. A special master was appointed by the state district court to hear the case, which involved 20,000 water users.[40] After four years of testimony and investigation, the special master concluded that the tribes of the Wind River Reservation were entitled to sufficient reserved water rights to meet the purpose of the reservation, using the PIA standard established in *Arizona v. California* (1963). In addition, the special master assumed that the purpose of the reservation was to serve as a permanent homeland for the Indians, and thus the reserved water could be used for many purposes, not just irrigation. The district court judge disagreed and decided that the sole purpose of the reservation was agriculture, and thus the water could be used only for irrigation.[41] This decision was appealed to the Wyoming Supreme Court, which upheld the lower court's ruling.[42]

This disagreement over the purposes of the reservation is not just legal hairsplitting. In an age when irrigated agriculture is rapidly losing its economic appeal as more profitable water uses become possible, limiting Indian water to irrigation forces upon them an economic anachronism; it freezes their quest for "the paths of civilization" to an age when the West was sparsely settled and a good hay crop was the best a person could hope for. Once again the court was trying to force Indian people to be a part of the New Eden, however tenuous it might be. On the other hand, the tribes won a right to 500,717 af[43] of water with a priority date that precedes Custer's Last Stand by eight years—not bad in a land where even a modest amount of water can provoke a serious altercation.

The Wyoming Supreme Court decision pleased no one. The state thought the decision awarded too much water to the tribes and argued that the tribes should receive only enough water so that the agricultural purpose of the reservation "is not entirely defeated" (apparently a partial defeat was acceptable).[44] The tribes disliked the decision because they did not want their water limited to irrigation and quantified solely on the basis of irrigation. Both sides appealed to the U.S. Supreme Court. In the meantime the tribes developed their own water code that, unlike Wyoming state law, recognized instream flow as a legitimate use. The tribes wanted to use their water for fish and wildlife habitat, river recreation, and traditional uses. In other words, they did not necessarily want to use it only to grow more hay. In the meantime tensions mounted as all sides waited for a declarative ruling from the U.S. Supreme Court. Threats of violence became common; one local Anglo declared that water rights would be "administered by Smith and Wesson."

There are moments in history when there is a palpable need for decisive action, when the yearning for resolution creates an opportunity to move to the next epoch. The decision of the U.S. Supreme Court in the Big Horn case was just such an opportunity—a potential landmark of historical magnitude—but the court chose instead to provide little insight or guidance. The court limited its review to the PIA standard. Justice O'Connor recused herself from the decision, but not before she expressed support for the Wyoming position.[45] The remaining eight justices split evenly, four to four, which had the effect of upholding the lower court's decision.[46] There was no written opinion, but the nature of some of the questions in the oral hearing made it clear that some justices are openly hostile to the Winters Doctrine. The following exchange occurred between Justice White and Mr. Minear, the assistant to the solicitor general, Department of Justice:

QUESTION [FROM THE BENCH]: You don't want the reserved right to ever be subject to diminution for non-use?
MR. MINEAR: That's, well, that is in the very nature of a reserved water right.
QUESTION: Well, it doesn't have to be.
MR. MINEAR: I think—
QUESTION: It certainly doesn't.
MR. MINEAR: Well, if there is a problem—
QUESTION: It's not a total exception as if it stood there on a plateau all by itself while all the appropriative rights went down to nothing. There— there is no doctrine of water law that elevates one water right over the other to that extent.
MR. MINEAR: But if the water was initially reserved for the reservation, it was set aside by Congress, then it seems as if Congress is the party that needs to worry if there are later shortcomings—
QUESTION: But, of course, the whole—the whole Winters Doctrine is just an implication of Congress. Congress never said in so many words, we're reserving a water right. That's just what this Court said Congress must have intended. So, Congress has never even spoken.[47]

In the words of Susan Williams, the American Indian attorney who represented the Wind River tribes, taking an Indian water case to the Supreme Court had become "very dicey."[48]

This legal saga did not end with the U.S. Supreme Court's decision. Legal conflicts over Indian water develop their own inertia, living on for decades as though they were indefatigable beasts that must be fed. A year after the Supreme Court decision the tribes attempted to use their water to maintain adequate instream flow for fish habitat. The state's chief water officer refused to honor the tribe's request, arguing that it violated state law. Then, in a move that surprised many observers, a state district court sided with the Indians and gave them the authority to administer their own water rights, which would permit them to use it for instream flow.[49] Finally it looked like the tribes would be free of the yoke of state control.

But their elation was short-lived. In a garbled, contradictory opinion the Wyoming Supreme Court reversed the district court and concluded that Indian water is best administered by Anglo state water authorities.[50] Legal scholar Eric Hannum succinctly described the decision: "The court's disposition of the case can be most charitably described as confusing. In five separate opinions the five Justices spun out a variety of rationales for their respective positions."[51] Justice Golden, in a scathing dissent, wrote that "All that is really clear from this narrow opinion is that the parties will continue to litigate their conflict."[52]

In sum, the Winters Doctrine created a concept of water acquisition and ownership wholly at odds with the prevailing western doctrine of prior appropriation. The two doctrines are contradictory in a number of ways: prior appropriation rights are based on diversion and use, while reserved rights do not require use; prior appropriation rights are based on state law, while reserved rights are created by the courts to meet the purposes of federal reservations; prior appropriation rights are quantified via a state permit system, while reserved rights do not require a state permit and are of indeterminate amount; and last but perhaps most important, the prior appropriation doctrine was designed to meet the needs of the leading political forces in the American West, primarily mining, ranching, and agricultural interests, while the main beneficiaries of the Winters Doctrine have been the small number of politically weak Indian tribes that managed to survive into the twentieth century. The New Eden had its own water doctrine, and Indian reservations had theirs; an epic conflict ensued.

The Song of the Raven

What is the legacy of the Winters Doctrine? By one estimate, probably excessive, there have been 4,000 cases that involved reserved water rights.[53] The result is a body of case law of "Talmudic complexity."[54] Currently reserved water rights play a role in sixty-three stream adjudications. A river of ink has been spilled, but how much water did Indian reservations actually receive as a direct result of *Winters*?

A good place to begin to answer that question is to return to Fort Belknap. After the *Winters* victory, BIA and Justice Department officials strongly urged that the irrigation project be finished as "rapidly as possible" to protect the tribes' newly won water rights.[55] At the time the tribes were actually irrigating only 11,800 acres out of 29,600 irrigable acres. But the project did not receive a boost in funding; quite the contrary, it was hopelessly underfunded. Fifteen years after *Winters*, the BIA's chief engineer wrote a telling letter to the irrigation engineer for Fort Belknap, describing the difficulty of obtaining funding for Indian projects, including Fort Belknap:

> I am sorry to say that we are not having any success in increasing our estimates this year. The Budget Committees have been very strict and instead of increasing have usually decreased our appropriations.
>
> I realize full well what you have to say in regard to the necessity of more money and I am rather of the opinion that it will be necessary to purchase more machinery not only for this project but for others, but I do not know how we will be able to do this until Congress gets a little more liberal in their appropriations.[56]

This condition never changed. At the beginning of the settlement era (early 1980s), the Fort Belknap project was "in an advanced state of deterioration," nine project units had been abandoned, and the tribes were irrigating only 5,000 acres—less than half of what was being irrigated at the time of the *Winters* decision.[57] Five years later the chairman of Fort Belknap testified before Congress: "I am sorry to report . . . that our current irrigation project is in disarray and of questionable economic benefit to our people at this time. The primary reasons for the . . . project being in this shape is inadequate funding and mismanagement by the Bureau of Indian Affairs."[58] There, in a nutshell, is the story of the entire BIA irrigation program. The Fort Belknap project, the focus of desperate urgency, became instead a monument to complacency and neglect.

The sad legacy of the Fort Belknap Project is important because it is so typical of the official attitude toward Indian water throughout the arid West. In 1920 the chief of Indian irrigation complained in his annual report that "the work of the Indian Irrigation Service has been seriously handicapped by lack of sufficient funds to carry on the work contemplated."[59] In 1928 a comprehensive survey of Indian irrigation found that "On many projects the acreage utilized by Indians is continually decreasing, while the acreage utilized by whites is increasing. . . . many of the Indian irrigation projects as contemplated are incomplete. They are being improved or extended from time to time as funds are made available."[60] Forty-eight years later the commissioner of the BIA made a similar statement: "Very candidly, a lot of the existing projects that we have were authorized and were never completed. So what we do is we try to keep the projects operational with what we have, and it is kind of giving enough money so that the project doesn't completely collapse."[61] In a 1996 interview, a BIA official summed up the agency's problematic performance: "Many projects are just subsistence systems, others have become defunct, and some have literally dried up. Quite frankly we haven't been running these projects very well."

The lack of adequate funding is reflected in the minimal growth of Indian agriculture since Winters. Although accurate data are nearly impossible to obtain, it appears that, from 1910 to 1977, the irrigated acreage on Indian projects increased from about 160,000 acres to 370,000 acres. In 1984 the Western States Water Council estimated that 625,981 acres of Indian land were being irrigated, which is only about 7 percent of the practicable irrigable acreage on reservations.[62] Ten years later a BIA official estimated that Indian irrigation had actually fallen in recent years, to 700,000 acres, due to a "lack of water because of non-Indian irrigation."[63] In other words, the PIA standard creates a water right for Indian tribes of approximately 46 million af, but they actually use only a small fraction of that amount.[64] In addition, most of this land is actually farmed by whites; by 1974, non-Indians were farming 71 percent of all the land in these "Indian" irrigation projects.[65]

The story of the BIA irrigation program is one of dismal failure. There is an old saying among BIA people: "We began our first irrigation project in 1867 and we've never finished one yet." In 1990 the Senate Select Committee on Indian Affairs held hearings on the BIA irrigation program. The following exchange took place between Committee Chairman Daniel Inouye and Patrick Hayes, Deputy Assistant Secretary for Trust and Economic Development, BIA, Department of the Interior:

> THE CHAIRMAN. In preparing for these hearings we came across the startling fact that of the 125 projects authorized, none have been completed. If we were to complete these projects and rehabilitate those that obviously need rehabilitation, what would be your estimate as to the cost?
> MR. HAYES. Just to give a very approximate estimate, Mr. Chairman, I would estimate it to be somewhere in the neighborhood of $700 million to $800 million to complete the projects.[66]

The BIA builds successful water projects the way the raven sings; it just doesn't happen. Despite many court victories, the BIA never delivered. This points out one of the great handicaps of the litigation strategy; no matter how many cases are won, only the U.S. Congress can appropriate money for water projects. As a Supreme Court justice pointed out, "On Indian reservations, as elsewhere, [i]t became clear a long time ago that the limit on the development of irrigated agriculture in the West was not water but money."[67] Thus the promise of Winters became a question of funding; would the Congress allocate sufficient funding to allow tribes to utilize their reserved water fully? The answer, history tells us, is an unqualified no. When it came to appropriating money for Indian irrigation, Congress was always short of funds. By one estimate, it would take nearly as much money to finish the BIA irrigation projects as has been invested in them since the inception of the program.[68] This nation has never made a serious commitment to develop irrigation on Indian reservations, even though agriculture was to be the lever with which to pry the "Indianess" out of American Indians and convert them into participating members of the New Eden.

There is an important relationship between the doctrine espoused in Winters and the absence of adequate funding. The Winters case clearly and explicitly did not limit the acquisition of Indian water rights only to those situations where no loss of water would result for Anglos. Indeed, Winters presented a very clear case where all water reserved for the Indians would by necessity be taken from Anglos. The Court pointed out that the desert land laws and other statutes were clearly subject to "existing laws," including Indian treaties. But the absence of funding for Indian irrigation created a de facto limit on Indian irrigation to avoid Anglo water losses. In essence, a no-injury-to-whites rule was imposed via funding restrictions. This kind of limit to reserved water rights did not appear in court decisions until the late 1970s, when a "sensitivity" test was suggested by Justice Powell in a dissent,[69] and later an economic feasibility requirement for Indian irrigation was suggested by the courts.[70] In case law, the "no injury" or "sensitivity" concept is relatively new to Winters cases, but in the highly contested politics of federal budgeting, it is as old as the Indian irrigation program itself. It is important to note that neither a "no-injury" test nor a realistic economic feasibility test has ever been imposed on non-Indian irrigation projects.[71] If they had, such projects would be rare indeed.

To a great extent, the paucity of funding for irrigation projects is typical of most Indian programs. But in the case of irrigation, there was the additional impediment of competition with the Bureau of Reclamation; any water allocated to Indians could not then be used to fuel the growth of the reclamation program. The Indians were up against the icon of western America, the purveyor of the New Eden that promised to quell the feral impulse of western water. The bureau was part of a larger political context that boxed in the Winters Doctrine and made its espousal an act of faith if not results. Ultimately this meant that the attainment of Indian water rights would have to move out of the courthouse and into this larger political context, which is the subject of the next chapter.

Conclusion

The nineteenth century saw the end of the first treaty era. In the American West, the treaty era flourished from about 1850 to 1871, when Congress unilaterally decided that agreements with Indians would henceforth be made as executive orders or acts of Congress. During the first treaty era, aboriginal lands were reduced to a fraction of historical usage; in exchange, the federal government set aside small remnants of former lands as reservations and promised to deliver certain goods and services to compensate for the land losses.

By the turn of the twentieth century the frontier had already become legend, and attention had shifted from acquiring land to developing water. In 1902 Congress passed the Reclamation Act, which put the mighty force and money of the U.S. government behind efforts to irrigate the west. Six years later the U.S. Supreme Court handed down Winters. These two epochal events set the stage for an unrelenting battle over water that continues to this day. Former Congressman Bill Richardson of New Mexico accurately described the intensity of this conflict: "There is no more divisive issue in the West than the dispute between Indians and non-Indians over water."[72] This bitter water war between western Anglos and Indian tribes continued unabated for eighty years. It is impossible to understand the appeal of negotiated settlements and the advent of the second treaty era without first understanding this long and frustrating struggle to obtain water for Indian reservations.

Indian tribes won many court battles, but Anglos nearly always ended up with the water. The biggest winners have been lawyers and corporate irrigators. The Supreme Court of Arizona described this apparent contradiction: "While the amount of water actually used by these entities [Indian tribes] may have been negligible until recent times, the magnitude of the right to use water on these lands has been far from negligible."[73] This gave rise to the phrase that Indians had "paper water" awarded by a court, but very little "wet water" that is actually used by tribal authorities. Rivers of ink have been spilled over the Winters Doctrine, but precious little water changed hands. However, the same cannot be said for the "white" water development programs of the Bureau of Reclamation and the U.S. Army Corps of Engineers. They are described in chapter 2 along with a discussion of the rise of negotiated settlements as a new way of resolving conflicts between Anglo and Indian water users.

Chapter 3 of the book assesses the claim that water settlements save time and money. Chapter 4 discusses the finality of the first fourteen settlements, and chapter 5 attempts to estimate how much water has been reallocated as a result of the settlements. Chapter 6 looks at the comity engendered by the negotiation process. Chapters 7 and 8 examine two major western water issues—environmental protection and water marketing—and how they have been affected by Indian water settlements. The final chapter provides an overall evaluation of the settlement policy and the future of the second treaty era.

2

A Vision of Good Faith

Destined by the Almighty

Derby Dam, on the Truckee River east of Reno, Nevada, was the concrete debut of the nascent Reclamation Service, the first structure to be built under the aegis of the 1902 Reclamation Act. The opening ceremony was held on a hot, dusty day in June 1905. Congressman Mondell, a principal supporter of the Reclamation Act, rose to give thanks for "the waters that today shall be turned from their natural channels to take their course through the canals which have been constructed to fructify the desert, to bring life where death now dwells and to make possible the establishment of the highest and the best and the most perfect institutions of civilization."[1] Not to be outdone, a Reno newspaper declared that, thanks to the new dam, "Lurking death will be banished from the alkali plains and the sand clouds of the arid wastes will give place to the wreathing smoke of civilization."[2]

What was all this talk about death? What was all this talk about civilization? Just downstream from the new dam was the site of an 1860 military engagement between white militia and Paiute Indians from Pyramid Lake; the Paiutes had won.[3] Perhaps the dam would accomplish what soldiers could not—the total subjugation of the Paiutes, who could now be displaced by the "highest and best" people.

Today it may be hard to imagine just how overtly racist the country was at the turn of the twentieth century. A high school geography text published in 1916 explained that there were two kinds of Indians: savages, who did not farm, and barbarians, who did (so apparently the Indian Irrigation Service was trying to convert savages into barbarians). This text went on to explain to its earnest readers that the white race was superior, and "being more advanced than the other races, the white race has conquered the weaker people and taken their lands from them, so that now they rule almost the whole world." This same text called the work of the Reclamation Service "one of the most important works in which our government is engaged."[4]

The early days of the irrigation movement are replete with racist sentiment. A speaker at the 1907 meeting of the National Irrigation Congress declared that the American West was "destined by the Almighty for a white man's country."[5] Four years later an official with the Reclamation Service explained that the West was where the "Aryan races" would coalesce into a "final race-type" that will "dominate the world."[6]

It was inevitable that the federal government's reclamation program would come into conflict with the "other" reclamation program—the meager effort to irrigate Indian lands. In many river basins of the West, water sources became fully appropriated early in the twentieth century. In the first treaty era, Indian tribes were usually allowed to retain only lands that no one else wanted —lands viewed as expendable. For example, the Uintah Reservation in Utah was set aside only after the government received a report that the land was so utterly useless that its "only purpose was to hold the other parts of the world together." But there was no comparable amount of slack water—water that no one wanted. Thus it was easier for the government to set aside land than it was to set aside water. The Reclamation Service, which was renamed the Bureau of Reclamation in 1924, greatly exacerbated this problem by aggressively developing water resources throughout the west. The bureau was abetted in this process by the U.S. Army Corps of Engineers, one of the oldest agencies in the federal government.

There is a dramatic contrast between the fortunes of the Bureau of Reclamation and the Corps of Engineers on one hand, and the BIA irrigation program on the other. While the latter suffered for want of even minimal appropriations, the government lavished money on Anglo water development for more than half a century, building not only thousands of projects, but also constructing one of the most durable political alliances in America.[7]

The great "iron triangle" political coalition of western water development began with a most grandiose promise: irrigation would pull restless, troubled people out of the teeming cities and convert them into the Jeffersonian ideal of the yeoman farmer; it would lead "the unsuccessful from the slavery of the city to the sovereignty of the country."[8] It was social engineering on a massive scale, designed to populate the New Eden with eternally grateful citizens. The National Irrigation Congress, the primary lobbying force behind the movement, was fond of pithy apothegms:

Save the forests, store the floods, reclaim the deserts, make homes on the land.

Make the desert bloom as the rose.

Put the landless man on the manless land.[9]

Originally designed to be self-supporting, the reclamation program quickly came to rely on eastern money and devolved into a system of petty pork barrel, multiple layers of subsidies, and political payoffs. The logrolling—the trading of political favors—began with the Reclamation Act itself. Eastern legislators opposed it, one calling it a "most insolent and impudent larceny."[10] To overcome this hostility, Senator Carter of Montana filibustered the appropriations bill for the Army Corps of Engineers, which had built many politically popular water projects in the East. Suddenly, many eastern legislators decided that western reclamation was not so bad after all. Thus began a complex ritual of vote trading for water projects that eventually spread the gospel of water development to every congressional district and state. Water projects became a favored vehicle by which legislators could bring home the bacon—using someone else's money—and then reap the rewards on election day.

The literature on western water development is voluminous, nearly all of it critical. With the exception of a few books written by those inside the iron triangle,[11] most authors heap scorn on the waste, inefficiency, and political cronyism that became the hallmarks of federal water development programs. The titles of these books speak volumes:

Muddy Waters, by Arthur Maass (1951)
Dams and Other Disasters, by Arthur Morgan (1971)
The Water Hustlers, by Robert Boyle, John Graves, and T. H. Watkins (1971)
Pork Barrel Politics: Rivers and Harbors Legislation, by John Ferejohn (1974)
The River Killers, by Martin Heuvelman (1974)
Killing the Hidden Waters, by Charles Bowden (1977)
A River No More, by Philip Fradkin (1981)
Nor Any Drop to Drink, by William Ashworth (1982)
Damned Indians, by Michael Lawson (1982)
Who Runs the Rivers?, by Barbara Andrews and Marie Sansone (1983)
Troubled Waters, by Rodney Smith (1984)
How to Create a Water Crisis, by Frank Welsh (1985)
Rivers of Empire, by Donald Worster (1986)
Troubled Waters, by Mohamed El-Ashry and Diana Gibbons (1986)
Cadillac Desert, by Marc Reisner (1986)
Endangered Rivers and the Conservation Movement, by Tim Palmer (1986)
A Life of Its Own: The Politics and Power of Water, by Robert Gottlieb (1988)
Overtapped Oasis, by Marc Reisner and Sarah Bates (1990)

Add to this list no less than four books with the title *Water Crisis*.[12]

The water policy critique need not be retold here, but two elements are especially relevant to Indian water rights. The first one concerns the Byzantine system of subsidies that have been lavished upon non-Indian water projects while Indian irrigators were told there was insufficient funding for their projects. It is important to realize that these multiple subsidies were set up during a time when Indian irrigation projects could not even muster sufficient funding to maintain dilapidated, half-finished projects. It is also interesting that opponents of reserved rights wanted to establish a stringent economic feasibility test for all Indian water uses — a test that would have strangled the Bureau of Reclamation's program. To be sure, Indian projects also receive subsidies, but these are due to treaty provisions that specify the government will provide certain services in exchange for the Indians' agreement to give up huge tracts of land and become peaceful farmers.

The second element of the reclamation program that is especially relevant to Indians is the point at which the two programs intersect. For the most part, the Indian irrigation program and the federal reclamation program coexisted as competitors, with the latter nearly always gaining the upper hand over the former.[13] But in a few instances a tribe held sufficient legal or political clout that the Bureau of Reclamation had to deal with them, and consequently a somewhat different relationship emerged. At times it has been politically expedient to incorporate Indian water development into a reclamation project to make it more palatable politically and resolve potential water rights problems. In the 1960s, agreements were signed with the Northern Utes of Utah and the Navajo Nation; both of these agreements involved reclamation projects and negotiated agreements that presaged the settlement era.

In Utah the Bureau of Reclamation wanted to build a massive project to divert water from the Colorado River Basin to the more populous Wasatch Front. The obvious source of water for this Central Utah Project (CUP) was the Uintah River Basin, which flows across the Uintah and Ouray Indian Reservation, home of the Northern Utes. The only way to ensure a water right for the project was to get the tribe to agree not to claim their reserved water rights. In 1965 the tribe and the Bureau signed a "deferral agreement" in which the tribe agreed to defer claiming and developing a major portion of its water in exchange for a Ute Indian Project, which was to be a unit within the CUP. The Ute Indian Unit was never built, but the CUP still took Ute water. In 1989 the Ute tribe declared the deferral agreement null and void, and three years later agreed to a new water settlement. The full story of this project and the Ute agreement is told in chapter 8.

The Navajo Nation also signed a water agreement in the 1960s. The Bureau of Reclamation wanted to build an interbasin transfer to take water out of the San Juan River and pipe it over the continental divide to the Rio Grande and hence to Albuquerque. But the Navajo Nation held potentially enormous reserved water rights to the San Juan, which flows through the reservation in an area with significant irrigable acreage. After many years of negotiations, an agreement was enacted into law that simultaneously authorized the San Juan–Chama Diversion for Albuquerque and the Navajo Indian Irrigation Project (NIIP).[14] Like the Ute deferral agreement, this arrangement also encountered problems: "Volumes have been written on the federal government's unfulfilled promise to the Navajo Nation. Although the SanJuan–Chama Diversion was completed in a timely manner, NIIP is over twenty years behind schedule and can only irrigate 60 percent of its total project acreage."[15] Judith Jacobsen explained why the promise went unfulfilled: "The combination of reclamation strength and Indian weakness yielded poor planning, chronic underfunding, undercapitalization, and insufficient training, all of which changed NIIP from the promised project."[16]

In sum, there has been a long and troubled relationship between Indian irrigation as provided by the BIA and the water development programs of the Bureau of Reclamation and the U.S. Army Corps of Engineers. The contrast in funding is stark, and the difference in results is of an order of magnitude. The Winters Doctrine simply could not compete with the New Eden. Put another way, the nation's moral commitment to the first Americans was overwhelmed by an unyielding belief in irrigation as a salve for the nation's growing pains.

This chapter explains how the highly conflictual relationship between Indian and non-Indian water programs evolved into an effort to find a more constructive relationship through negotiations. A contrast is drawn between litigation and negotiation, the latter being an alternative form of conflict resolution with unique properties.

From Deadliest Enemies to a New Era

In the nineteenth century the godfathers of the New Eden aggressively pressed Congress to transfer Indian lands to white ownership. The results for Indian people were catastrophic. By 1875, nearly 166 million acres of land had been set aside as Indian reservations, but by 1934 this acreage had been reduced to 52 million. Much of the loss was due to the Allotment Act of 1887, which divided reservation trust land into 160-acre parcels and sold the remaining "surplus" land to Anglos. Other Indian lands were lost through the creation of national forests, federal reservoir and dam sites, and rescissions of previous treaties, statutes, and executive orders that created reservations. In nearly every case these land losses were unilaterally imposed on tribes without their participation or consent.

Most losses of Indian land in the West occurred in the nineteenth century and the first two decades of the twentieth. Beginning with the more enlightened policy of the FDR administration, land losses were curtailed, and some lands were actually restored to Indian ownership during the depression when bankrupted farmers and ranchers were only too happy to find buyers for their lands. Stopping the hemorrhage of land loss was part of the Roosevelt administration's larger strategy of recognizing the permanence and autonomy of Indian tribes. No longer were Indians to be the "vanishing race."[17] Instead, they would gain a significant amount of control over their own destiny by developing modern tribal governments according to the 1934 Indian Reorganization Act. Finally it appeared as though Native Americans might have a future as Indian people rather than as Anglo imitators.[18]

Not everyone was comfortable with this notion, but they held little sway within FDR's Interior Department. Indian opponents had to wait for the Eisenhower administration and a new policy with the lugubrious title of "termination." The termination policy attempted to attach a time limit to treaty obligations, as though a sunset clause had been written into each treaty. At about the same time, the Indian Claims Commission began to hear cases arising out of treaty violations. However, the policy of the commission, even in the most flagrant instances of land theft, was to award money to tribes rather than return stolen lands. Termination and the Indian Claims Commission were, in essence, contrasting efforts to mitigate the impacts of the first treaty era.

By the end of the 1950s the policy of termination had clearly become a demonstrable failure, both morally and politically, and the federal government began searching for a new approach to what had been called for a century "the Indian problem." But it was not until 1975, with the passage of the Indian Self-Determination and Education Assistance Act, that federal Indian policy finally began to have a modicum of coherence. There was a growing recognition that Indian policy could be improved if Indian people had a role in its formulation.

In addition to the new policy of self-determination, other events were changing attitudes toward Indian policy. Several Indian organizations had risen to prominence, including the National Congress of American Indians, The National Tribal Chairman's Association, the Council of Energy Resource Tribes, and the Native American Rights Fund. At the same time a series of events occurred that garnered widespread media attention; the rise of AIM and the occupations of Wounded Knee and Alcatraz, the Trail of Broken Treaties, and the trial of Leonard Peltier brought the demands of Indian people into the homes of average white America. In 1977 a special commission was established to review Indian policy and report to Congress. This commission made more than two hundred recommendations for change.[19]

By the end of the seventies, the federal government had finally begun to recognize Indian tribes as semi-autonomous governments that had a right to control their own destinies. But a change in attitude at the federal level only resolved part of the problem. It was the states, especially western states, that had long been the most vitriolic opponents to Indian land and water rights.

Since the beginning of this nation, there has been a high level of conflict between Indian tribes and the states in which they reside. Late in the nineteenth century the Supreme Court noted that the people of the states where Indians live are "often their deadliest enemies."[20] This animosity has continued through the years, with the federal government in the official role of trustee for the tribes, but often acting more like an agent of the states that are antagonistic to tribes. In this unequal contest, Indian tribes often did not fare well, especially in regard to water.

The first real change in the federal government's approach to Indian water rights came late in the Carter administration. In 1977, Jimmy Carter issued his famous "hit list" of wasteful water projects that he wanted to cut from the budget. He quickly discovered that the old iron triangle of western water interests still wielded a big club; Carter was viciously attacked by western legislators and governors. One congressman said Carter's project cuts were based on "ignorance, intransigence, and obduracy."[21] Reeling from the criticism and facing a difficult re-election bid, the Carter administration became more sensitive to the priorities of western leaders.

One concern these leaders repeatedly voiced was the possible impact Indian tribes could have on western water allocations. The last thing these Anglo leaders wanted was a substantive victory that would allow tribes to develop and use their water resources and thus use water desired by western farmers and growing cities. Indian tribes were also looking for new solutions. They were fed up with eighty years of empty court victories. With a few exceptions, the Winters Doctrine had not provided them with much water.

The Carter administration began working on an alternative to protracted litigation that relied upon consensual negotiation leading to a formal settlement. The Reagan administration, even more responsive to western interests, began to pursue the settlement strategy vigorously. After a slow start the negotiation alternative began to produce settlements; in the ensuing years seventeen water settlements were signed, most of them since 1988.[22]

This settlement policy gave rise to a cautiously optimistic view that "A new era has emerged in response to the limitations of paper water rights. Tribal governments are increasingly turning from courtroom battles to practical efforts to translate their paper rights into tangible benefits for the reservation."[23] The deputy attorney general for Colorado declared that negotiated settlements were a way of "averting a water rights war."[24]

Can the settlement policy actually fulfill such a promise? Can centuries-old enmities be assuaged by a new approach to resolving conflict over water? In order to answer that question, which is the central goal of this book, it was first necessary to examine the past in chapter 1 and this chapter; we do not know if policy has improved unless we first know what was gained through past policies. Then we need a thorough understanding of the objectives of the new process and how they are going to be achieved. This chapter examines the settlement policy by discussing the process itself: what does a "good" negotiation process look like? Then it identifies the expected outcomes of that process: what are the elements of a "successful" settlement?

Good Faith Bargaining

What is a negotiated settlement? What kind of bargaining takes place? How does it compare to other methods of achieving an outcome? What decision-making procedures are used?[25]

There are a number of ways to resolve conflict. Most public conflict is resolved through a competitive political process. Other conflicts take place within the confines of the judicial process. And occasionally, when these methods fail, opponents resort to violence. All three of these methods have been used in the struggle over Indian land and water. The "Indian wars" lasted for several hundred years, an enormous and complex legal doctrine was developed by the courts, and the political process produced innumerable laws regarding Indian people. None of these methods yielded significant amounts of water for Indian reservations.

Within the last twenty-five years an effort has been made to develop a different approach to resolve conflicts over natural resources, often labeled alternative dispute resolution (ADR), that emphasizes direct participation, consensus building, collaborative problem-solving, and a focus on interests rather than positions. Roger Fisher and William Ury turned these ideas into the bestseller *Getting to Yes*.[26] As the conceptual foundation for ADR improved, its popularity and application broadened dramatically.[27] It has been used to resolve conflicts ranging from divorce to international disputes.[28] ADR centers and institutes sprang up across the country and government agencies developed their own conflict resolution capabilities. It was only a matter of time before these new procedures would be applied to one of the more vexatious public conflicts, the water war between Indians and Anglos.

There are numerous proponents of the negotiation/settlement approach to resolving conflicts over Indian water. Most of them contrast the new approach with the failure of past litigation strategies: "The costs of litigation can be tens of millions of dollars for each side and can perpetuate bitterness with non-Indian communities. Thus, parties to many of these Indian water rights conflicts are opting for the negotiating table, as they grow acutely aware of the immense financial burdens and lost opportunities caused by lengthy litigation. Negotiated solutions also have the capacity to deal with practical problems of using and developing common water resources to the advantage of both Indians and non-Indians."[29] This emphasis on practical solutions that can be tailored to fit specific situations is a prominent theme in the settlement literature. Courts are adversarial in nature, producing winners and losers, and generating a great deal of animosity. But settlements create the opportunity to establish constructive relationships: "The most valuable result of a negotiated settlement is the establishment of commercial and governmental relationships which remain after the negotiations are concluded. In most cases, water rights negotiations are the first substantive opportunity for the local non-Indian community to begin to understand and appreciate the needs and capabilities of their Indian neighbors."[30]

However, negotiated settlements are not appropriate for all conflict situations, including some of the current battles over Indian water rights: "Negotiations potentially offer Indian and non-Indian entities more timely clarification of water rights, in a non-adversarial setting, and give all parties greater control over the eventual outcome. However, negotiations are not a panacea. Unless *basic conditions* are set forth concerning the power differentials between the negotiating entities, the existence of a power base from which to negotiate, and the entities' ability to understand and advocate their own interests, negotiations may not be an effective mechanism for the resolution of disputes" (emphasis mine).[31]

The potential success of negotiated settlements is influenced by how well these "basic conditions" are met. Researchers have found many attributes of the conflict-resolution process that affect the outcome and hence the success of the negotiation. There are five attributes of the process that are particularly relevant to Indian water rights negotiations. These five procedural attributes establish a standard—an ideal—of what a "good" negotiation should look like. It is nearly impossible to meet all of them in all situations, but the ADR literature emphasizes them as factors that significantly contribute to the success of negotiated settlements. The ensuing chapters provide a sense of how well Indian water settlements meet these standards.

First, negotiators need to know what the alternatives to negotiation might bring them.[32] ADR works best when participants see it as their best hope for a favorable solution. This requires an understanding of what might be won or lost by each party in various conflict-resolution venues. Peterson Zah, former chairman of the Navajo Nation, made note of this: "The Beginning point in any negotiation is the knowledge of what you have and what your opponent has. Without that knowledge, any negotiation is a charade."[33] In regard to Indian water rights, the primary alternative to negotiation has been litigation. Without a doubt, past litigation has been a disappointment to all concerned. If we compare the promise of negotiation with past litigation, then it appears to be the best available alternative. In addition, recent court trends do not bode well for Indian claims to water. As Walter Rusinek has noted, "the road ahead for reserved water rights may be risky."[34] Of course, no one can truly predict future trends in case law or court personnel, nor can we assume that Congress will not intervene in some way. However, for the best-available-alternative standard to be met, negotiators must always be cognizant of possible trends in case law and the possibility that at some future point, courts may be more receptive to Indian reserved water claims.

A second attribute concerns the probability that settlements can be successfully implemented,[35] which requires that settlements be adequately funded, that all major issues be resolved, and that all parties agree on the interpretation of the settlement. It also requires a procedure for working out post-settlement difficulties and ensuring appropriate follow-up.

A third attribute of successful negotiations concerns the need for full participation by all affected parties. The literature on ADR universally cites the need for every significant stakeholder to be at the table.[36] But for Indian water rights cases, this is virtually impossible due to the sheer complexity of issues and the number of affected parties. In the Big Horn cases there were 20,000 parties. In the case that led to the Southern Arizona settlement there were 70,000 parties. The Gila and Salt River cases involved more than 80,000 parties. And the Snake River Basin adjudication attracted 175,000 claims.[37] John Folk-Williams suggests this problem may be resolved by creating a continuum of parties depending upon the impact the settlement will have on them.[38] However, if an important player is left out — or walks out — the settlement is likely to be plagued with future problems.

A fourth attribute concerns procedure. In all negotiations the first item on the agenda must be the process of negotiation itself. In any dispute-resolution effort, the design of the procedure to be used is nearly as important as the dispute itself.[39] In Indian water negotiations there are two sets of procedures that must be agreed upon: the rules of negotiation and the process by which the settlement is administered.

And finally, all negotiations must be consensual. One major difference between litigation and negotiation is the degree of coercion; no one has ever been subpoenaed to a negotiation. All negotiations must be entered into freely: "Negotiation is a voluntary process involving two or more individuals or groups who seek to attain some or all of their objectives through mutual consent. . . . Decisions cease to be negotiated when they are imposed on the participating parties by an outside authority. For negotiation to exist, the parties must believe that they are participants by choice rather than by compulsion."[40]

In sum, for a settlement to have a significant chance of success, all parties must view negotiation as a voluntary process that presents opportunities that are not available through other dispute-resolution venues — opportunities that are realistic and achievable.

If these conditions are met, then what can negotiators expect to gain from a settlement? What are the expected outcomes of negotiating rather than litigating Indian water rights conflicts? The literature on negotiated settlements identifies four expected advantages to that process:

— Time and Money. Litigation over Indian water rights can drag on for decades, sometimes generations, and consume enormous amounts of money in legal fees and preparation costs. The expectation is that a negotiated settlement can be reached more quickly with a concomitant reduction in legal costs.

— Finality and Certainty. A quantification of all water rights can remove the big question mark of reserved water rights that might be claimed in the future and allow all parties to proceed with the knowledge that their water rights are protected by the settlement. The objective in a settlement is to resolve all outstanding water issues, not just those that involve narrow legal questions.

— Wet Water. Settlements need not be limited to purely legal issues. This scope allows them to involve a much wider array of issues and solutions. This flexibility can result in the commitment of financial resources and the development of water resources, leading to wet water rather than merely the paper water victories that so often accrue from litigation.

— Comity. After decades of open hostility and legal confrontation, a settlement can bring parties together to work out a solution that offers something for everyone. Indians and Anglos become partners in a process rather than adversaries in a court case. The hope is that old enemies will begin to view one another as neighbors.

In the chapters that follow, each of these expected advantages is discussed in detail in order to assess the extent to which the settlement policy has lived up to its promise. No settlement can achieve perfection in all four of these areas. However, compared to the constraints of prolonged litigation, settlements offer the possibility of a significant improvement over the past.

Conclusion

There is a stark contrast between the federal government's abject parsimony when funding Indian water development and its gratuitous generosity when funding non-Indian water development. For decades the Winters Doctrine remained a hollow promise, and the BIA's Indian irrigation program became a symbol of the federal government's lack of commitment. In the meantime, the water development program for non-Indians continued at a dizzying pace.[41] Big dams and reservoirs were perceived as the vital core of western development, the essential base ingredient of the New Eden. An estimated 30,000 dams were built to divert 475 million af of water in the seventeen western states.[42] No expense was spared as western politicians used federal money to create an irrigation empire—an empire that often stopped at the reservation boundary. Today the Bureau of Reclamation operates 348 reservoirs that provide water for ten million acres of farmland and 31 million people.[43] In addition, the U.S. Army Corps of Engineers operates another 218 dams in its three western divisions.[44] But the BIA has never finished an irrigation project.

The appeal of negotiated settlements rests largely on this history; almost anything would be an improvement over the past. Non-Indian water users became tired of having the threat of Winters hanging over their heads like an anvil on a string. And Indian tribes were tired of winning hollow victories in court and fearful that their only allies, the courts, might turn against them. Pushed by fear, frustration, and a sense that the whole western water situation was slipping from their grasp, whites and Indians sat down at the table and began talking. The dark shadow of 500 years of war, genocide, and broken promises lay across the table; could the negotiators somehow overcome this shadow with a new vision of the future?

Can settlements replace this legacy of enmity with a new era, magically taming old animosities? The search for a panacea is as old as the human race— the elixir that miraculously melts away all problems. This search has always proven futile. Water settlements are not a panacea, although some people have perhaps oversold them as the magic bullet of western water. The beginning of the settlement period was characterized by a heady combination of naiveté and optimism. It was perhaps the first time since the New Deal that there was wide-spread hope on reservations that life just might get a little better. Suddenly there was talk of solutions, of "neighbors" working things out.

But Indian water policy will always be more complex than that. It is a policy that is pushed and shoved from all directions as well-meaning whites, anti-Indian racists, entrenched bureaucrats of both races, and 500 separate and unique Indian tribes all attempt to steer Indian water their way. Perhaps no other policy milieu is subjected to such panoply of interests. In the final analysis, the struggle over Indian water rights is merely a reflection of the larger struggle between two disparate races. Federal Indian policy has always been a tug-of-war between high-minded moral commitment and the incessant clamor of political reality at its grittiest level; a calling for what is right, versus what is merely opportunistic. Settlements reflect this continuous interplay between politics and principle, just as in the first treaty era. Thus, the second treaty era is to a great extent a result of the inconsistencies of Indian policy from past eras, entangled in the struggle between two divergent sets of priorities. It is best to always keep in mind the political and historical context of settlements; rather than seek a perfect blend of harmony and commitment, it is wise to view the settlement era in realistic terms, which means several things.

First, settlements are often characterized as win/win propositions, as though there are no costs, no sacrifices. The win/win notion makes settlements look appealing, but it does not capture the actual reality of bargaining over the West's most precious resource. Rather, it is much more accurate to think of settlements as a give-and-take political process. Congressman Kyl of Arizona alluded to this aspect of settlements in speaking on behalf of the San Carlos settlement:

> Madame Speaker, this is a good and fair settlement. As is usual in any negotiations, some give-and-take was required from all parties. In the end, however, everyone is better off. The tribe gives up damage claims against the United States and other parties, and reduces the amount of its water claim. In return, it avoids costly and lengthy litigation, and gets early use of its water as well as the funding to help develop its water resources and economy. Non-Indian participants give up water and cash, but gain the certainty they need to plan for future growth and development. The United States makes a contribution, but is relieved of damage claims by the tribe. With the settlement, the United States will have fulfilled its responsibilities to the tribe.[45]

In every settlement each party will be expected to give up something. The extent of this sacrifice will be a reflection of the relative political and legal positions of the parties. A good negotiator will give up only what is necessary in order to gain something of perceived greater value. That is the nature of negotiation. Thus every party to a settlement must begin the process by thinking about what they are willing to sacrifice in exchange for a set of benefits.

A second point concerns negotiators. Settlements are still largely negotiated by lawyers. Thus some of the preconceived notions and limitations of client-based representation are still found in settlements. Settlements, for all their promise, can still become contests between people who want to win. A former Hill staffer, who worked on numerous settlements, became disillusioned by the process: "There's nothing worse than when young lawyers get nasty. When you negotiate you believe both sides will act in good faith, but young lawyers seem to view winning as more important than the settlement." This sentiment can be applied to some, but by no means all, of the people who negotiate. Many dedicated attorneys have tirelessly devoted their energy to finding solutions to these problems. But we must remember that settlements still take place within a decision-making framework with inherent limitations, vested interests, and self-serving actions. Settlements may nurture a feeling of neighborliness, but do not expect a love-in.

And finally, there is still widespread disagreement about the wisdom and promise of settling water rights. A broad range of sentiment has been expressed:

We own the water, period. What we're really talking about [in settlements] is the state and the feds taking more of our resources.[46]

Water settlements . . . have apparently been seen by Congress during the 1980s not as ends in themselves but as a means to advance the more basic goal of enabling tribes to develop economically toward self-sufficiency.[47]

In the end we're going to be losers. We always end up being the losers.[48]

Settlements are the key to economic development and self-determination on reservations.[49]

In negotiations there is winning, but the best you can do is get half of what you want.[50]

In some cases tribal decisions are being driven not by the fact that negotiations are so much better, but because the results of litigation are potentially so much worse.[51]

Settlements are one of the best things to happen to Indian country in the last fifteen years.[52]

Talking about negotiations and settlements, Indian tribes have suffered through those settlements and negotiations. We know what has happened.

But tomorrow holds another day. Let's look at it with our decent minds and hearts so that you and I can live together as human beings.[53]

There will never be an absolute consensus that negotiations will lead to a brighter future. But at least settlements present possibilities that are not attainable through litigation — and were inconceivable in the first treaty era.

Vignette: From the Bear to the Snake

On a bitter cold day in January 1863, an encampment of Northwestern Shoshone people slept quietly beside the Bear River just north of the Utah Territory. The first hint of dawn was glowing over the mountains to the east when a sudden fusillade of bullets ripped through the tepees. The massacre of Bear River had begun. Men, women, and children were shot as they ran from their campsites, many of them falling into the frigid waters of the Bear. The attacking army units, lead by Colonel Patrick Conner, tried to surround the camp and shoot the inhabitants as they fled. Within minutes hundreds of Shoshone people went down. One of the soldiers described what happened: "[The soldiers] with one impulse made a rush down the steep banks into [the Indians'] very midst when the work of death commenced in real earnest. . . . The fight lasted four hours and appeared more like a frollick than a fight."[54] Conner claimed his men killed 224 warriors, burned the group's food supply and shelters, and left the surviving women and children to fend for themselves. Other witnesses reported that as many as 400 Indians were killed, including many women and children. Twenty-two soldiers were killed.[55]

Today the Bear River massacre site is a private hay farm. When white people die in battle we create a national monument; when Indian people die in battle, we put the land to seed. There is a small stone obelisk next to the road near the massacre site. A plaque on the obelisk blithely describes the Shoshones as "guilty of hostile attacks on emigrants," and says ninety "combatant women and children" died in the melee. The Boy Scouts and the Daughters of the Utah Pioneers placed this plaque in 1932.

On a warm, sunny day in September 1996, I attended a celebration convened by Shoshone-Bannock tribal officials in the powwow arena on the Fort Hall Reservation. The festivity was called the "Water Rights Agreement Commemoration." After a decade of negotiation and legal challenges over the Snake River, the Fort Hall Water Rights Settlement had been finalized by a court decree.

All the principal tribal officials were there, as well as numerous officials from the state of Idaho, the federal government, and several water agencies. Fred Auck, tribal member, welcomed the guests with a prayer of thanks that all the parties had finally been able to resolve their differences and make peace. Lionel Boyer, the master of ceremonies, called it the start of a new relationship between the Shoshone-Bannock people and the Anglos who surround them. The ceremony continued with four special dances, followed by an honor song. After the speeches and dancing, the whole crowd moved to the tribal bingo hall for a buffalo stew feast. The hall was packed with tribal members and a smattering of white visitors, who looked quite conspicuous in the sea of brown faces. The mood was upbeat and hopeful, and as I sat eating my buffalo stew I could not help but marvel at the contrast between this event and the tragic encounter on the Bear River 133 years ago.

The Snake River drains nearly all of southern Idaho, and forms the northwestern boundary of the Fort Hall Indian Reservation. Like most western rivers, the Snake has been the subject of fierce conflicts over water use. The Fort Bridger treaty of 1868 established the reservation and strongly encouraged the two tribes that lived there, the Shoshones and Bannocks, to "commence farming" upon government-authorized "improvements." The treaty promised that the President of the United States would "provide for protecting the rights of the Indian settlers in these improvements."[56] A BIA irrigation project was authorized in 1907, but was never fully developed, and the president did a very poor job of protecting the rights of the Indian farmers, especially in regard to water.

In 1985 the state of Idaho and the tribes entered into a government-to-government agreement to attempt to negotiate their differences over water rights. This negotiation ultimately led to the passage of the 1990 settlement act. It is one of the more creative settlements and relies on a number of innovative arrangements, including a tribal water bank, the use of federal storage space, and a recognition of the importance of maintaining instream flows for habitat preservation, recreation, and aesthetics. As with any settlement, it is not perfect, and there were detractors. But thus far the problems have been ironed out and the court decree is in place.

Lionel Boyer was on the tribal council when the discussion of a water settlement began. I met with him in his office at Fort Hall in an old, creaky frame building that used to be the BIA hospital. It is now the Tribal Fisheries Department, and Lionel is the tribes' Fisheries Policy Representative. He wears his hair in long graying braids, which are tied together at his chest. He is soft-spoken yet quite forceful in expressing his opinions. His father was tribal chairman in the fifties when the tribe signed an early form of water settlement called the Michaud Agreement.

Lionel acknowledged the imperfections in the settlement but offered a generally upbeat assessment: "In the negotiation the tribes came out on the positive end. It was something they said we had to do; if we hadn't we would have been left without any water. So in essence it was a positive move." Mr. Boyer hopes the water settlement will solve a long-standing problem on the reservation; Indian people are often the last on the ditch and by the time the water reaches them the quantity is inadequate. "I gave up farming because I couldn't get water. My dad fought with that problem too; they used to lock his headgate so he couldn't get water. The amount of watering time allocated to tribal members wasn't enough. In my case I had to go about a mile to turn the headgate on. By the time the water got to my fields, it was time to end."

For the future, Lionel sees a different approach to the use of water. He wants to see the tribe use its water for instream flows: "The water should be provided for the natural resources — for the benefit of the natural rivers, fish and game. Instream flow is an important use." He also expressed concern for the quality of water on the reservation. Some of the groundwater along the Snake River is now polluted due to pesticide saturation. Mr. Boyer wants to see that problem solved.

Kesley Edmo provided a less sanguine view of the settlement. I met him at tribal headquarters, where he sat smoking next to a "no smoking" sign. He is bent with age and uses a walker, but is as independent and strong-willed as ever. He was on the tribal council for 33 years.[57]

"When the negotiations first began, we went down to the Justice Department. They were going to tell us what to do with our water. We decided to tell them what we wanted to do with our water." At that point in the interview Mr. Edmo laboriously turned his head and stared at me. "You know, we're first in time."

"Yes, I know," I replied.

"I like telling white people that." A trace of a smile appeared.

"Did you support the settlement?" I asked.

"There was a referendum on the settlement. It passed, but not by a big margin. The rest of the council went to Washington to sign the settlement, but I didn't go because a lot of members opposed it, and I was representing them."

Keith Tinno, the vice chairman of the tribes, was more positive: "It's a good agreement, it's not excellent, but it's not bad. The water we agreed to was pretty much the same as the water we've had in the past under the BIA, but now it's in the tribes' name."

One of the water issues that is obviously important to tribal members is the preservation of the wetlands along the Snake, an area known as the Snake River bottoms. It is lush in grass and riparian habitat, and supports a healthy population of bald eagles. There are several springs in the area, and the tribe's youth organization built a wooden fence around some of them to keep out cattle.

Gail Martin, the tribe's cultural research director, explained to me that the tribe has a buffalo herd that sometimes grazes the bottoms, and tribal members go there to cut native grasses. "We don't want this area developed, we want it left in a natural state," she said. For Ms. Martin, the value of the settlement is that it gives the tribe the water and authority it needs to protect the reservation's riparian environment in a manner that fits the needs of the tribe.

For many tribal members the real measure of the value of the water settlement is whether it solves common day-to-day problems; their support for it is contingent on seeing practical and immediate results. One problem on the reservation, which was mentioned by several tribal members, concerns the rotation schedule for irrigation water. According to tribal members, they are last on the rotation schedule and often get shortchanged. Venus Mitchell spoke eloquently of this problem. She is a 77-year-old tribal member and still actively farms on the reservation. She lives alone in a remote part of the reservation called Lincoln Creek.

"When I was a little girl, I dreamed of owning a hundred cattle. Well, now I do. I grow mostly hay, but last year I grew some peas because I heard they were good for cattle. But I'm always short of water. I'm last on the ditch. Do you know what they call the ditch?" she asked.

"No, what do they call it?"

"Little Indian Ditch," she said, smiling. "They call it Little Indian, but we're the last ones on the ditch to get water, and by the time it gets to me somebody has used too much, or the water has been lost into the ditch."

I asked why the tribal members were placed last in the rotation. Mrs. Mitchell did not hesitate to answer.

"The Whites pay O&M [operation and maintenance charges] but the Indians don't, so the BIA favors them."

"Why don't you complain about it?"

"Oh, I do, but those BIA people don't have ears." Mrs. Mitchell expressed hope that the new settlement will solve her water problem. As I got up to leave, she opened a large container on the kitchen table and slid it toward me. "Here, take some buffalo jerky, and take some extra for your friends."

Gail Martin expressed reserved optimism that the settlement may indeed solve the rotation problem. The settlement provides $7 million for a new water management plan, which presents an opportunity to change the current watering schedule. Ms. Martin also indicated that the tribe at some point would like to assume management of the entire irrigation project, but that may take some time.

Resolving these conflicts over water may take more than a single settlement. Animosities run deep. One tribal member told me her husband has threatened to shoot an Anglo farmer who keeps turning off the water at their headgate. "My husband practically sits on the headgate. He has to or we won't get our water."

In regard to the future, many tribal members expressed concern for both the quantity and quality of water on the reservation. Genevieve Edmo, the tribes' land use director, made this point clearly: "We have to have water to survive, and it has to be good quality water. I would hate to see the river die. It is slowly dying now because of all the stuff that is flowing into it. We must keep the water spirits going and pray for them. As soon as the water spirits are gone the river is dead. When life in the river is gone, the river is dead." Perhaps the settlement will provide an opportunity for the Shoshones and Bannocks to keep the river alive.

This vignette began with a description of the Bear River Massacre—one of the darkest chapters in American history, and then described the festive commemoration of the Snake River settlement. The stark contrast between these two events clearly demonstrates how Indians and Anglos can fundamentally change the way they relate to each other. The settlement era is an opportunity to explore new ways to build relationships, new ways to avoid conflict, and new ways to approach old problems. The *potential* for significant progress on age-old water conflicts is the promise of the second treaty era, to move from the Bear River mentality to the Snake River mentality.

3

Decades and Dollars

A Legal Steal

In the nineteenth century the internecine war against the Indians continued relentlessly throughout the West. In Arizona the conflict was particularly intense due to the paucity of arable land and water. As a result, a series of bloody massacres took place. One of the earliest occurred in Canyon del Muerto — the Canyon of the Dead, so named because many Navajos were shot to death there in 1805 by Spanish soldiers.[1] Many years later, in 1871, a peaceful band of Apaches, mostly women and children, were nearly wiped out by an attack at Camp Grant. And the repeated massacres of the peaceful Yavapais gave Arizona three gory place-names: Skull Valley, Bloody Basin, and Skeleton Cave. The perpetrators of these crimes were often hailed as heroes; they were performing the important task of cleansing the land of Indians so that white settlers could farm the bottom lands along Arizona's few rivers and streams.

In the broad valleys of central Arizona the farmers found what they were looking for — flat, arable land that needed only water and the plow to produce an abundant crop. Indian people were already living there and had been farming successfully for centuries. It became necessary to displace them. Three tribes were in the way; the Yavapais, the Pimas, and the Apaches.

The Yavapais were labeled Apaches, even though they were in no way related to Apaches, and forcibly relocated to the San Carlos Apache Reservation. Only later would they be allowed to return to small parcels of their aboriginal lands.

The Pimas in the region were gradually forced off their farms by aggressive whites through what the Indian agent called "Nothing more or less than a legal steal."[2] At that time the fate of the Pima Indians was in the hands of Irvin McDowell, a former Civil War general whose bungling had resulted in the

Union's humiliating defeat in the first battle at Bull Run. Fortunately, in regard to the Pimas, McDowell exercised better judgment; he wrote to his superiors that the Pimas were "susceptible of being civilized"[3] and therefore worth rescuing from greedy settlers. Eventually reservations were established for the Pimas in the Gila River Valley, but the theft of their water continued.

The Apaches of central Arizona also suffered at the hands of local whites. In 1863 the Indian agent concluded that the Apaches, "in contending with a race who, under the circumstances, can feel no sympathy with them, . . . must soon be swept from the face of the earth."[4] Somehow the Apaches persevered until General William Tecumseh Sherman, a man not known for humanitarian impulses,[5] was moved to suggest that a reservation be created for the Apaches because "there is an implied condition that they should not be permitted to starve."[6] Many people in the region disagreed with that assessment, but eventually a reservation was set aside at San Carlos. However, that did not prevent local whites from diverting the water flowing across the Apache reservation. In 1880 the Indian Commissioner commented that, in Arizona, there was a "prevailing opinion . . . that Indians have no water rights which white men are bound to respect."[7]

The ruling in the Winters case had little initial impact on the water rights of the Pimas, the Yavapais, and the Apaches of central Arizona. But gradually, through a series of court victories and a growing sensitivity to the injustices of the past, Indian water rights gained recognition. By the time the massive Central Arizona Project (CAP) was initiated in the 1970s, the water rights of American Indians could no longer be ignored. The days of the legal steal were over.

In 1978 the state of Arizona filed suit to determine the water rights of all parties in the Gila River basin. The Gila River meanders across the entire width of central Arizona. The main stem and its tributaries provide the only surface water for an enormous region that encompasses Phoenix, huge agribusiness farms, numerous mines, and eleven Indian reservations. The case covered 65,000 claims filed by 22,000 parties. A greater water rights nightmare could hardly be imagined. Anglo farmers and miners, and the cities and towns in the region, greatly feared that the Indian tribes might win the lion's share of the water rights in the case. Suddenly there was widespread interest in negotiating with Indian tribes rather than summarily stealing their water.

The prevailing notion was that both time and money could be saved if the tribes' water rights could be settled — and thus limited — through negotiation rather than prolonged litigation. The push to settle Indian water claims in Arizona helped initiate the federal policy of negotiation for all Indian water claims throughout the nation.

The desire to save time and money has been a prominent theme in all negotiations. The first settlement act, Ak-Chin, declared that "it is the policy of Congress to resolve, without costly and lengthy litigation, the claims of the Ak-Chin Indian Community for water based upon failure of the United States to meet its trust responsibility."[8] Similar language appears in most of the other settlements. A sufficient number of settlements have been passed now to assess how much time and money have actually been saved; do settlements live up to this claim? First this chapter will compare how long it takes to negotiate rather than litigate Indian water rights claims. Then the chapter will examine the relative costs of settlements and litigation.

Aamodt Dammit

In 1966 Lee Aamodt, a scientist from Los Alamos, New Mexico, joined his non-Indian neighbors in a court case to clarify their water rights. Some Anglos in the area viewed the nearby Nambe Pueblo as a potential threat to their water supply. More than a quarter of a century later the governor of the Nambe Pueblo offered his opinion of that case: "It's been going on for twenty-seven years and it's going to continue for another twenty-seven years."[9] This case, *New Mexico v. Aamodt*, is one of the longest running cases in the federal court system. Whole generations of lawyers have come and gone during this litigation, and the issue is still unresolved. People working on the case are so frustrated with the lack of progress that they routinely use the rhyming epithet of "Aamodt Dammit."

Aamodt is not an isolated example; water conflicts on many reservations recur over and over, going through a succession of court cases. The water rights for the Pyramid Lake tribe have been in court sporadically since 1913. A similar situation developed on the San Carlos Reservation. These court cases seem designed to employ lawyers for long periods of time, like a kind of litigious Rock of Sisyphus that keeps rolling back down the interminable hill of water law.[10]

Much of the impetus for negotiating settlements grew out of frustration with the glacial progress of Indian water cases. The Reagan administration, in announcing its preference for negotiation in 1982, noted that one of the cases then being litigated was first filed in 1915. Reagan's secretary of the interior, James Watt, noted that they wanted to settle the fifty Indian water cases then in the courts "quickly through negotiated settlements."[11] The objective was to "speed the settlement of Indian water claims."[12] In hindsight it appears particularly naive to assume that the most complex, contentious, and long-lasting lawsuits in the land could suddenly be settled "quickly," but the Reagan/Watt statement was an accurate reflection of the hopes of many westerners who had grown weary of the bitter water feud between Anglos and Indians.

Two years after Watt's announcement, a much more realistic assessment was provided by the Interior Department's assistant secretary for water and science: "These issues historically have taken years to resolve, and the impression that this program [of negotiating settlements] will resolve the 50+ cases quickly would be inaccurate and counterproductive."[13] Although negotiation may be less time-consuming than some litigation, it would be a mistake to assume that negotiations can be completed quickly. Quite often settlements take many years to negotiate. Peter Sly notes that "the weakness of the negotiation process is its lack of structure, which can consume time and effort at high cost without measurable results."[14]

There are numerous examples. In 1982 the Reagan administration began to actively encourage tribes to negotiate. According to a 1982 Department of the Interior memorandum there were four negotiations that were already "proceeding" at that time. It is worth noting how much additional time it took to complete each of those four settlements:

Fort Peck, settled in 1985 (three years)
San Luis Rey Mission Bands, settled in 1988 (six years)
Pyramid Lake, settled in 1990 (eight years)
Yakima, still unresolved

In 1980 the Department of the Interior began conducting "technical studies to support water rights negotiations" on 44 reservations. Twenty years later only seven of those 44 reservations have signed water settlements.[15]

When Secretary Watt announced his negotiation policy in 1982 he ordered the BIA to select "candidate tribes" that were "ripe" for negotiation. BIA selected five tribes. Again it is worth noting how much time has been spent in these negotiations:

Warm Springs, still unresolved
Northern Cheyenne, 1992 (ten years)
Fort Berthold, still unresolved
Uintah and Ouray, 1992 (ten years)
Southern Utes, 1988 (six years)[16]

In 1979 the state of Montana established the Montana Reserved Water Rights Compact Commission to facilitate negotiation. At the time many observers thought it would expedite the settlement process and serve as a model for other states. But in 1985, six years after the Commission was formed, one author expressed the frustration felt by many: "Although Montana's negotiation process could conceivably be more efficient than litigation, to date this efficiency has yet to be demonstrated."[17] That record has improved with the passage of time; three reservations have completed settlements in Montana—

Fort Peck, Northern Cheyenne, and Rocky Boys. The Crows have an agreement with the state but it has yet to be approved by Congress.[18]

On the other hand, some settlements have been achieved in a comparatively short time. The Salt River Pima-Maricopa settlement was signed after slightly more than two years of actual negotiations. The Colorado Utes signed an agreement four years after negotiations began; two years later that agreement was ratified by Congress. Fort Hall and Fort McDowell required five years of negotiations.

A review of the first fourteen settlements provides an indication of how much time elapsed between the initiation of negotiation and the passage of a settlement act:

Ak-Chin. Litigation was prepared in 1976 but not filed. An inadequate settlement was passed in 1978, and a second settlement became law in 1984, eight years after legal action was initiated.

Tohono O'odham (Papago). The original case was filed in 1975. A settlement was passed in 1982 but the original lawsuit has never been dismissed due to problems with the settlement. A technical amendment was passed in 1992.

Fort Peck–Montana Compact. Litigation was filed in 1979, and a compact between the state and the tribe was signed in 1985.

San Luis Rey (the Mission tribes). The settlement, passed in 1988, grew out of lawsuits filed in 1972.

Colorado Ute. A lawsuit was filed in 1976. Negotiations began in 1984, and a settlement act became law in 1988.

Salt River Pima-Maricopa. The first case was filed in 1974. Negotiations began late in 1985 and resulted in a settlement in 1988.

Fort Hall. A general adjudication was initiated in 1985. A settlement was signed in 1990, although the lawsuit was not dismissed until 1996.

Fort McDowell. Five years of negotiation led to a settlement act in 1990.

Fallon Paiute-Shoshone/Truckee-Carson–Pyramid Lake. This combined settlement became law in 1990. The Fallon settlement was an attempt to resolve a series of past injustices that had been dealt with ineffectively in a 1978 statute.

The Pyramid Lake settlement was part of a long-running water conflict between the tribe, local irrigators, and the Reno metropolitan area.

Jicarilla Apache. Negotiations took place sporadically for eight years, eventually yielding a settlement in 1992, with technical amendments in 1994. A final court decree was entered in April 1999.

Northern Cheyenne. Formal negotiations began in 1982. The settlement was passed in 1992, and a final court decree was entered in 1995.

Northern Ute. This act, passed in 1992, grew out of the failure of the government to keep promises made in the 1965 deferral agreement. The accompanying compact with the state of Utah has yet to be ratified.

San Carlos Apache. The general adjudication for the Gila River was filed in 1975, but this tribe's water right troubles began long before that. A settlement was first introduced in 1990 but did not become law until 1992, and a minor technical amendment was passed in 1994.

Yavapai/Prescott. Another Gila River case, the settlement became law in 1994.

Clearly, it can take a long time to negotiate an Indian water settlement. Also, it is not really possible to accurately compare litigation and negotiation in regard to the time they typically require because the latter is often a result of the former. Indeed, negotiations appear to make the most notable progress when a lawsuit hangs over the heads of the parties; litigation forces all parties to consider the possibility of losing in court as an alternative to negotiation. And once an agreement has been ratified it may not signal the end of the process.[19] Many reservations are experiencing problems implementing and finalizing their settlements — the subject of the next chapter. If we include prenegotiation litigation, and the time necessary to renegotiate and successfully implement settlements, the entire process becomes time-consuming indeed.

Negotiation is not necessarily a time-efficient alternative to litigation. Both negotiation and litigation have the potential to absorb many years of effort. However, negotiation has proven to be an effective tool in resolving at least some Indian water conflicts in a time frame that looks favorable when compared to the many horror stories of endless litigation. Perhaps the most relevant contemporary comparison is with the Big Horn court battle described in chapter 1. A few years of negotiation certainly look preferable when placed in that context. On the other hand, some negotiations have dragged on for years with little progress; thirteen tribes that are currently engaged in formal negotiations appeared on the 1980 list of forty-four tribes described above; twenty years is a long time to negotiate the "speedy" settlement of an issue. In the contentious realm of Indian water conflicts, speed is a relative concept.

Cheaper by the Dozen

To many people, the issue of Indian water rights is a matter of justice; the United States is duty-bound to honor the treaties it signed with Indian nations. But for others, it is simply a matter of money; prolonged litigation generates costs for all parties. In the early 1980s a group of wealthy western businessmen, each from a major corporation, formed the Western Regional Council and began pushing for a termination of all Indian water claims based on the Winters Doctrine. It was their view that such claims were stalling economic development in the West. Once again the Indians were in the way. The solution proposed by the Western Regional Council was for Congress to pass a law that unilaterally imposed deadlines and specific limits. Then, with the Indian water rights problem out of the way, economic development on non-Indian lands could continue apace.

It did not happen that way. A wall of opposition arose to block such a blatantly unfair solution. What happened next was something of a surprise. The two opposing sides came together and decided that all parties might benefit if these issues could be resolved on a case-by-case basis. Following Secretary Watt's 1982 announcement of his policy of negotiating agreements, an unlikely assortment of people sent him a letter lauding his "excellent start." The letter was signed by representatives of the Western Regional Council, the Council of Energy Resource Tribes, the Western Governors' Policy Office, the Native American Rights Fund, and the National Congress of American Indians. Indians hoped to get money to develop their water resources and reservation economies, Anglos hoped to get clear title to water for economic development, and all sides wanted to save money on lawyers and court cases.

As part of the push for negotiations, there was a near-universal assumption that negotiations could save money. The exorbitant cost of the Big Horn adjudication loomed overhead, reminding everyone that millions could be spent on lawyers and still not resolve the conflict. John Thorsen, who later became the special master in the Gila River adjudication, wrote in 1985 that "most observers agree that it costs much less to talk than to sue."[20] From a congressional perspective, settlements look like a good deal: "Regardless of budgetary constraints, water settlements are a . . . member of Congress' dream come true."[21]

There are several questions concerning the money question. First, is negotiation truly cheaper than litigation? A second question concerns the distribution of benefits; who is actually receiving the financial payoff, if there is one? And third, which parties are bearing the financial burden? Each of these questions will be addressed in this chapter. But first it is worth taking a look at some numbers simply to understand the overall spending context.

In recent years, funding for Indian programs generally has not fared well. In constant dollars, per capita federal expenditures for American Indians fell from $7,000 in fiscal year 1975, to below $3,000 in fiscal year 1998.[22] Funding for the BIA has been a consistent target in recent years. For fiscal year 1996 House Republicans wanted to cut the BIA budget by nearly a third. After persistent lobbying, the cuts were reduced to 8 percent. For succeeding fiscal years BIA appropriations have remained essentially static. The Clinton administration consistently asked for increases, and the Congress has just as consistently pared funding from the administration's requests. For fiscal year 2000, the administration requested $1.9 billion and complained that "a procession of Congressional budget cuts have inflicted serious damage to the BIA's administrative structure."[23] Congress appropriated $1.8 billion.

In regard to Indian water, the Congress has appropriated the required funding for all the settlements except one (Northern Ute) and continues to fund the negotiation teams, albeit at a reduced rate. The overall funding picture for Indian water programs can be seen in tables 3.1 and 3.2.

Table 3.1 includes both the requested and actual expenditures for the federally funded water settlements for fiscal years 1990 to 1999. The fiscal years are in a row across the top of the table. The requested budget, identified by an "R" following the number of the fiscal year, is how much money was requested in the president's budget. Just to the right of that figure is the amount of money actually appropriated by Congress and signed into law, indicated by an "A" following the number of the fiscal year. Generally, the Congress has fully funded the settlements. The one exception, the Northern Ute settlement, was much more expensive because the government's legal exposure was tremendous due to the failure of the government to honor an agreement signed in 1965 (more on this in chapter 8).

Indeed, when the situation calls for it, Congress is willing to spend more money on a settlement than was requested. Thus, while Congress has been parsimonious with other Indian programs, it has spent the money necessary to keep settlements on track.

Table 3.2 compares spending on Indian water in four different categories.

Table 3.1 Indian Water Settlements Funding Requests (R) and Appropriations (A), Fiscal Years 1990–1999 (in millions of dollars)

Settlement	90R-90A	91R-91A	92R-92A	93R-93A	94R-94A	95R-95A	96R-96A	97R-97A	98R-98A	99R-99A
Tohono*	12.7-12.7	0	0	0	3.2-3.2	2.3-2.3	3-1.5	0	0	0
Colorado Ute	5-19.5	15-14.9	15-15	0.62-0.62	0	0	0	0	0	0
San Luis Rey	5-32.4	0	0	0	0	0	0	0	0	0
Salt River	5-23.7	23.8-23.7	0	0.1-0.1	1.4-1.4	0	0	0	0	0
Fort McDowell	—	—	23-23	0	2-2	0	0	0	0	0
Fort Hall	—	—	12-12	5-5	5.2-5.2	0	0	0	0	0
Fallon	—	—	3-3	8-8	11.2-11.2	11.2-11.2	8-8	8-8	0	0
Pyramid Lake	—	—	25-25	8-8	8.7-8.7	8-8	10-10	12-12	3.5-3.5	2.5-2.5
Utah Utes	—	—	—	—	58.9-17.2	62.3-20.7	25-25	25-25	41.5-25	31-25
San Carlos	—	—	—	—	38.4-38.4	0	0	0	0	0
Jicarilla	—	—	—	—	2-2	2-2	2-2	0	0	0
Northern Cheyenne	—	—	—	—	0	22.7-16.9	25.6-25.6	15.4-15.4	5.5-5.5	0
Yavapai	—	—	—	—	—	0.3-0.3	0	0	0	0

Source: Interior Department Budget Office

Note: The Fort Peck Settlement is not included because it did not require federal funds. The Ak-Chin settlement is not included because it had already been fully funded by 1990.

*By FY1990, $44 million had already been appropriated for the Tohono O'odham settlement.

Table 3.2 Federal Funding for Indian Water Rights and Resources, Fiscal Years 1985–1995 (in millions of dollars)

Fiscal Year	Water Resource Program	Water Neg/Lit	NIIP	Settle-ments
1985	$7.1	$4.3	$9.9	$62.5*
1986	$8.8	$10.4	$0.9	$0.0
1987	$9.0	$2.9	$5.0	$0.0
1988	$9.0	$2.9	$3.5	$10.7
1989	$9.0	$6.9	$10.0	$88.3
1990	$9.2	$6.9	$10.0	$88.3
1991	$10.3	$9.8	$17.9	$38.6
1992	$9.9	$10.6	$16.3	$86.0
1993	$9.9	$10.5	$15.2	$29.1
1994	$7.9	$15.7	$25.7	$98.3
1995	$7.9	$14.5	$26.4	$61.3
1996	$7.9	$11.9	$25.5	$72.1
1997	$7.9	$11.0	$25.5	$60.4
1998	$7.9	$11.0	$25.5	$34.0
1999	$8.0	$11.0	$25.5	$27.5
Total	$129.7	$140.3	$242.9	$680.1

Source: Office of Management and Budget, Accounts 34020 and 34420, and Budget Office of the Department of the Interior.

*This is a total of spending on settlements for FY1980–1985.

The first column displays expenditures for water resources programs on Indian reservations.[24] The second column is the amount of money spent on the process of negotiation and litigation, primarily attorney fees and preparation studies. The third column lists annual appropriations for the Navajo Indian Irrigation Project (NIIP), which was authorized by statute in 1962. NIIP is by far the largest water project undertaken on an Indian reservation that was built to serve Indians (in contrast to the many large projects that serve primarily non-Indians). The final column on the right of table 3.2 totals the actual expenditures listed in table 3.1 (plus FY 1980–89), and thus provides a picture of how much the federal government has spent on the water settlements; it does not include the modest amount of money that states and local entities have contributed to the settlements, or indirect expenses (discussed below).

There are several trends evident in these tables. First, the total amount of money spent on Indian water each year is a minuscule part of the federal budget. Trying to balance a $1.8 trillion budget by cutting Indian water programs is like trying to save the *Titanic* by bailing with a teaspoon. Second, table 3.2 shows only actual appropriations; the amounts requested by the administration are not shown as they are in table 3.1, but an analysis of the budget requests reveals that Congress is much more willing to make cuts in the Indian water programs that are not the result of settlements. The discussion of beneficiaries below explains why this is so.

Third, the most obvious lesson from the data in these tables is that the settlements have dramatically increased spending on Indian water and related programs. For 130 years the Indian water development program has been a tragicomedy, but suddenly the federal government has found the wherewithal to spend money for Indian water. Perhaps this is the greatest legacy of the water settlement era. Some have argued that the settlements represent a sellout for "token wealth" similar to selling great tracts of land for a few glass beads.[25] But compared to historic spending for Indian water, the settlements have dramatically increased the tribes' funding. Spending for settlements built to a crescendo in the early 1990s but has tapered off since then. However, with twenty-five tribes currently at the negotiation table, spending may once again increase.

In the last fifteen years the federal government has spent a little less than a billion dollars on the thirteen federally funded water settlements (Fort Peck was not federally funded). Additional funding was made available through state cost-shares and accounts in the Bureau of Reclamation budget, bringing the actual total to approximately $1 billion in direct costs. Is this cheaper than litigating those cases? In 1981 the Department of the Interior estimated that it cost an average of $3 million to litigate an Indian water rights case.[26] If the Interior Department estimate is accurate, the thirteen settlements would have cost the federal government $39 million. The $3 million estimate is probably too low—the Big Horn case makes that point well.[27] Also, that estimate does not include the state's litigation costs. A 1984 study by the Western States Water Council surveyed the litigation costs incurred by several western states and concluded that "a great deal of money has been expended litigating Indian reserved water rights claims."[28]

Still, settlements are not cheap. Federal policymakers, even those fervently in support of negotiated settlements, have long worried about the costs of the settlements. Budget conscious officials in the administration, particularly the Office of Management and Budget (OMB), have long contended that the criteria for spending should be based on legal liability, that is, no settlement should cost more than the federal government's legal exposure to claims and damages. Others argue that the settlements are simply part of the government's larger trust responsibility and should help fund long-term goals such as tribal economic development.

The first Bush administration tried to respond to both of these views when it developed the 1990 Criteria and Procedures, which set up guidelines for negotiations. They limit settlement funding to two objectives: "calculable legal exposure — litigation cost and judgment obligations if the case is lost" and "costs related to Federal trust or programmatic responsibilities."[29]

Advocates of settlements have never been comfortable with the "legal exposure" criteria and have routinely ignored it. There is widespread agreement that settlements have exceeded that limit. This agreement has led some people to conclude that settlements are more expensive than litigation. According to a justice department attorney, "It's actually cheaper to litigate because we can win a case without the big output by the federal government for the settlement, which often calls for a big outlay." An OMB official also thought that negotiation was more expensive: "You are better off to keep it in court. It's cheaper." An Interior Department spokesperson made a similar point: "I don't think negotiation saves any money, and maybe even costs more money than litigation. If you break even you're in pretty good shape."

Funding settlements beyond legal exposure was often necessary in order to generate sufficient political support: "I think if the government tried to limit its costs to litigation exposure, there would be very few settlements."[30] But gradually this increased level of spending began to focus attention on cost. The Reagan and Bush administrations opposed a number of settlements because of their cost. And the current emphasis on budget cutting has engendered even more scrutiny. A House subcommittee staffer recently commented that "Now OMB may be thinking that it may be less expensive to litigate. In the late 1980s we did a bunch of settlements, and the cost got people's attention." A water attorney with the BIA made a similar statement: "The budget situation is more complicated now. We used to throw money at settlements; later OMB and others said no to that."

So far this discussion has centered on the costs of implementing settlements — the output of the process. A related question concerns the costs of that process; is the negotiation process cheaper than trying a case in court? Many observers believe that extended litigation is a necessary prelude to negotiation: "Although some proponents of negotiation extol it as an alternative to the courts, nothing settles a dispute better than the combined force of the strong arm of the court . . . and active negotiation."[31] John Folk-Williams notes that, "Often the necessary precursor to negotiation is a litigation strategy aimed at winning recognition of the power of one or more parties. Such recognition may occur only after prolonged litigation."[32]

In the early years of the Reagan administration an Interior Department report explained that "frequently the non-Indian competing water users are not interested in reasonable negotiations and the threat of litigation is needed in order to get them to the bargaining table."[33] An Interior Department official emphasized that point: "We should litigate at the same time that we negotiate; people then take you more seriously. One drives the other." In other words, the costs of litigation should be considered part of the procedural costs of the negotiation strategy. These are not competing costs, but cumulative costs.

In addition, the cost of preparing for negotiation is virtually the same as preparing for a court case, so even if litigation does not precede negotiation, all the studies and preparatory work still have to be completed: "Settlement negotiations, like litigation, are costly and time consuming because they usually require hiring experts and lawyers and preparing technical studies."[34] As one observer noted, "In litigation the money goes to lawyers; in negotiation it goes to engineers and economists." The costs of conducting the actual negotiation are also high. All parties must hire attorneys and sometimes engineers and economists, and occasionally facilitators, often at great expense.

These procedural costs are sufficiently high that the BIA has not been able to keep up with the demand. By the early 1990s tribes were literally lining up for federal negotiation teams, but the Department of the Interior did not have the money to field all of the requested teams. One tribe complained that "Inadequate water rights negotiation funding has been an obstacle to progress in our dispute as it is for other water rights disputes around the country."[35]

In short, it is doubtful that settlements actually save the federal government money. The question then becomes, "Is settlement funding spent in a more productive or useful fashion?" Defenders of settlements point out that litigation throws money at attorneys, but settlement funding can be allocated for many useful goals, including tribal economic enhancement, water and land development, and cultural preservation. Are settlements serving the larger goal of the trust responsibility? Who are the primary beneficiaries of the settlement funding?

Who Benefits?

Every settlement is unique, just as every Indian tribe is unique. But there are certain trends in the settlements—common devices used to assuage age-old hatreds and purchase the good humor of objectionists. Typically this is some combination of water and money, and, occasionally, more abstract benefits concerning rights or privileges. In regard to pecuniary benefits, the most common benefit for Indian tribes is a trust fund. The list below identifies the dollar amount and the purposes of these trust funds:

Ak-Chin. The two settlements for this reservation did not establish a traditional trust fund. Instead, the settlement pays damages of $15 million, to be used for "general community purposes," provides one-time grants totaling $3.4 million, and pays $1 million for a water conservation fund. In addition, the federal government agreed to pay project operation and maintenance costs in perpetuity.

Tohono O'odham (Papago). Provides a $15 million tribal trust fund, a cooperative fund consisting of $5.25 million in federal funds, and an equal amount from state and local sources (this fund was extended by the 1992 amendment).

Fort Peck–Montana Compact. No federal funding.

San Luis Rey (the Mission tribes). Contains a $30 million tribal development fund.

Colorado Ute. Provides $17.5 million tribal development fund for the Southern Utes and $32 million for the Ute Mountain Utes.

Salt River Pima-Maricopa. Provides $33.5 million for a community trust fund ($3 million from the state of Arizona) and $17 million for the rehabilitation of existing water facilities.

Fort Hall. Provides a $10 million tribal development fund.

Fort McDowell. Provides a $23 million water development fund.

Fallon Paiute-Shoshone/Truckee-Carson–Pyramid Lake. This combined settlement generated $43 million for the Fallon Paiute-Shoshone settlement trust fund, $40 million for Pyramid Lake for an economic development fund, and $25 million for a fisheries fund.

Jicarilla Apache. Provides $6 million for a water resources development trust fund.

Northern Cheyenne. Provides $21.5 million for a reserved water rights settlement trust fund, of which $11.5 million must be loaned to the state of Montana to refurbish the Tongue River Dam.

Northern Ute. Provides $125 million for a tribal development fund.

San Carlos Apache. Provides $41.4 million for a tribal development fund (this includes $3 million in funds from Arizona).

Yavapai/Prescott. No trust fund.

These trust/development funds are an unprecedented investment in Indian country. But this money did not come without a price. The government has negotiated a peace by treating all stakeholders to a piece of the pie. Like a fine liqueur served at a dinner party, federal money has lubricated the social interaction of negotiation and settlement. It could be argued that every settlement except Fort Peck, San Luis Rey, and Yavapai/Prescott has been settled by simply pouring federal money into the equation.[36] This way the set of beneficiaries includes Anglos as well as Indians, and everyone has an incentive to reach an agreement.

It is a matter of politics. Indian settlements are politically feasible only if money is spent on mitigating their impact on Anglos. Such an approach meets the mandate of the no-harm rule described in chapter 1. Anglos may have to give up control over some water, but they are compensated in return. There is a certain degree of justice in this.

But funding for Anglos sometimes goes beyond simple compensation. Sometimes Indian settlements have been used in the age-old strategy of the "Indian blanket," which refers to tying a dubious Anglo project to an Indian program in hopes that the added political support will help push an otherwise unacceptable Anglo expenditure through Congress. One example is the San Juan–Chama Project, which simultaneously authorized the Chama Project for Albuquerque and the Navajo Indian Irrigation Project. Among the settlements the most obvious example is the Animas–La Plata Project in Colorado. That project was politically moribund until it was attached to an Indian water settlement. Suddenly, an old-fashioned pork barrel project was being touted as the savior of the Utes.

In a similar vein, the Central Arizona Project has, over time, evolved from a whites-only project into one claimed to have great benefits for Indians. Even the Central Utah Project, which diverts water away from the Uintah and Ouray Reservation, was sometimes promoted as a pro-Indian project because one of its small components provided some benefits to tribal members. These examples of the Indian blanket involve the construction of new projects, but sometimes the blanket is used to cover other special favors, such as loan forgiveness or a reduction in water charges. All of these cost the government money, so the Indian blanket has the effect of dramatically increasing the costs of settlements.

Of course, this increased funding does not go to Indians, but it does create a kind of political insurance for settlements; western legislators, who are quite adept at pushing their pet projects through the sausage-making process in Congress, will remain staunch supporters of settlement funding as long as the Indian blanket keeps their Anglo constituents warm. John Duffy, former chairman of the Interior Department Working Group on Indian Water Settlements, made this point quite succinctly: "The settlements will continue to be funded because they have the same political strength as all other western issues — more senators per capita than anyone else. These settlements were designed to have large non-Indian components. They are indeed wrapped in the Indian blanket."[37] This practice may be why Congress is more willing to fund settlements than other Indian water programs.

The political imperatives of the Indian blanket raises an interesting question: How much of the benefits of Indian water settlements are actually allocated to non-Indians? Christopher Kenney of the Department of the Interior offered this opinion: "Most of the cost [in settlements] is to mitigate impacts on Anglos, that is a big part of the cost."[38] Herb Becker, former director of the Office of Tribal Justice in the Justice Department, made the same claim: "In the past, the big money in settlements went to satisfy non-Indian interests. Politics is supporting that process."[39] A budget official in the BIA pointed out that, even though Congress cut the overall BIA budget, the water settlement funding got through relatively unscathed. His explanation: "Arguably these settlements benefit the non-Indians the most, so the congressional delegation sees a win/win situation in funding these settlements."

It is difficult to quantify the relative Anglo and Indian benefits in the settlements. The mere fact that the issue is settled creates a benefit for all parties. However, the Anglo benefits that directly impact federal expenditures, taxes, and fees can be identified:

— The Ak-Chin settlement of 1984 pays $9.4 million to non-Indians for their loss of water, and according to the House report, they also receive $11.7 million in additional benefits. The Congressional Budget Office cost estimate for the 1984 act estimates that the government will lose $25.3 million in long-term reclamation loan obligation discharges.[40]

— The Tohono O'odham (Papago) settlement relies on the federally funded CAP, which also provides numerous benefits to non-Indian communities.

— The Colorado Ute settlement relies on the Animas–La Plata Project, which was originally estimated to cost $458 million in federal funding. The cost of the scaled-down version that was approved in 2000 is estimated at $343.8 million (see chapter 4).

— The San Luis Rey settlement specified that no federal funding could be used to develop a new water source to meet the requirements of the settlement. The All-American Canal will be lined to produce the necessary water; the funding will come from the state of California.

—In the Salt River Pima-Maricopa settlement, the federal government acquired 22,000 af of water from the Mohawk irrigation district for use in the settlement. The federal government valued that water at $14 million, but the district demanded $66 million.[41] The final agreement paid the district $9 million up front and provided a number of lucrative contract amendments to the district, including Reclamation Reform Act waivers.

—The Fort Hall settlement forgave some repayment obligations.

—The Fort McDowell settlement hinged on the purchase of water from the Harquahala Valley irrigation district. The price was not specified at the time of the settlement, but the Congressional Budget Office estimated total losses of federal revenue at $26 million.[42] In contrast, the General Accounting Office analyzed the settlement benefits that would accrue to the irrigation district and found they totaled $124 million. The GAO report concluded that the Interior Department "did not adequately protect the federal government's financial interests."[43] The final deal gave the district $9 million up front and forgave the district's 9(b) loan under the Colorado River Basin Project Act.

—As part of the Pyramid Lake settlement, the secretary is authorized to help the Truckee-Carson Irrigation District study ways to improve water use efficiency to help the district meet its obligations to other water users, including Indian tribes.

—The Northern Cheyenne settlement relied upon federal funds to refurbish a dam owned by the state of Montana. The settlement provides money for the tribe, which must then lend $11.5 million to the state for the dam's repairs.

—The settlement for the Northern Utes in Utah was part of a larger bill that authorized an additional $1 billion for the Central Utah Project. CUP supporters argued that this massive project would help resolve Indian water claims.

—The San Carlos settlement contained an unusual form of payoff to non-Indians. In exchange for their loss of potential (not actual) access to the water used to meet the tribe's needs, the non-Indian contractors are exempted from ownership limitations and the full-cost pricing provisions of federal reclamation law. This means they will pay $57 per acre-foot rather than $250 per acre-foot, and their repayment obligations are reduced (once the settlement is finalized).

—The Yavapai/Prescott settlement authorized the secretary to purchase the CAP contract of the city of Prescott.

The net effect of these payoffs to non-Indians is to significantly increase the costs of settlements. It is nearly impossible to ascertain the total amount of non-Indian benefits in the settlements, especially if the enormous cost of the Indian blanket projects is included. But it is clear that the federal benefits accruing to non-Indians is quite substantial and may indeed exceed the benefits to Indian people. This leads to a third question: Who pays for the settlements?

Who Pays?

When the settlement era began, many tribal leaders were elated. Finally, the federal government was investing in Indian country, and tribes were receiving funding to help them build their water infrastructure and economies. But after several years of settlement funding, a disturbing trend began to develop. In the 1980s and early 1990s, when most settlements were passed, the federal deficit was rising to unprecedented levels. Congress and OMB chose to deal with the deficit by attempting to impose a kind of tit-for-tat budgetary rule. In the parlance of economics, this is called "zero-sum," meaning that any additional money added to the budget had to be matched with a reduction in spending of equal amount in some other part of the budget.

Thus, the important question became, "For every additional dollar spent on settlements, what other programs would be cut by the same amount?" For the Office of Management and Budget, the answer was clear; the cuts would come out of other line items in the BIA budget. In a 1990 interview an OMB official, who wished to remain anonymous,[44] explained their thinking: "OMB's position in general is that the Department of the Interior is the department that must take care of the Indians. Indian settlements must compete internally and externally with other funding needs. The advocates of negotiation look upon these settlements as a moral obligation, a trust responsibility. We look upon them as competing with other demands, as a program. . . . Where's the money come from? It comes from the same pot that finances everything else. . . . Something else will have to be cut a like amount; it's zero-sum." This statement leaves open the possibility that settlement funding could come from other Interior Department programs, but politically this is highly unlikely. The BIA is the weakest agency in the Interior Department; it is difficult to imagine that Congress would cut dollars from, say, the National Park Service or the Bureau of Reclamation just to fund Indian water settlements. From a political standpoint the easiest place to cut is other BIA programs. A Senate staffer familiar with the process affirmed this in a 1990 interview: "In the budget climate we are in, if there isn't money specifically set aside for a settlement, you can be sure it comes out of the hide of other Indian programs. Overall, Indian country does not gain from these settlements when that happens. Congress sets aside an amount for all Indian programs. If a water settlement takes $3 million, I can assure you that the money comes out of other Indian programs. That's how Congress appropriates the money." In other words, there is no net gain in Indian country as a result of the settlements; money has been diverted from Indian housing, Indian education, and other trust responsibilities to fund the water settlements. Perhaps this is why other Indian water programs have stagnated. Eddie Brown, former assistant secretary for Indian Affairs, called it "a tax on other Indian programs."[45] John Echohawk, director of the Native American Rights Fund, was even more expressive: "It's crazy and it's unethical but that's what happens when the budget people take control. They just want to balance the books. It is unethical to pay us out of our own money."[46] Timothy Glidden, counselor to the secretary of the interior in 1992, opposed federal funding for the repair of the Tongue River Dam (the Northern Cheyenne settlement) because it would contribute "to an inequity upon all Indians. . . . other Indians will suffer from the loss in budget to the Department of the Interior."[47]

Neither the Reagan nor Bush administrations demonstrated any desire to solve this problem. Senator Inouye brought the matter to the attention of the Senate in 1989, asking for a budgetary provision that would ensure that "funding for such settlements be allocated in a manner that does not adversely affect other Indian programs."[48] But it was not until the Clinton administration came to power that an effort was made to correct the funding problem. For fiscal year 1994 Secretary Babbitt created a separate line item in the BIA budget specifically for "implementation of enacted Indian land and water claim settlements" with an appropriation of $200 million.[49] BIA budget requests state that the purpose of this line item is "to provide a separate source of federal funds to implement the provisions and intent of each water settlement, with the goal of establishing a viable homeland for affected Tribes."[50] The hope is that, by separating out the money for water settlements, it would stop the raiding of other Indian programs.

Has it been successful? In a 1996 interview, an OMB official answered that question: "Do the settlements come out of other Indian programs? Yes. If a chunk is allocated to a settlement, it must come out of other Indian programs; there must be an offset, if it is discretionary spending, and all water settlements are." A water attorney with the BIA reached the same conclusion: "From a practical perspective, it is a zero-sum thing. Congress wants to spend only so much. There is x billion dollars available for Indian programs, so the settlements have to come out of that. Babbitt's separate line item makes things tidier; does that change perceptions? I doubt it. We perceive one size of pot."

The tendency to rob other Indian programs to pay for water settlements has increased as Congress and the president worked to balance the federal budget. And despite recent budget surpluses, the problem perseveres and has possibly gotten worse. Michael Jackson, staff attorney for the Senate Indian Affairs Committee, recently complained that it was a "very untenable option [to have] the United States Government try to fund its legal liabilities to Indian tribes by cutting Indian programs benefiting all tribes. I submit that that's unconscionable and it's the wrong way to go."[51] Robert Anderson, special assistant to the secretary of the interior, was less pointed but agreed there is a problem: "We need to be more creative to figure out mechanisms through which we can ensure that appropriations for Indian settlements do not unduly tax the BIA's budget. It's going to be difficult to justify taking money out of some other portion of the federal budget."[52]

This problem has become so severe that funding for settlements has been partially choked off because there is no room for cuts in other Indian programs. In exasperation a number of settlement proponents have proposed that a mandatory fund (meaning non-discretionary money) be set up to guarantee that money will be available for settlements without robbing other Indian programs. A proposed bill would authorize $250 million to "fence off" settlement money from the annual fight over discretionary expenditures, similar to a court of claims judgment fund. In a letter to the Senate, the Western States Water Council explained why such a step was necessary: "Under current budgetary policy, funding of land and water settlements is considered to be discretionary, with the result that no settlement can be funded without a corresponding reduction in some other discretionary component of the Indian Department's budget. The practical effect of this budgetary policy is to preclude the funding of land or water settlements. It is virtually impossible for the Administration, the State or the Tribes to negotiate settlements knowing that they will not be funded because funding can occur only at the expense of some other Tribe or essential Interior Department program."[53] The latest incarnation of this legislation is S. 1186, "The Fiscal Integrity of Indian Settlements Protection Act of 2001." The continuing effort to pass such legislation makes it evident that this serious problem persists.

The net effect of this zero-sum policy on Indian country was succinctly summarized recently by Pam Williams, chief counsel for the interior secretary's water office: "Water settlement spending has had a devastating effect on the BIA because historically it comes out of BIA funding. We have been successful in shifting some of the cost to the Bureau of Reclamation, but only a small part of it."[54]

This raises a troubling possibility. If settlement funding comes from other Indian programs and a substantial portion of the settlement funding goes to compensate Anglos and fund the Indian blanket, then the settlement policy has become in effect, at least in part, a vehicle to funnel Indian money to non-Indian westerners; monies that would have gone into the BIA budget have instead been used to pay for both Indian and non-Indian benefits in water settlements. Anyone familiar with the history of Indian policy knows there is plenty of precedent for this, but it is certainly disturbing to see such a diversion of funds in a policy that is supported by so many Indian leaders—a policy that is supposed to bring real change to Indian country. An explicit accounting needs to take place; what cuts were made to fund settlements, and what percentage of settlement funding actually goes to Anglos? Without an answer to these questions, it is impossible to determine the relative success and fairness of the settlement policy.

Conclusion

There are many reasons why politicians support settlements. For some, it is an effort to honor trust responsibilities; for them, it is a moral stand against the failed policies of the past. For others, it is yet another way to funnel federal money to their western constituents; for them, the greater the cost and the wider its distribution, the better. Still others support settlements because they fear what the courts might do to them; for them it is a way to take the initiative away from the courts and exercise control over an issue that is important to voters. These three groups can be labeled as the moralists, the pork barrelers, and the controllers. What are their incentives in regard to saving time and money via the settlement policy?

For all of these interests, there is an incentive to save time. Every politician would rather deliver the goods sooner rather than later. Thus it is probably true that the settlement policy saves time relative to litigation. This does not mean, however, that it offers a quick solution. The settlement process can be painfully slow and frustrating. In most cases, achieving a settlement takes years, but achieving a final court decision may take decades.

Does the settlement policy save money? Let's look at each of the three groups of participating politicians. First, the moralists would prefer to spend as much money as is politically feasible on Indian people via the settlement process. Their goal is to meet trust responsibilities and ameliorate past injustice, and the past-due bill is enormous. For the second group, the pork barrelers, there is even more incentive to spend large amounts of money, especially if they are using the Indian blanket to cover dubious pet projects. These politicians are particularly interested in distributing benefits outside the reservation—that is where they will find most big campaign donors, voters, and well-heeled interest groups. The controllers also have an incentive to spend more rather than less. Federal funding is the fuel that powers the settlement engine; the more money that is available, the greater the likelihood that a settlement will be reached and the matter will not be settled by a court. In short, the politicians most interested in supporting the settlement policy have few incentives to actually save money.

And indeed, it is quite evident that settlements do not save money, at least compared to the relative measure of strict legal liability. This is especially true if tangential costs are considered, such as prerequisite litigation; preparatory technical, historical, and legal studies; the Indian blanket; and associated political costs. The real value of the settlements lies not in their parsimony, but in the manner in which the money is spent. Instead of spending money on lawyers and court expenses, the government is spending it on the people of the West. Indian reservations get funding for activities that directly benefit tribal members, and non-Indians receive a whole panoply of goodies ranging from big water projects to special deals on water rates, loan repayments, and contracts. In the language of political science, the conflict has been resolved by bringing the opposition into the circle of beneficiaries — co-optation via allocation. Everyone but federal taxpayers and other Indian programs wins. Is there a net monetary gain in Indian country? It is highly doubtful. But there is a net gain in the non-Indian communities in the West.

Vignette: Cheyenne Spring

It was the grass that brought the buffalo, and the buffalo that brought the Indians to the Great Plains. The land was so luxurious in grass it could support millions of grazing animals. This is, or at least was, America's Serengeti, a land teeming with all varieties of wildlife. In a long-ago era, when human life was tenuous, the abundant game of the Great Plains made this area a desirable place for a home. Of course, "home" meant a million square miles of roaming territory. It was a land worth fighting for. Once the plains Indians acquired the horse, they began to know a freedom that we can only dream about today. It was a footloose, expansive freedom that fit the land perfectly.

The Northern Cheyenne Reservation is but a remnant of those once-vast lands. Still, it is imposing, and retains many of its indigenous qualities. The landscape is so open and spacious that it might more properly be called a spacescape. Sandwiched between the infinity of sky and the earth's crust is a thin veneer of grass that stretches across the undulating hills like a tight-fitting piece of clothing. An occasional cluster of lodgepole pines protrudes from the hill-sides. The wind, which knows this land well, moves the grass in waves, making it hiss. The contrast in color between the loden green of the pines and the soft beige of the grass seems to give the land an extra visual dimension. Place these colors on a palate of gracefully curving hills occasionally punctured by jagged rock outcroppings, and you have a scene of austere beauty.

I am sitting on a mesa top at the site of the battle of the Rosebud, which oc-curred eight days before Custer's fateful rendezvous on the Little Bighorn. In this all-day battle, Sioux and Cheyenne warriors stopped General Crook's col-umn, preventing them from reinforcing Custer. Today the battlefield is a state park, purchased from private owners by the state of Montana with coal royal-ties. Except for two horseback riders on a distant ridge, I am utterly alone. This is a land of buttes and mesas, with pine and scrub growing sparsely where the slope affords an increase in water and shade. Huge, rolling expanses of yellow prairie grass spread out in all directions. One of the soldiers who fought here described the prairie as "undulating as billows of mid-ocean."[55] It would be a great place to hide in ambush.

A month ago, I walked the battlefields of Gettysburg, ambling across the mile of open land where Pickett's men charged into history. There, the blue-clad soldiers fought for a noble cause, and on that blistering hot day in July 1863, slavery in America was effectively eliminated. But here in 1876, a mere thirteen years later, the blue cavalry fought for a cause that stands in ignomin-ious contrast to the ideals of the Civil War. Here, they fought to steal a land from its people. They were not the first, of course. The Shoshone lived near here at one time. They were pushed into the mountains to the west by the Crow, who were in turn pushed westward by the Sioux and Cheyenne. It was indeed a land worth fighting for.

Not far from the Rosebud battlefield, in the next valley, huge earthmovers are rearranging the topography around a reservoir on the Tongue River. The earthmovers are building a road in order to repair a dam that will provide water for the Northern Cheyenne Reservation. Today, the Northern Cheyenne are fighting a battle for water, and, like the Rosebud fight 120 years ago, they have won a victory.

It is somewhat amazing there are any Cheyennes still living. The Southern Cheyenne somehow survived Colonel Chivington's massacre at Sand Creek in 1864 and Custer's sneak attack on their village on the Washita in 1868. The Northern Cheyenne had fought alongside their Lakota Sioux allies in many battles. In 1877, starving and greatly reduced in numbers, they conceded defeat and were ordered south to Indian country (present-day Oklahoma). By that time Indian country had become something of a giant, open-air concentration camp for many different tribes.

In the hot, fetid conditions the Northern Cheyenne soon began to sicken and die. They faced a stark choice; they could stay and slowly perish, or attempt an audacious escape and try to return to their homeland on the northern plains. They chose to flee. Their epic journey became one of history's most tragic episodes. Many died along the way, killed by soldiers and the elements. But a few managed to return north and eked out a feeble existence along the Tongue River in south-central Montana. It was not until 1884 that an executive order officially created the Northern Cheyenne Indian Reservation. By that time many settlers had flooded into the Tongue River valley to homestead, and the government had to buy land from them in order to create the reservation.

At that time no effort was made to ensure there was a water supply to the new reservation. Thirty years later the Miles City water decree, which clarified the water rights to the region, gave the tribe a minute portion of the waters of the Tongue River. In that litigation the U.S. government failed to file Winters Doctrine rights for the tribe.

The tribe remained virtually without water for fifty years. In 1975 tribal chairman Edwin Dahl decided to do something about it. His friend Ernie Robinson explained what happened: "Edwin was a visionary; he was great at solving problems. He wasn't a lawyer, but that didn't stop him. The tribe couldn't afford its own lawyer back then, so Edwin just filed the case himself."[56] The state of Montana reacted by filing for a general stream adjudication to resolve the question of who owned the waters of the Tongue River basin.

But by that time, western states were getting worried about Indian water claims. Most states simply reacted in opposition, but Montana tried something different. In 1979 the state legislature created the Montana Reserved Water Rights Compact Commission. Among western states this was a fairly audacious move. Most western states at that time did not even want to acknowledge that federal reserved water rights existed; they talked about Indian water *claims*, never about Indian water *rights*. But Montana, in creating the commission, clearly signaled that it was ready to deal with the problem through open and direct negotiations.

At first the Cheyennes were hesitant. Shackled by mistrust and cruelty's long remembrance, they were leery of negotiation. Finally, in 1980, they began official talks with the commission. It took eleven years of on-again, off-again contentious discussion, but in 1991 the state and the tribe signed a water compact, which was approved the following year by Congress.

The key element of the compact is a novel plan that looks a little bit like a shell game; the federal government gives the tribe $21.5 million for a trust fund, the tribe then takes about half of that sum and lends it to the state, and the state then allocates that money to repair and enlarge its dam on the Tongue River, which in turn provides water storage for the tribe. It sounds circuitous, and some people in the federal government objected to the hand-offs, but the key to successful negotiation is to get resourceful—be imaginative—and no one will accuse the negotiators in this settlement of lacking those qualities.

The repair and enlargement of the Tongue River Dam solved a score of problems. This earthen dam, built in the 1930s, had become unsafe. A flood in 1978 had seriously compromised the spillway; another flood of that magnitude could wash out the dam and create a catastrophic flood that could wipe out several communities. Senator Burns of Montana called the rehabilitation of the dam "the No. 1 water project of the State of Montana."[57] By enlarging the dam's spillway, the capacity of the reservoir will be increased by 20,000 af, which provides a new source of water for the tribe. It also removes the threat of a dam failure and the threat that the tribe will claim other water that is currently used by Anglos.[58] Everyone wins. Of course, a large infusion of federal cash made it all possible.

Another innovative part of the settlement involves the Bighorn River, which flows across the Crow Indian Reservation which in turn abuts the western boundary of the Northern Cheyenne Reservation. The federal government built Yellowtail Dam on the Bighorn River on Crow lands.[59] The settlement gives the Northern Cheyennes 30,000 af of water storage in the Bighorn reservoir "for use or disposition by the Tribe for any purpose." How did the Cheyenne manage to gain access to water that was on another reservation? The answer to this question goes to the heart of the negotiating process; any combination of deals is possible. When I posed this question to one of the Northern Cheyenne water managers, he answered mischievously: "Oh, we took the Crow by surprise. We've been doing that for centuries." Keep in mind that the Crow and the Cheyenne are traditional enemies (the Crow were the trusted scouts for the Seventh Cavalry).

But the reality of the deal is more complicated than that. The Crow tribe had a few objectives it wanted to meet, so the tribe used the settlement negotiations as leverage. The Crows established several conditions that would have to be met before they agreed to allow the Northern Cheyennes to establish rights to Bighorn water. This is pretty clever bargaining since the water behind Yellowtail Dam is, technically speaking, federal water and not tribal water. The foremost problem the Crow wanted to resolve concerned a land dispute between the two tribes. The Crows said they would agree to the water settlement if a fair settlement of this land problem could be reached—presumably with federal money to buy out one side or the other. The Crow also insisted on placing a ten-year moratorium on the Northern Cheyennes' right to market the water from Bighorn reservoir.[60] The Northern Cheyennes agreed to this moratorium, and it was written into the final settlement. Once again the negotiators had demonstrated their creativity.

The tribe's new water storage behind a rehabilitated Tongue River Dam, combined with the Bighorn water, Rosebud Creek, and other sources, totaled more than 90,000 af in the settlement. When the Tongue River Dam enlargement was finished in June 1999, the threat of a catastrophic flood was eliminated. And the Anglo water users in the area no longer needed to worry about a different kind of catastrophe—a big legal victory for Indian reserved water rights. In addition, the Crows got a promise from the Montana congressional delegation to resolve a hundred-year old land dispute. Did all this save a lot of time and money? Probably not, but to the beneficiaries of the settlement, it looks like a real bargain.

The small hamlet of Lame Deer is the tribal headquarters of the nearly 600,000-acre Northern Cheyenne Reservation, which is surrounded by huge open-pit coal mines and a ring of towns named after generals who did their best to exterminate the Cheyenne and their Lakota Sioux allies. In a large room in the tribal headquarters building, an enormous sign with foot-tall letters hangs across one end of the room: "Home of Senator Ben Nighthorse Campbell." Below that sign a half-dozen people work in the tribe's Department of Natural Resources.

Their director, Jason Whiteman, is an energetic, outgoing man who passionately believes in his tribe and its water settlement. He has more than just enthusiasm, however; he understands the realpolitik of western water. The settlement is not perfect, but it solved a lot of problems for the tribe and gave them a clear, guaranteed source of water.

Mr. Whiteman also knows the frustrations of implementing a complicated water settlement. The tribe has experienced difficulties drafting a tribal water code, which is mandated by the settlement. And the legal requirement to write an environmental impact statement (EIS) for the Tongue River Project created all sorts of problems. The tribe hired a firm to do the EIS, but it made little progress, so the tribe had to find another consultant. The final EIS finally came out in March 1996, but in the meantime work on the project stopped. The development fund created by the settlement has been a source of conflict among tribal members; after much wrangling, the tribal council set up an ad hoc committee to develop scenarios of how to spend the money.

The settlement also experienced problems gaining acceptance among tribal members. A tribal referendum was held to approve the settlement, but an insufficient number of tribal members voted. Llevando Fisher, tribal president, made the best of it: "I want to thank the people for their support during the January 1993 referendum vote for the Water Compact. Even though we were short of a 30 percent voter turnout, I was confident of your blessing to move forward with perfecting the Water Compact. The voting turned out solidly in favor of the Tribe finally getting ownership to a large amount of water in the Tongue River, Rosebud Creek, and Bighorn River."[61]

As with all settlements, not everyone was pleased with the final outcome. Most of the complaints concern water quality—an issue that some tribal members feel should have been addressed in the settlement.

Harriet Little Bird, a tribal elder and member of the tribe's cultural commission, met with me at the elders' center in Lame Deer. She had hoped the settlement would address the water quality problems. Ms. Little Bird stared at her hands as she began talking. "In the Muddy Creek district of the reservation, bad water from the wells is making people sick. Now they have to haul water. They think it went bad because ARCO was blasting underground mines. And the water in the rivers—it used to be good, we could swim in Rosebud Creek and the Tongue, but now it's no good. You can't even drink it. I thought the whole reservation was going to get clean water out of the settlement." At that point Ms. Little Bird looked at me and smiled broadly. "A swimming pool for the kids would have been nice too."

I asked her if she thought the tribe got a good settlement, despite the absence of a swimming pool.

"We don't all think the same. Some think it was good, some don't. But more people thought it was good, so it happened."

Claudine Cano is the director of the elders' center. She is college educated and articulate, and she's not afraid to express her opinion. I asked for her perception of the settlement. She looked directly at me as she spoke. "How can you put a price on water? Why do you negotiate something that is already yours? That water was ours from the treaties. And why did we give the state $11 million to fix their own dam—and the loan was without interest! What's going to happen twenty years from now? It might look good now, but not later. I strongly feel that this is our land. We fought our way back to here; that's how we returned home. Then we were confined to a small reservation. Then they turn around and say; we'll negotiate with you on your water. I can't understand their thinking."

For both Ms. Little Bird and Ms. Cano, distrust of the settlement is rooted in history. Ms. Little Bird explained. "My great-great grandmother's brother was Black Kettle. Look what happened to him. There have been a lot of things like that."[62]

Claudine Cano made a similar point: "I see a need for an established amount of water, but how can it guarantee that we will always have our water when always in the past they didn't keep their promises. There has been so much injustice in the past. There is just no trust there."[63]

Butch Sootkis, a member of the tribe's cultural commission, agreed to accompany me to the Tongue River Project construction site. As we drove through the reservation, he pointed out which houses had good water and which had bad water. I posed the same question to him; what do you think of the settlement? "The tribal council got a lot of cussing out because of the water settlement. Many people believe they gave away our water rights. But we didn't really have any choice, and we didn't have any money. And when the White Man decides he's going to do something, then it's going to happen."

Butch introduced me to Dennis Limberhand, the tribe's labor relations representative on the project, and Ernie Robinson, the tribe's coordinator for the project. They took me on a tour of the construction site. Both men reflect the dual nature of their cultural environment; they both wore plastic construction hats with their long traditional ponytails down the back. They explained that the dam was not being raised, only the spillway. This minimizes the environmental impact and cost of the project, but still increases the capacity of the reservoir, giving the tribe a total of 20,000 af of storage. New concrete facing on the downstream side of the dam will prevent failure during flooding.

I asked them to pose for a picture next to the new spillway construction. I fumbled with the controls of my camera for a moment as I focused on the full-length profile of the two men with the spillway behind them. Then Dennis said, in a tight voice, "Hurry up! We can't suck it in all day!"

The word "settlement" is a bit of a misnomer. Many issues remain unresolved after the ink dries, especially when a final court decree is required. In the case of the Northern Cheyennes, the final court decree was not approved until July 1995. It is somewhat amazing that, out of thousands of water users, only ten objected to the pending decree.

Jason Whiteman explained how the tribe dealt with that problem: "We went out and talked to each one of them. All of them were ranchers, including Soap Creek Ranch—one of the biggest ranches in Montana. We told them this was a chance to get federal support. Eventually all the objections were withdrawn."

Judge Loble's memorandum opinion for the final court decree contained a very succinct statement of the nature of negotiated settlements: "It's possible that different people might have differing opinions on the individual components of the Compact. Some might say 'It's too much' and others might say

'It's too little.' But taken as a whole, the Compact represents a fair settlement of a difficult problem. . . . In summary, this Compact resolves issues that began over one hundred years ago. . . . [It] validates the confidence reposed by the 1979 Legislature in the Reserved Water Rights Compact Commission and the Northern Cheyenne Tribe that good faith negotiations can achieve solutions to difficult problems."[64]

Did the Northern Cheyenne settlement save time and money? In a sense, this vignette demonstrates that a lot more is at stake than time and money. This settlement involved a complicated shell game with federal money, a state dam, and Indian water. Compared to litigation, it probably did not save the federal government money, but it may have saved the state of Montana a considerable sum. Like all settlements, the issue of time and money is a relative question concerning the value of what is gained, compared to what is expended.

4

Eternity on the Block

For All Time

Permanence has always been an elusive goal in American Indian policy. Throughout U.S. history the government has sought to establish a workable, long-term relationship with Indian people that would withstand the test of time. And time is no small matter; Indian policy is the oldest political issue on the continent, what Charles Wilkinson calls a "time-warped field."[1] Throughout that long history the dominant Anglo population has repeatedly sought to finalize a solution to the "Indian problem."

The language of permanence is found in most official documents dealing with American Indians. The Northwest Ordinance of 1787 was one of the first official Indian policies issued by the fledgling government of the United States. It stated: "The utmost of good faith shall *always* be observed toward the Indians; their land and property shall *never* be taken away from them without their consent; and their property, rights and liberty shall *never* be invaded by Congress" (emphasis added).[2] When the Osage came to Washington to visit President Jefferson in 1804, he promised them, "No wrong will *ever* be done you by our nation" (emphasis added).[3] In 1834 Congress passed an act to create a "permanent Indian frontier" along the Mississippi River.[4] However, this policy was soon abandoned as white settlers pushed west. Then a "permanent" Indian country was established for the exclusive use of Indian tribes; this land was later opened for settlement and became the state of Oklahoma.

The language of permanence is clearly evident in the individual treaties of the first treaty era. Although very few treaties contained the famous phrases "as long as the rivers shall run" or "as long as the grass shall grow," permanence was a predominant theme. The treaty with the Cherokees promised *"perpetual peace and friendship"* (emphasis added).[5] When the U.S. Army began treaty deliberations with Chief Red Cloud of the Sioux, the commanding officer began the proceedings with this statement: "What we want your people to remember is that this treaty is the last one, not made for a day, but *for all time*" (emphasis added).[6] In the 1868 treaty between the Navajos and the United States, the Navajos agreed to "make the reservation herein described their *permanent home*" (emphasis added).[7] The Fort Bridger treaty with the Eastern Shoshone and Bannock tribes declared, "From this day forward peace between the parties to this treaty shall *forever* continue" (emphasis added).[8] Clearly, permanence was promised; unfortunately, it was rarely honored.

The impermanence of the promises made in the first treaty era caused great loss to Indian tribes when "final" land cessions were inevitably followed by demands for more cessions. But in water rights cases, permanence has often worked against tribes. Many Indian water rights cases came to judgment early in the twentieth century when the government was notoriously inept or unwilling to forcefully press for reserved water rights. As a result, many early court decrees did not adequately protect Indian water rights. Years later, when the political and social climate had changed and tribes began to hire their own attorneys, some of the tribes that had been inadequately represented in these early court cases went back to court to rectify the injustice. But the Supreme Court decided that certainty and permanence were more important than justice for Indians, and let the flawed court decisions stand.[9] David Getches describes what this meant for tribes: "The effect of the Court's decision is to bind Indians to determinations in stream adjudications in which they are represented by the United States government, even if the government's advocacy was weak, incomplete or compromised by a conflict of interest."[10]

By comparing nineteenth-century land treaties with early twentieth-century water rights cases, an obvious double standard becomes apparent. The "final" land cessions of the first treaty era were almost never permanent, but the finality of unfair court decisions regarding water rights has been elevated to an important legal principle; this inequity creates a problem for Indian people in the second treaty era.[11] In both situations the dominant Anglo society benefited at the expense of Indian people. Thus, policy "permanence" for Indian people can either be a protective shield against future incursions, or an anachronistic albatross.

Despite the Supreme Court's attempts to achieve finality in water rights adjudications, the goal proved to be very elusive. Many water rights conflicts simply continued in one forum or another. Problems were rarely solved, only mitigated or delayed. When the policy of negotiating settlements was first being developed, one of the primary goals was to finally put an end to the maddening litany of conflict. The promise of permanence offered something to all sides.

Indian tribes feared that their water rights would succumb to the same process that gradually reduced their land holdings. Perhaps the best way to prevent future raids on Indian water was to enter into an agreement with those parties most likely to engage in such raids. And Anglo water users sought certainty in water rights to free them of the threat of future Indian water claims. Thus, "finality and certainty" became a favorite catch phrase of the second treaty era, just as permanence "for all time" had been a prominent theme in the first one.

How are finality and certainty achieved? In a word, quantification — an official tally of water rights that is authorized by statute or court decree (or both). John Weldon writes, "Probably the primary reason for the growing number of water rights adjudications and Indian water rights settlements in the West is the pressing need of both Indian and non-Indian parties to achieve certainty as to their respective shares of a scarce natural resource. The quantification of Indian reserved water rights is crucial to the accomplishment of this goal."[12] For Anglo water users, quantification was an obvious solution. The entire structure of western water rights, anchored in the Prior Appropriation Doctrine, is based on the specific measurement of individual water withdrawals that can be sustained over time. Such rights are permanent and fixed as long as they are in use. The great thorn in the side of this system has been federal reserved water rights, which are contingent upon future uses to meet the purposes of federal land withdrawals. The Supreme Court of Arizona put it bluntly: "To solve the conflict and uncertainty that reserved water rights engender, we must quantify them, for we may not ignore them."[13] Settlements provide a venue for quantification and thus hold out the hope for an end to this conflict.

For tribes, the quantification of their rights is more of a mixed blessing. It means giving up the open-ended promise of the Winters Doctrine and settling for whatever they can get in the hard bargaining of the negotiation process. It is also contrary to cultural perceptions of water as an indivisible community resource. Dan Decker, an Indian attorney, made this point succinctly: "Measuring our water — our lifeblood — just runs contrary to our traditional ways. But states think differently. They don't appreciate these cultural concerns."[14]

So why do tribes want to quantify? As chapter 1 pointed out, the courts have become more hostile to Indian water claims; the holdings in the *Big Horn* and *Lewis* cases indicate that some judges and justices want to replace the practicable irrigable acreage standard with a more restrictive approach.[15] Tribes are especially worried about the prospect of state courts quantifying their water rights. Quantification via a settlement looks increasingly better as the alternative — litigation in state courts — looks increasingly worse. A prominent American Indian attorney made this point recently: "For many tribes, the choice is the lesser of the two evils. I'm convinced there are still many tribes that, if given the choice, would not quantify at all. They resent having to do that. They resent the McCarran Amendment and the *San Carlos* case [which resulted in state court adjudication]."[16]

The bottom line is this: both Anglo water users and tribes hope to achieve a certain level of finality and certainty by quantifying their water rights via a negotiated settlement. This raises two questions. First, have the settlements achieved that goal, and second, is the pursuit of finality an appropriate objective for settlements?

Finality Finally?

The literature on alternative dispute resolution emphasizes the need for "durable resolutions" to conflict.[17] How well this goal is achieved depends on two variables; the nature of the settlement itself and the success with which the settlement is implemented once it becomes law. To evaluate the extent to which negotiated water rights settlements have achieved finality, it is helpful to look at each settlement separately:

Ak-Chin, Arizona, 1978, renegotiated 1984. The original Ak-Chin settlement contained serious shortcomings regarding water sources that made its implementation impossible. These problems were addressed successfully in the 1984 settlement. In 1992 an amendment to the settlement gave the tribe the right to market water locally; the tribe has leased some of its water to Del Webb, a local developer. The remaining settlement water is used on the tribe's 20,000-acre farm. By all accounts this settlement has been successfully implemented.[18]

Tohono O'odham (Papago), Arizona, 1982, amended 1992. The original lawsuit that inspired the settlement has not been dismissed due to continuing conflicts involving allottee rights. The irrigation project promised in the settlement remains unfinished. An internal BIA memo, written in 1999, said, "BOR [Bureau of Reclamation, builder of the irrigation project] doesn't know what to do." Major portions of the settlement are now being re-negotiated, eighteen years after the original settlement was signed. Negotiators say a revised settlement is nearing completion. It should also be noted that this settlement applies only to the Santa Cruz and Avra-Altar Valley basins, but parts of the reservation extend into other river basins. This settlement is discussed in greater detail in the vignette in chapter 6.

Fort Peck–Montana Compact, 1985. The original settlement provided no mechanism for water marketing—a significant disadvantage to the tribe. A bill was introduced in 1993 and again in 1994 to remedy that problem, but downstream states prevented its passage.[19] A frustrated Senator Baucus complained in 1994 that "We have delayed the implementation of the Fort Peck Indian Tribe–Montana Compact for far too long."[20] No bill has been introduced since then. The compact is still in the Montana Water Court process due to questions regarding the legal standing of objectors and the review process.

San Luis Rey (the Mission tribes), California, 1988. This was, until quite recently, a settlement without a water source.[21] The solution to that problem became ensnared in a massive conflict over California's Colorado River overdraft. In 1996 Secretary of the Interior Babbitt indicated that a resolution of the settlement's water supply problems must be "an essential component" of the plan to solve the overdraft issue.[22] A bill introduced in 1998 to solve the settlement's water source problems failed to pass.[23] A technical amendment to the settlement provided for the payment of accumulated interest to the Mission tribes.[24] A plan to provide water for the settlement by lining the All-American Canal was integrated into the "4.4" agreement that was signed in 1999.

Colorado Ute Settlement, 1988. This settlement was mired in political controversy for more than a decade. A second law, essentially a resettlement, was signed in 2000 (explored in detail in the vignette at the end of this chapter).

Salt River Pima-Maricopa, Arizona, 1988. This settlement is considered to be fully implemented. However, critics charge that the settlement left many problems unresolved: "In a significant way, the [settlement] package totally fails to resolve existing litigation, in essence substituting new claims and potentially increasing federal exposure over that existing in the face of pending claims."[25]

Fort Hall, Idaho, 1990. This settlement has been fully implemented. A number of objections to the court decree were filed. Some of the opposition to the settlement and resulting decree came from non-Indian irrigators who are part of the on-reservation irrigation project.

Fort McDowell, Arizona, 1990. This settlement has been fully implemented. Some problems arose when archaeological sites were discovered in the new farm, but the sites were fenced off and other lands were added to compensate for them.[26] See the vignette in the following chapter.

Fallon Paiute-Shoshone/Truckee-Carson–Pyramid Lake, 1990. An internal 1999 Interior Department memo explained that these settlements "provide a policy basis for resolving certain water and other resource issues affecting many areas in the Truckee and Carson River and Lake Tahoe Basins."[27] In other words, the settlements provided a beginning, rather than a conclusion, to numerous negotiations that are still in progress. The Pyramid Lake settlement is covered in detail in the vignette in chapter 7.

Jicarilla Apache Water Settlement Act, 1992. The implementation of this settlement has been slowed by a number of problems due in part to the Endangered Species Act. The tribe has yet to complete a water conservation program and is still building an administrative structure to manage its water. However, the long-awaited court decree was issued in April 1999, following the publication of the San Juan River flow recommendations. Certain provisions in the act were recently extended via an amendment.[28] The draft supplemental EIS for the Animas–La Plata Project states, "Interior will facilitate discussions between the Jicarilla Apache tribe and other parties with interest in the San Juan River Basin to develop options of obtaining 25,500 af [per year] depletion as authorized under the Jicarilla Apache Tribe Water Rights Settlement Act."[29] Thus, progress is being made, but the settlement is not yet fully implemented.[30]

Northern Cheyenne Reserved Water Rights Settlement Act, 1992. The completion of the Tongue River Dam improvements in July 1999 brought this settlement to fruition. The tribe is still working on a Tongue River Reservoir plan of operation and a tribal water code. An issue that has yet to be resolved is the Bighorn River storage agreement; both the Northern Cheyenne tribe and the Crow tribe have an interest in that basin.[31]

Ute Indian Rights Settlement Act, 1992, PL 102-575. This settlement was accompanied by a separate compact, which has yet to be approved by either the State of Utah or the tribe. Thus the water rights of the tribe remain unquantified. See the vignette in chapter 8.

San Carlos Apache Tribe Water Rights Settlement Act, 1992, amended 1994. This settlement settled practically nothing, leaving nearly all important issues for future negotiations. Furthermore, there were built-in contradictions: "Section 3711(a) (7) anticipates that provisions in the agreement originally proposed to Congress might be in conflict with the Act as passed."[32] The act authorized the secretary of the interior to execute agreements to bring the settlement to fruition. This resulted in a great deal of continuing conflict and "marathon negotiation sessions."[33] Agreements had to be reached with Phelps-Dodge Mining Company and a score of towns, irrigation districts, and individuals. The special master in the case noted that "Congress appears to have authorized the continuing negotiation of the agreement. . . . those subsequent negotiations were neither completely successful nor harmonious."[34] The act had to be extended twice to facilitate continued negotiations. Objections to a proposed settlement were recently overruled, clearing the way for final court approval of the agreement.

But even a final agreement will not mean an end to water conflicts involving the San Carlos Apaches. The framers of the original act noted that the settlement would "settle the Tribe's claims to water as against all parties except the Gila Valley and Franklin Irrigation Districts . . . , and the San Carlos Irrigation and Drainage District and the Gila River Indian Community downstream."[35] To make matters worse, it is unclear who is actually a party to the settlement (the act lists eighteen); according to the special master, "These provisions have the complexity of a tax code. Woe to the future court and water commissioner who will actually have to try to apply these provisions."[36]

Yavapai/Prescott Indian Tribe Water Rights Settlement Act, 1994. This settlement is fully implemented.

In sum, of the fourteen settlements reviewed, six have been fully implemented, providing a fairly high degree of finality. Five settlements have experienced extended difficulties and have yet to offer any sense of finality. And three of the settlements have been implemented but certain outstanding problems remain unresolved.

Many of the problems described above can be attributed to language in the settlements themselves; no matter how earnest the parties might be, some settlements simply did not resolve important conflicts. But even if a settlement act was fairly well constructed, numerous problems have appeared in the implementation stage. So many settlements have encountered problems that the federal government began fielding "implementation teams" in 1990 in an effort to get them back on track. By 1995 there were a dozen implementation teams in the field, absorbing nearly as many resources as the original negotiation teams.[37] Furthermore, the time required for implementation keeps increasing. As John Duffy, the former chair of the interior working group on settlements, put it, "We have a large number of settlements that are not settled."[38] Finality is proving ever more elusive.[39]

Pushing a Rope

Given the problems that some settlements have encountered, it is reasonable to ask if finality and certainty are appropriate, realistic goals. If finality is the goal of all parties, why is it so difficult to achieve?

First of all, negotiation is a political process, and politics is always fickle. Changes in personnel and policy make finality difficult if not impossible.[40] At the federal level, discontinuity has long been a problem in water rights negotiations. Peter Sly notes that "In the past, Interior has had difficulty resolving internal conflicts about reserved rights negotiations. Positions on reserved rights negotiations changed with administrations, and there was little consistent policy concerning even agreements that had been concluded."[41] Similar problems exist at the state and local levels. In Arizona the state legislature changed the laws pertaining to general stream adjudications while several negotiations were in progress.[42] Such efforts do not stop with the passage of a settlement act; both sides attempt to interpret the settlement in their favor. A justice department official complained that "tribes and states often try to change settlements after they've been negotiated and passed into law; it goes on forever."

These problems are exacerbated by the complex linear nature of the negotiation process; there are numerous obstacles along the way, and the end product may look quite different from the original agreement. This process can be so frustrating that negotiators often resort to humor in trying to describe what it is like to spend months working out an agreement, and then take it to Congress only to have numerous parties tear at it "like buzzards at a road kill." One tribal member said it was like "trying to nail Jell-O to the wall." A justice department attorney likened it to "pushing a rope." A tribal attorney said it was like "trying to put toothpaste back into the tube."

This process may leave some parties disenchanted and willing to challenge the settlement. Judy Knight-Frank described what happened to the Colorado Ute settlement: "We had language in the settlement that gave us what we wanted, but that got watered down because so many people wanted something."[43] Another problem is a result of potentially different perceptions of the issues, which can be due to contrasting cultural traditions, differences in the use and meaning of language, and the inevitable influence of bias and self-interest. Dan Decker has encountered these problems: "All too often we get up from the table, and we have a different understanding of what we have agreed to."[44] In short, "There is a great distance separating the assertion of permanent resolution in the language of an agreement and the achievement of actual stability."[45]

These problems raise the troubling question of whether it is even possible to achieve true finality in water rights cases. Dan Tarlock argues convincingly that finality is an "illusion" that can never be achieved.[46] Carla Bennett makes a similar point: "It seems clear that no water right is ever truly certain."[47] These authors attribute the lack of finality to the vagaries of policy, law, and government. But nature plays a role too; water is nature's most unpredictable resource: floods, droughts, global warming, El Niño, melting/freezing ice caps. Is it not pure hubris to attempt to overlay such a fickle resource with a "permanent" grid of expectations? A case from history makes this point well; the negotiators of the Colorado River Compact of 1922 assumed an annual flow of 15 million af and allocated the river on that basis. But alas, they based their flow measurements on a series of wet years; the normal average flow is considerably less. Seventy-five years later we are still saddled with a critically important water compact that is based on a hydrological fallacy.

Even if it were possible to achieve finality and certainty, is it truly desirable? Will it provide justice? Many westerners assume that certainty will provide them with the assurance they need to develop the West's last remaining water resources with confidence in their rights. But there are two significant disadvantages to finality, one that affects the entire society and one that places the burden directly on Indian tribes.

The first disadvantage is the lack of flexibility engendered by "final" water rights determinations. Who is sufficiently prescient to know that a "permanent" water regime set up today will not become an outdated liability in the future? Finality ties the hands of water policy makers; to change what has been regarded as "final" usually results in a bitter, emotional political battle with significant costs, long delays, and a set of perceived victims. It sets the status quo in concrete, sometimes literally. Again history provides a lesson; the prior appropriation doctrine worked well in the nineteenth century, but it has become an anachronism in the New West. Today, progressive reforms in water policy are continually stifled by this antiquated doctrine that works against conservation, instream flow, riparian habitat protection, water-borne recreation, and the rational pricing and marketing of water. A continued insistence on finality in water settlements begs to create a similar situation in the twenty-first century. Today's successes can easily become tomorrow's failures unless we have the ability to adjust policy to correspond to changes in society, government, and the environment. The West is changing at an unprecedented rate just as settlements attempt to lock water rights into a static system.

A second reason finality may be undesirable concerns the impact it has on Indian people. For Indians, the price of settlement is the forfeiture of the single most powerful weapon they have wielded in the second treaty era: the Winters

Doctrine. It is important to remember that water settlements are a give-and-take process. For Indian tribes, the "give" consists of a permanent forfeiture of the right to claim reserved water rights. The settlements are very clear regarding rights Indians must relinquish:

Ak-Chin

"The Ak-Chin Indian community shall agree to waive, in a manner satisfactory to the Secretary, any and all claims of water rights or injuries to water rights of the Ak-Chin Indian community, including both ground water and surface water from time immemorial to the present . . . [and] waive any and all claims of water rights or injuries to water rights . . . which it might have in the future" (1978 Act).

Tohono O'odham (Papago)

The tribe "executes a waiver and release" of "any and all claims of water rights or injuries to water rights . . . any and all future claims of water rights" (1982 Act).

Fort Peck–Montana Compact

Article 1: "The basic purposes of the Compact are to determine finally and forever all rights of the Assiniboine and Sioux Tribes of the Fort Peck Indian Reservation . . . and to settle all claims by the Tribes and by the United States on behalf of the Tribes." Article IX: "The Tribal Water Right confirmed in Article III shall be final and conclusive . . . the Tribes and the United States as trustee for the Tribes hereby relinquish forever any and all existing and future claims to water from any source and for any purpose" (1985 Compact).

San Luis Rey (the Mission tribes)

The law takes effect only when all the parties, including the five Mission bands, "have entered into a settlement agreement providing for the complete resolution of all claims, controversies and issues" in the pending case and the FERC proceeding (1988 Act).

Colorado Ute (Animas–La Plata)

Language in the act refers to the 1986 agreement: "The Tribes are authorized to waive and release claims concerning or related to water rights as described in the Agreement" (102 Stat. 2978). The agreement states, "The Tribes, and the

United States as trustee for the Tribes, shall waive any and all claims to water rights within the State of Colorado not expressly identified in the Final Consent Decree" (1988 Act).

Salt River Pima-Maricopa

Section 10: Claims Extinguishment: Waivers and Releases. "There are extinguished . . . claims for water rights includ[ing] all claims under Federal and State laws. . . . The Community is authorized . . . to execute a waiver and release of all present and future claims of water rights or injuries to water rights (including water rights in ground water, surface water, and effluent), from time immemorial to the effective date of this Act, and any and all future claims of water rights. . . . The benefits realized by the Community under this Act shall constitute full and complete satisfaction of all monetary claims against the U.S. for any damages alleged to accrue" (1988 Act).

Fort Hall

"The Tribes and the United States shall be deemed to have waived and released any and all water rights or claims to water rights of the Tribes, its members and its allottees from any source within the Upper Snake River Basin." The tribes also waived the right to sue for lands inundated by American Falls Reservoir (1990 Act).

Fort McDowell

"The benefits realized by the Community's members under this Act shall constitute full and complete satisfaction of all members' claims for water rights or injuries to water rights under Federal and State laws (including claims for water rights in ground water, surface water, and effluent) from time immemorial to the effective date of this Act, and for any and all future claims of water rights (including claims for water rights in ground water, surface water, and effluent) from and after the effective date of this Act" (1990 Act).

Fallon Paiute-Shoshone/Truckee-Carson–Pyramid Lake

Fallon: No funding released until "the Tribes have released any and all claims they may have."
Pyramid Lake: The settlement provisions are contingent upon the dismissal with prejudice of four court cases and one administrative proceeding, all filed on behalf of the tribe. The Fishery Fund will not be released until "The Pyra-

mid Lake Tribe has released any and all claims of any kind whatsoever against the U.S. for damages to the Pyramid Lake fishery" (1990 Act).

Jicarilla Apache

The settlement "is intended to provide for the full, fair, and final resolution of the water rights claims of the Tribe" (1992 Act).

Northern Cheyenne

The purpose of the settlement is to "achieve a fair, equitable, and final settlement of all claims to Federal reserved water rights" (1992 Act).

Northern Ute (Utah)

The tribe "shall waive . . . any and all claims relating to its water rights covered under the agreement of September 20, 1965" (1992 Act).[48]

San Carlos Apache

"The benefits realized by the Tribe and its members under this title shall constitute full and complete satisfaction of all members' claims for water rights or injuries to water rights under Federal, State, and other laws (including claims for water rights in ground water, surface water, and effluent) from time immemorial to the effective date of this title. . . . [The tribe is authorized to] execute a waiver and release, except as provided in the Agreement, of all claims of water rights or injuries to water rights (including claims for water rights in ground water, surface water, and effluent), from time immemorial to the effective date of this title, and any and all future claims to water" (1992 Act).

Yavapai/Prescott

"The benefits . . . under the settlement agreement and this title shall constitute full and complete satisfaction of all claims by the Tribe and all members' claims for water rights or injuries to water rights under Federal and State laws . . . from time immemorial to the effective date of this title, and for any and all future claims of water rights" (1994 Act).

The only settlements that do not expressly prohibit future reserved water claims are Pyramid Lake and Northern Ute. The Pyramid Lake settlement was not a

Winters settlement, but rather an endangered species settlement; the Northern Ute settlement placed the Winters forfeiture language in a separate Ute Water Compact.

Taken as a whole, the clear objective of the settlement policy is to lay to rest the Winters Doctrine *forever*—that is a long time. This requires that tribes signing water settlements must speculate about their future water needs and then set that speculation in concrete. Pamela Williams of the Office of the Solicitor, Department of the Interior, very aptly described this challenge: "We have to find out how much water a tribe is going to need, not for just today, but for all times, and that is the scary part of it."[49] Is it reasonable to assume that tribal leaders—or anyone—can predict what kind of water needs a tribe will have in a century or two?

Looking back at the first treaty era, did anyone at that time have the faintest idea what reservations would look like at the end of the twentieth century? At that time the government assumed Indians would all become hay farmers; now irrigated agriculture is in demise, and reservations want water for instream flow, habitat protection, cultural preservation, high-tech industry, tourism, casinos, new housing, and off-reservation water leasing. Reservation economies are nothing if not unpredictable; just fifteen years ago did anyone anticipate that gaming would be a major revenue source for tribes?

Part of the tribes' quest for certitude via settlement appears to be a belief that the Supreme Court will never again be receptive to Indian rights. But the current high court is not immortal. Some day Rehnquist will retire. Even Scalia may begin to age some day (and Thomas is sure to follow his example). Yet the settlement policy seems predicated on the assumption that anti-Indian justices will be glaring at them from the bench *forever*. A friendlier Supreme Court could reverse the trend toward state court adjudication and recognize a wider array of uses for reserved water. At some point the high court may even embrace the homeland concept advocated by many Indian law specialists. A settlement that looked good under a Reagan-dominated court may look like a desperate bargain under a progressive court. But the forfeiture language in most settlements will prevent tribes from taking advantage of a more enlightened court.

On the other hand, states are proceeding with river basin adjudications, which include reserved rights for Indian reservations. Tribes may not have the luxury of ignoring them in hopes of a friendlier venue in the future; like time, a river basin adjudication waits for no one. It is unlikely that a future Supreme Court, no matter how pro-Indian, will overturn completed general stream adjudications.

But focusing on current appointments and the near future is still shortsighted. Will the federal bench remain relatively hostile to Indian reserved water rights for a century? For two centuries? One of the most important elements in a successful negotiation is knowing the alternative; negotiators must be able to compare one outcome with another in order to ascertain which is best.[50] We have a fairly good idea where the courts stand today; what alternative will they offer in the distant future?

Conclusion

The current Supreme Court probably will not emasculate the Winters Doctrine, but it could significantly limit its application and utility as a guide to quantification.[51] Some of the justices are hostile to reserved water rights, and there is a widespread belief that the federal bench at all levels is significantly less supportive of Indian rights than in the past. In addition, state courts, which now have jurisdiction over basin-wide adjudications that include Indian rights, are perceived as even more hostile. As the solicitor general of the Interior Department put it, "Going to court today is a crap-shoot."[52] This attitude has given rise to a sense of urgency among tribes that they must settle now while they have the opportunity or face a hostile court.

There is another dynamic that pushes tribes to settle now rather than wait for a more propitious court, and it concerns demographics and economics. The West is filling up with people, its cities are burgeoning, and the demands for water are escalating. In the eleven western states—where all of the settlements have taken place thus far—the population grew from 41.8 million in 1980 to an estimated 59.3 million in 1999.[53] There is a "last chance" attitude among many people that tribes must take what they can get today or be swept asunder by this new wave of "settlers." They do not want to see their water go the way of their land; they do not want the second treaty era to be a succession of losses like the first treaty era. This attitude is certainly understandable given the long history of cessions and the threat of state court adjudications. Perhaps optimism is not realistic in the gritty water wars of the contemporary West.

Nevertheless, the quest for finality demands a prophetic insight that we do not possess. An alternative approach would be to recognize that water is inherently unpredictable, and flexibility rather than certitude should be the guiding principle. No statutory promise of finality can substitute for a greater commitment to our trust responsibility. It would be better to have an enlightened Indian policy than to trap both Indian and non-Indian water users into a twentieth-century use regime as we enter the new millennium. But perhaps that is asking for too much. Perhaps the settlements are a statement that we will settle for the latter in the absence of the former.

Vignette: River of Lost Souls

There was a time when the entire western slope of the Colorado Rockies was Ute country. These mountain people were able to live in a traditional style long after other tribes had been rolled over by the juggernaut of Anglo settlement. However, they still had a long history of contact with Europeans. They signed their first treaty in 1670 with the Spanish. They signed a treaty of friendship with the United States in 1849, just a year after the United States acquired the area by force from Mexico.

Once the Ute lands became part of the United States, the typical pattern of the first treaty era emerged; each treaty authorizing a "final" land cession was followed by more treaties and more cessions. In 1874, in an effort to justify the land theft, the *Denver Tribune* editorialized that the state should be cleansed of all Utes because they were "actually practicing communists" and "the government should be ashamed to encourage them in their idleness and wanton waste of property."[54] Eventually the Ute lands in Colorado were reduced to two reservations in the southwestern corner of the state,[55] the Ute Mountain Ute Reservation, comprised of 557,000 acres, and the Southern Ute Reservation, which encompasses 310,002 acres. There are numerous streams and rivers that cross the reservations. The Spanish gave one of these watercourses the ominous name of Río de las Animas Perdidas — River of Lost Souls. In typical Yankee fashion the Americans truncated the name to the Animas River.

The Southern Ute Reservation is beautiful country. The lower elevations are mostly rolling hills of grass and sage, dotted with trees. As the ground rises gradually the grass gives way to pinyon pine and juniper. The San Juan Mountains, gleaming in snow, grace the skyline to the north. Cattle obviously thrive here. Farmhouses are widely dispersed, but growing less so every year as the area around Durango grows at an exponential rate.

The little town of Ignacio sits in a small valley about 20 miles south of Durango. The sign at the city limits proclaims it to be a "tri-ethnic community." A Catholic church dominates the north end of town. The Abel Atencio Community Center sits in the center of town, and the usual array of minute marts, video rentals, and packaged liquor stores line the main street. The tribal headquarters complex is just north of town. There, old decaying BIA buildings,

surrounded by huge cottonwood trees, are intermixed with newer tribal buildings. The tribe's casino, built in a bold Indian motif, is just south of the tribal
offices.

The seat of power on the Southern Ute Reservation is in a building that
looks something like a 1970s-era high school. In the hallway outside the tribal
chairman's office is a large plaque titled "Southern Ute Indian Tribal Veterans."
The names are divided into the various wars that have called Americans to duty.
The Frost family has obviously made a substantial contribution: Andrew Frost
in the First World War, Billy Frost in the Second World War, Harvey Frost Sr.
and Raymond Frost Sr. in the Korean Conflict, Clement Frost and Ray Frost
in the Vietnam War, and Ray Frost Jr. and Jack McClure Frost in the present
era. But today the Frost family is fighting a different kind of battle. Clement
Frost, the tribal chairman, is an outspoken proponent of the Animas–La Plata
Project. His brother, Ray Frost, is his principle antagonist. The 1988 Colorado
Ute water settlement has rent this family right down the middle.[56]

The Animas–La Plata Project (ALP) is a superlative example of a water
project that was contrived when federal money was easier to get than a credit
card. The ALP was designed to solve a "problem," as defined by irrigation
farmers and their allies in the Bureau of Reclamation; the best water was in the
Animas valley, but the best farmland was in the La Plata valley. So, after several
ideas were offered and rejected, they settled on a scheme to suck water out of
the Animas River, pump it 525 feet up a mountain, store the water in a two-
dam reservoir above Durango called Ridges Basin, and then pump it another
300 feet uphill to a series of farms in the La Plata River valley. The pumping
would consume enough electricity to power a city of 60,000. The principle use
of the water would be to grow alfalfa (a low-value crop) and wheat (a surplus
crop) at high altitude.

How could such a preposterous idea even get off the drawing board? The
answer is simple: the raw, high-stakes play of western water politics. In the mid-
1960s several states in the Colorado River basin, especially Arizona, wanted to
build a series of giant federal water projects. Their first hurdle was to get the
legislation past Congressman Wayne Aspinall of western Colorado. Aspinall,
known by the sobriquet "Mr. Reclamation," was chairman of the House Interior Committee, and nothing could get through the committee without his
approval. He indicated a willingness to approve the Central Arizona Project
and other projects, but only if western Colorado got five new projects. This kind
of pet-project exchange, known as logrolling, had become a common practice
when authorizing water projects. A deal was struck in 1968, and the ALP and
four other west slope projects were authorized. Of these, the ALP was arguably
the weakest, and it progressed the slowest. By the time of President Carter's

1977 "hit list" of America's most wasteful water projects, the ALP was not far enough along to make the list; two of its sister projects did, however.

The ALP languished for twenty years, unable to muster sufficient political support to overcome its obvious inadequacies. In the meantime, the Utes in Colorado filed claims for federal reserved water rights to the seven rivers and streams that traverse the two reservations. It was clear to everyone that they had a strong claim and might very well win the lion's share of water: "The state of Colorado has estimated the potential effect of outstanding Indian claims on non-Indian water rights and predicted that all non-Indian irrigation in the Mancos and la Plata River drainages could be eliminated if Colorado Ute Tribal water rights claims were fully exercised. During dry years, the Tribes would exercise senior water rights to virtually all available water on numerous rivers and streams in the San Juan River Basin. It was estimated that more than 34,000 acres of land irrigated by non-Indians could be adversely impacted if a settlement of Tribal water rights claims was not achieved."[57] In short, the Utes had a strong case, but a series of federal court decisions forced the tribes into state court, which made them wary of trusting their water future to a potentially hostile decision-making venue.[58] At that point both the Utes and local non-Indian water users began to view the ALP as their salvation. Politically this made the ALP completely dependent on a resolution of Ute water claims; as an untitled Interior Department document put it, "without the tribal claims on Animas–La Plata water, ALP is without legs, without a future."

By that time the settlement era was in full swing, and local water interests came up with the idea that a settlement could resolve the Indian water rights case and jump start the moribund ALP; all they needed was $600 million from the nation's taxpayers. The federal government saw things differently. By the mid-1980s the federal deficit was skyrocketing, and the Reagan administration had initiated the policy of cost sharing for water projects, which requires local project beneficiaries to absorb a significant portion of the costs.

After two years of negotiations between the tribes, state and local entities, and the federal government, an agreement was reached that divided the project into two phases. Phase 1 would be financed primarily by the federal government and would build the primary components of the Ridges Basin system. Phase 2 would be built later at the expense of state and local entities, and would include the water delivery system for the Utes' irrigation. The agreement also used water from the Dolores Project, another federal water project about fifty miles west of the planned ALP, to provide drinking water to Towaoc, the tribal headquarters of the Ute Mountain Utes.

Because the agreement was dependent on federal money and federal projects, it had to be authorized by an act of Congress. Congressman Bevill, attempting to convince his colleagues to vote for the proposed settlement, spoke of it in revealing terms: "This is not just a Western water project. It is an opportunity to restore dignity and the heritage of our Native Americans in a manner that is in peace with their non-Indian neighbors."[59] Apparently "our" Native Americans had no dignity or heritage until ALP came along. In 1988 Congress passed the Colorado Ute Settlement Act, which ratified the 1986 agreement and reauthorized the ALP.

We often conceive of settlements as the culmination of a long political conflict that, after years of debate, is resolved with "finality and certainty" when the parties agree to settle. But in this case, the settlement merely intensified the political battles over the ALP and the impact it would have on the environment, the budget, endangered species, and the Ute reservations. The controversy over the ALP and the accompanying settlement has all the hallmarks of an interminable struggle; the only permanent aspect may be the fighting. This struggle is very complex, involves numerous players, and has become quite personal for a number of people.

The long debate over the ALP demonstrates the perils of basing an Indian water settlement on a large federal water project. There is a score of problems: environmental impacts, economic and budgetary considerations, and conflict among Indian people. Each of these will be addressed.

Environmental problems have plagued the ALP for a long time. The project as originally conceived would have built a large dam and reservoir on the Animas River; these were moved to Ridges Basin to avoid the impact of an on-stream placement. After the settlement was passed, the project ran into endangered species problems. Before construction could begin, the U.S. Fish and Wildlife Service issued a "jeopardy" biological opinion for the endangered Colorado squawfish (now called the Colorado pikeminnow) that is native to the San Juan River.[60] Both the Animas and the La Plata Rivers flow into the San Juan. This effectively put much of the project—especially phase 2, which has the Indian benefits—on hold while a seven-year study is completed (the environmental problems are discussed in further detail in chapter 7).

The second set of problems concerns economics. Opponents claim it is a waste of the taxpayers' dollar; proponents claim it is the cheapest way to resolve the water claims of the Ute reservations. As with many water projects, it depends on how the benefits and costs are calculated. The Bureau of Reclamation has a long history of figuring benefits and costs in a manner that exaggerates the former and minimizes the latter. For example, if the ALP's benefit/cost ratio is calculated using the bureau's old method, the ratio is 1.4:1. This method assumes a discount rate set unrealistically low, assumes all kinds of "indirect benefits" (which are no longer permitted in modern calculations), and does not count the interest subsidy, crop subsidies, or opportunity costs. Independent benefit/cost analyses arrive at a much different conclusion. The benefit/cost ratio using a modern discount rate, and not including indirect benefits, is a dismal .36: 1. In other words, for every dollar the federal government pays for the project, it gets only 36 cents in return. If the multiple subsidies and interest costs are included, the ALP looks like an exercise in fiscal absurdity.

The project supporters counter that the biggest dollar benefit of the project comes from the settlement of the Indian water claims, which would cost millions in court costs if it were litigated: "None of the Reclamation analyses, even the $1.4 to $1, includes ANY dollar values for the Indian water rights settlement — a negotiated agreement in lieu of long and expensive litigation."[61] This perspective assumes that building the ALP is the only way to honor the Utes' water rights.

Another economic problem concerns the limited ability of the farmers to pay back their share of the project. Opponents point out that their "ability to repay project construction costs to the treasury would be minimal. Of the $7,600 irrigation investment per acre, only approximately $500 would be returned to the treasury over the fifty-year interest free repayment period provided for in the Federal Reclamation law. The loss to the Federal treasury would be equivalent to $1 million per farm."[62] ALP supporters point out that any money that cannot be repaid by the farmers is covered with funds generated by federal hydroelectric power. This is, of course, simply another kind of subsidy for farmers, paid for by people who use federally generated energy in the Colorado River basin.

In 1994 the inspector general of the Interior Department completed an economic analysis of both the ALP and the neighboring Dolores Project, and concluded that neither was cost-effective. In regard to ALP, the inspector noted, "The Animas–La Plata Project as currently formulated would not be financially feasible under existing Reclamation law and policy. . . . We believe that the irrigation component of the Animas–La Plata Project should be reexamined given that project irrigation is apparently neither economically justified nor financially feasible. We estimated that the elimination of the non-Indian irrigation component of the Project could result in construction cost savings ranging from $134 million to $171 million."[63] To a great extent, the argument over the economics of the project hinges on a political, not economic, question: Is this a project built to honor the nation's commitment to the Utes, or is it a thinly veiled charade to get one last pork barrel water project through Congress? If it is the former, then a strict economic calculus is irrelevant; if it is the latter, then the benefit/cost calculus is critically important. It is the debate over this question that has led to the third major problem with the project; the bitter fight among both Utes and non-Indians over the true nature and purpose of the ALP.

The Colorado Ute settlement provides a resolution to the water claims of both the Ute Mountain Utes and the Southern Utes. The former have been relatively pleased with the settlement. They received a much larger development fund than the Southern Utes, and they finally got a pipeline to Towaoc, which had been trucking in its water for the past forty years. That pipeline was part of the Dolores Project, and it is now in place. The Ute Mountain Utes have used their bargaining position to gain funds for a new 7,800-acre irrigated agricultural project. An internal Interior Department memo described it as "nonviable," but the Colorado delegation is so desperate for political support for ALP that they have been willing to spend millions on the Ute Mountain Ute farm (more than $15 million thus far).

The big controversy is on the Southern Ute Reservation, where a bitter and highly personal struggle has divided the reservation into two camps. The faction that supports the settlement and the ALP has been led, until recently, by former chairman Clement Frost. Prior to that, the project was promoted for a quarter century by long-time chairman Leonard Burch and tribal attorney Sam Maynes. They worked closely with the local non-Indian water district, which Maynes also represented. On the opposing side is a tribal faction led by Ray Frost and several other tribal members who call themselves the Southern Utes Grassroots Organization. They are allied with four environmental groups: the Four Corners Action Coalition, Taxpayers for the Animas River, the Sierra Club, and Sierra Club Legal Defense Fund.

In 1986, when the tribal council endorsed the water agreement, it provided an explanation to tribal members of why it supported a settlement with the ALP as the linchpin:

> The Tribal Council of the Southern Ute Indian Tribe decided to negotiate for the Tribe's Winters reserved water rights. The focus of the Tribal Council in these negotiations is the Animas–La Plata Project. The Tribal Council of the Southern Ute Indian Tribe has unanimously supported the Animas–La Plata Project for over twenty years because the Project represents the best hope for the Tribe to become financially secure through the development of the Tribe's natural resources. The Tribe already benefits from the Vallecito Project [a small reservoir north of the reservation]. The Animas–La Plata Project will provide similar irrigation water and, in addition, it will supply needed industrial water. The Tribal Council of the Southern Ute Tribe views the water supply provided to the Tribe by the Project as a valuable substitute for the Tribe's reserved water rights on the Animas and La Plata Rivers.[64]

For many years the Southern Ute Tribal Council, led by Chairman Burch, supported ALP. But by the time of the 1986 water agreement a number of dissenters had appeared. A petition to recall five council members passed by one vote, including a vote from a tribal member who was in prison and voted by proxy. The prisoner's vote was successfully challenged, which made the vote a tie, which meant the recall failed. This recall was the beginning of many electoral battles where the main issue was ALP. In 1990 Ray Frost tried unsuccessfully to unseat Chairman Burch, but he did manage to gain a council seat in 1993. That same year, Guy Pinnicoose, a long-time member of the council and a former ALP supporter, challenged Chairman Burch, but again Burch held his seat.

Recently the Southern Ute Grassroots Organization (SUGO) advanced a proposal that they would like to see substituted for the ALP. It calls for "redirected moneys from the ALP to establish a *Ute Legacy Land and Water Fund* that would enable the two Colorado Ute Tribes to buy back senior water rights and land. . . . The idea is that all water obligations that remain outstanding under the 1986 Colorado Ute Indian Settlement Agreement would be alternatively satisfied by acquisitions made through the fund." SUGO estimates that their proposed legacy fund would cost one-third of the amount needed to complete phase 1 of ALP. They do not want to abandon the 1988 settlement; rather, they want to amend it by substituting the legacy fund for the ALP.[65] The SUGO approach has been complemented by environmental groups that also want to find an alternative to ALP.[66]

Another enduring source of conflict over ALP is whether it is truly an Indian water settlement, or merely an old-fashioned water project cloaked with the Indian blanket. Congressman George Miller, a persistent critic of ALP, made the latter claim during the debate over the settlement: "Let's be honest about what we are buying if this bill is enacted. Are we really buying an Indian water rights settlement? . . . We are buying a Bureau of Reclamation water project. . . . we are buying a water project that will benefit non-Indian alfalfa farmers much more than it will ever benefit the Ute Mountain Utes and the Southern Utes. I believe this bill is flawed because it forces the American taxpayer to settle legitimate Indian water rights claims by bootstrapping construction of a $600 million water project that will primarily benefit non-Indians."[67] More recently, a Bureau of Reclamation official made a similar claim: "I call it Jurassic pork. They say it's for the Indians, but it's clearly a developer's project, and taxpayers are going to pay for it."[68]

In the midst of all this controversy, the governor and lieutenant governor of Colorado began working on alternative formulations of ALP in an effort to satisfy all parties. That effort, which bears their names and is known as the Romer/Schoettler process, developed both a structural and a nonstructural alternative. Other scaled-down proposals and variations were proposed. Funding for the ALP barely survived the last few years as Congress searched for ways to cut the federal budget. In 1998 Congressman John Kasich, chairman of the powerful House Budget Committee, added the ALP to his "Dirty Dozen" list of corporate welfare programs he wants to cut.[69] On the other hand, old water projects seldom die. A congressional aid recently described the politics of funding the ALP: "No matter how illogical the economics of this project might be, no matter how fraught it is with environmental problems, it is almost impossible to kill it."[70] In 2000 Congress amended the 1988 settlement and authorized a scaled-down version of ALP.[71]

Sam Maynes is Mr. ALP. To call him combative is an understatement. He would make a great and loyal friend, but an implacable enemy. I met with him at his home on the outskirts of Durango, Colorado. The house sits on a rise above the Animas River, which flows past in a graceful horseshoe curve. There is still a lot of pastureland along the river, but new homes are sprouting up everywhere.

Mr. Maynes spent his formative years in Durango, where his father ran a tavern. During World War II they temporarily relocated to California, where their closest neighbor was Russell Means, who was destined to become the controversial leader of the American Indian Movement (AIM). The Maynes family returned to Colorado, where Sam attended law school, then began practicing in the Durango area. In 1965 he became the attorney for the Southwestern Water Conservation District of Colorado and has represented water interests ever since. He has also represented the Southern Ute tribe for twenty-nine years.

Much of the criticism of ALP is directed at Sam Maynes, but he seems to enjoy the role of project lightning rod. He has been accused of a conflict of interest—a charge that was not upheld in court (he points out that the tribe has a separate water attorney that negotiated the settlement). He has also been accused of railroading the Southern Utes into supporting a project that is not in their best interest. In response to this accusation, he notes that the tribe supported ALP before he became tribal attorney: "Everyone says this bad white lawyer is hoodwinking the Utes, but the Utes are proud and fierce, and they would not let me tell them what to do."

His argument is simple and straightforward: the ALP, regardless of its alleged faults, is the Utes' best hope of ever getting funding for water development and permanent storage rights. He notes, "Both tribes early on recognized that these projects [ALP and Dolores] were their best shot for getting water." And both projects have the incidental advantage of providing water to the Anglo water districts in the area—which Maynes represents.

He recited a litany of hurdles that supporters of the Dolores and ALP projects have faced, including "Carter's goddam hit list that alienated everyone"; the National Environmental Policy Act (NEPA), which he called the "big tomahawk for environmentalists"; a "nasty lawsuit" over the creation of a special water district for ALP; and then, "up jumped the devil, cost sharing." Sam and many others in the area had hoped the 1988 settlement would resolve these problems and the project could go forward.

They were mistaken. "We've been waiting ten years now, and the government still hasn't delivered on its promises." Sam reserves his greatest vitriol for environmentalists: "I am really bitter about the Sierra Club Legal Defense Fund. They have done a great disservice to the Indians. If ALP goes down the tubes, will the Sierra Club be there to help the Utes?"

Toward the end of the interview, Mr. Maynes summed up his attitude about water development: "I know about farmers. I think irrigated agriculture is a good thing. I grant that it is subsidized water, but it's just a question of who gets the subsidies; if it's the other guy's subsidies, it's no good, if it's yours, its okay." For Sam Maynes, water development for irrigation is always a good investment of the taxpayer's money.

Isabelle Eagle is a respected elder in the Southern Ute tribe. She and her husband have spent their entire lives on the reservation. They live in a modest HUD home just outside of Ignacio. I phoned Mrs. Eagle and made an appointment. When I showed up at her door I was a complete stranger, but she greeted me with a smile and invited me in. We sat at her kitchen table.

As we talked it became obvious that Mrs. Eagle was well versed in the arcane ways of water policy. She talked about acre-feet, reserved rights, and payback schedules. I asked her how she became so well informed.

"I'm always asking questions. Some people don't like to be questioned, especially elected officials. We Native Americans are supposed to be quiet, especially women, but that's just not my nature."

Mrs. Eagle explained that her opposition to ALP evolved over time. "I gradually became aware that something was brewing, that something just didn't quite fit. When you read about what the water lawyers and the proponents say, you can't help but wonder what they are not telling you. Somebody was selling us a bill of goods. They said it over and over again, like they were brainwashing us. People that want money spent for something need to brainwash the public; people in this country are fed this stuff all the time."

Mrs. Eagle was also aware of the environmental impact of the project. "[The Bureau of] Reclamation didn't consider the wildlife and the health of the rivers. My Indian spirit was always with the river. I hated to see it die, I hated to see it dammed up. All those things living in the river would be suffering."

But Mrs. Eagle was also concerned about what the tribe gave up in the settlement and the problems of delivering water to the reservation. Phase 1 of the project did very little for the Southern Utes other than provide storage in the proposed Ridges Basin Reservoir, which is a considerable distance from the reservation. The facilities to deliver that water to the reservation were moved back to phase 2, which was not federally funded.

"I found out we had done a trade-off, and we had to give up our claims to those rivers just to get water stored up there [in Ridges Basin]. Then people started to say, how are we going to get that water down here? The White Man has promised a lot of things. I don't believe in this settlement. I feel in my bones that we didn't get what we should have."

At the end of the interview I asked her about the future; what does she think might happen? She sat silently for a moment, then began to speak quite softly with her eyes closed. "My main concern is that this whole business will mortgage our land. I think it is part of a government policy to stop Indians from being Indians and owning lands, because those lands have resources. What's the word you call that in English? Oh yes, genocide. Just put it all into a larger perspective and you can see it heading that way. First they'll take our water, and then they'll take our land. For us it will be a catastrophe."

As I got up to leave, Mrs. Eagle tapped me lightly on the arm. "Remember," she said with a smile, "I'm not a leader; I'm just against that project."

Leonard Burch, chairman of the tribe for twenty-seven years, has spent nearly his entire professional life fighting for ALP. No longer chairman but a member of the tribal council, Mr. Burch is still an adamant supporter of the project. He and Sam Maynes have been friends for a long time — they played basketball together in high school — and they have worked for decades to bring ALP to fruition.

"I've been involved with the project since the planning that took place in the late fifties and early sixties. When the first authorization act passed in 1968 we thought, by golly, we are on our way; we're going to have a project that actually delivers water."

A lot has happened since then; building the project is not one of them. One of the most controversial elements in the reauthorized ALP was moving the Indian component to phase 2, which was not federally funded. Mr. Burch defended that plan. "Who's going to pay for phase 2? Well, we'll have to work this thing out. It's not determined yet who is going to pay for it. It's on down the road after we get the reservoir built."

I asked him why the tribe consented to move most of its benefits into phase 2.

"We got into cost sharing. They had us over a barrel. We said fine, we need the storage. We want wet water stored for the future of our tribe."

For Leonard, it was important for the tribe to work in harmony with local Anglos. He noted how the tribe had collaborated on two other projects, Vallecito and Lemon Reservoirs. "We saw how a reservoir is important to irrigation and working with the neighbors. So we have a history of working with the other people to build projects that serve the land. This got us started on ALP."

In contrast to Mr. Burch's steadfast support for ALP, Guy Pinnicoose changed his mind about it several years ago. He was on the tribal council for fifteen years. Initially he supported the project and the settlement but later became a persistent critic. He ran against Leonard Burch in the 1993 election for chairman; he lost narrowly after a campaign that was dominated by the debate over ALP.

Mr. Pinnicoose is now out of politics but remains a vocal critic of ALP. "I was against the project because of the money. We can't afford it. We should have leased the water downstream and made some money off it, but they wouldn't let us do that."

The most visible opponent of ALP is Ray Frost. He is no longer a tribal council member, but he serves as chairperson of SUGO, the Southern Utes Grassroots Organization. He lists a score of problems he sees in the settlement: "We had senior water rights on all the rivers. Now we have become junior water holders. By building the reservoir off-reservation it makes us lose out. Only four tribal members live along La Plata, which is where the new water will go. And this project just makes the surplus crop problem worse."

Like Mr. Pinnicoose, Ray Frost is concerned that the tribe will not be able to afford the water from the project if and when it is delivered. "Who is going to pay for Phase 2? There is no backing from anybody. We'll have an enormous bill to pay through cost sharing. The beneficiaries, if there are any, will be paying for it for the rest of their lives."

Mr. Frost is sympathetic to the environmental groups that oppose the project and has worked closely with them. "If the settlement had been done right it would be built already. But the environmental stuff was not done right — that's what stopped the project. The Sierra Club just used existing law."

Ray also expressed his view of the Romer/Shoettler process. "Hopefully they'll look at the Ute Legacy Fund. Then we might have a chance to move forward. We should have a public discussion of this, followed by a tribal referendum. There has never been a referendum on the project."

The final supplemental EIS for the ALP listed ten alternatives, which represented five basic approaches with variations:

> 1. Build the project as recommended by the Bureau of Reclamation in 1996, which would have two phases, a full-size reservoir, and a large irrigation component, with an eventual total water depletion of 149,220 af. It

is basically the original project with the first phase divided into two stages in order to meet the limit of 57,100 af depletions required by the U.S. Fish and Wildlife Service. The second stage would then exceed that limit. The cost estimate for this project, using a new formula imposed upon the bureau, added salinity and lost power production to the costs, bringing the total cost to $847.7 million.

2. The reconciliation plan (ALP-Light), developed by Romer-Schoettler, would build a 260,000-af reservoir, provide irrigation water to both Ute and non-Indian farmers, and refrains from de-authorizing any project features. The cost estimate for this alternative is $290 million, which is unrealistic if the cost of the full project is $847.7 million.

3. The Clinton administration proposal (ALP-Ultralight) to construct a 90,000-af off-stream reservoir and limit non-Indian project water to municipal and industrial uses—to be paid for by the beneficiaries. To meet the tribes' water allocation guaranteed in the settlement, they would receive nearly 80 percent of the stored water (19,800 af apiece), and a water acquisition fund would purchase the rest from willing buyers. All project features not a part of this plan would be deauthorized. The estimated cost is $170 million.

4. The Animas River Citizens' Coalition proposal is a nonstructural alternative that would purchase irrigation lands and associated water rights and use that water to satisfy the tribes' water allocations as set forth in the settlement. This alternative grew out of the SUGO proposal, outlined above, and is backed by SUGO and four environmental groups. Rough cost estimates place it around $170 million.

5. The Citizens Progressive Alliance proposal would allow the Ute tribes to market their water downstream, which would generate considerable revenue for the tribes and create benefits of instream flow, increased hydropower production, and reduced salinity in the Colorado River basin. The cost to the federal treasury would be negligible, but downstream interests fiercely oppose it (more on this in chapter 8).

The draft supplemental EIS that came out in January 2000 recommended the administration proposal with modifications and assumes that the Southern Ute tribe will develop a coal-fired power plant that requires a 27,000 af diversion.[72] In the meantime, several congressmen tried to short-circuit that process by introducing legislation to decree their favored alternative. Senator Campbell and Congressman McInnis pushed for passage of a bill that would authorize ALP-Light (the reconciliation plan). They tied this bill to the Chippewa Cree settlement in hopes of improving its chances for passage.[73] But the Chippewa

Cree settlement became law without ALP. Anti-ALP legislation was also introduced; twenty-nine House members introduced a bill to completely deauthorize ALP and instruct the secretary of the interior to enter into new negotiations with the Ute tribes.[74] All of this activity prompted former Southern Ute tribal chairman Clement Frost to complain, "My tribe has been caught in a terrible political web."[75]

A final supplemental EIS, issued in July 2000, was followed by a record of decision two months later. The settlement amendment passed by Congress later that year accepted the preferred alternative, with some minor modifications, and added a pipeline to Shiprock, New Mexico, to mollify the Navajo Nation.

Before I left the Southern Ute Reservation I stopped in a small cafe in Ignacio for a cup of coffee. The man in the next booth began talking to the waitress about the sparse rain they had received that spring. I introduced myself and asked him if he thought ALP would finally solve the region's water problems. He slowly shook his head. "Oh, god, what a mess."

The Colorado Ute settlement is a clear illustration of what happens when major issues are not resolved in a settlement. In this case, the "cure" was as bad as the problem. Finality will always be elusive when significant problems are left unresolved, including problems created by the settlement itself.

5

The Cup of Living Water

Paper Water

In the final pages of *Black Elk Speaks*, the elderly Lakota holy man Black Elk gives thanks to the Great Spirit: "You have given me the cup of living water and the sacred bow, the power to make life and to destroy."[1] The Great Spirit had provided the cup of living water, but the New Eden had taken it away. A century later the federal government began encouraging Indian tribes to negotiate settlements so they could acquire water. Are settlements the new source of the cup of living water?

Indian tribes — America's first irrigators — were not always water destitute. Some tribes diverted and applied large amounts of water before encroaching settlement pilfered the water supply. A case in point is the Pima Indians of the Gila River Reservation in central Arizona. During the latter half of the nineteenth century the tribe grew prosperous from its large irrigated farms. Then the waters of the Gila were diverted upstream from the reservation, and the Pimas' fortunes declined precipitously. Arthur Davis, who later became a commissioner of reclamation, described the situation as a "grave wrong against peaceful and industrious Indian tribes."[2] Today the Gila River Pimas are engaged in a long, difficult negotiation in an attempt to regain some of their lost wealth.

Of all the reasons to negotiate, perhaps the most convincing is the opportunity to turn back a century of water loss and return ancestral waters to Indian people. Or, in the more arcane language of negotiations, a settlement can provide "wet water" rather than the mere "paper water" won in court. David Getches writes, "Negotiation is a more promising vehicle for reaching a meaningful, practical resolution that provides the Indians with deliverable water and non-Indians with genuine certainty."[3] An OMB official made a similar point: "The big advantage of settlements is that you free up the resource; the Indians get some wet water and the Anglos get the cloud removed." An Indian attorney argued that "The goal that everyone should have is getting wet water."[4] Thomas McGuire summarized this prominent theme: "In the now-familiar discourse over water settlements, the Indians are about to get 'wet water.'"[5]

The possibility of regaining lost waters is a powerful incentive for tribes to negotiate. A negotiated settlement looks quite appealing when it holds the promise of finally rectifying years of water losses. For example, the tribal council of the Southern Ute tribe attempted to generate support among tribal members for a proposed settlement by referring to wet water: "The Tribal Council made the decision to negotiate for the added purpose of obtaining results which may be unavailable through litigation. Litigation will secure the Tribe only paper water rights, whereas the outcome of the negotiations will be 'wet' water the Tribe can put to use."[6]

Of course, all water is wet, and to an equivalent degree. Yet everyone involved in Indian water negotiations uses this term like a mantra despite its hydrological shortcomings. However, the term appears to mean different things to different people. The most common usage embodies some form of artificial diversion and application. Thus, wet water is "delivered water instead of 'paper' rights defined through a decree but not realized through engineering systems."[7] Nunez and Wallace define wet water in terms of its flow and quality: "A key objective facing Indian tribes when confronting negotiations is to secure a reliable supply of 'wet water' to fulfill the Winters rights of the reservations. The desired characteristics of this supply of water are that it be reliable (meaning free from interruptions in supply, including drought) and that the water be of appropriate quality."[8] Others define it in terms of funding for water resource development,[9] with an emphasis on "federal construction moneys to obtain firm water rights ('wet water') against an uncertain economic and political future."[10]

But there are other possible interpretations. One author defines wet water in terms of its leasing potential: "Tribes can now turn what was litigated 'paper' Winters rights into 'wet' Winters rights which often can be marketed to enhance economic development and self-sufficiency."[11] Marketing water does not necessarily require a diversion on the reservation, so this definition of wet water focuses on economics rather than engineering.

To others, wet water is simply a more solid, defensible right than the tenuous rights based on *Winters*: "Wet water can also be a kind of water in the middle. Indians have a property right. Maybe it's not wet, but it's moist. Some day, they can put that water to use, even though they can't now. At least we extinguish the doubt about Indian water rights."[12] In other words, wet water is a water right backed up by statute, which increases the possibility that it can some day be developed.

In another perspective, wet water is any water that remains in its natural watercourse, flowing across the reservation unimpeded. In this view, it is water not diverted by upstream users and is used for instream flow, habitat, aesthetics, spirituality, and all of the ineffable qualities that are found in a living river.

Given the great interest in wet water, it is worth looking closely at each settlement in an effort to determine how much water is actually being used by Indian people as a result of the water settlements.

Wet Water

The promise of wet water is at the crux of the settlement policy. The most prevalent meaning of this term focuses on diversion and actual use. This use often entails either new water development construction, efficiency measures, or a reallocation of supply from an existing water source. The survey below examines each of the settlements in an attempt to assess the amount of wet water that has accrued to Indian tribes as a direct result of the settlement policy. It compares the amount of water the settlement tribes were using at the time of the settlement to the amount they are using today. It also identifies the potential for future wet water resulting from the settlements. The water figures are for annual diversions; annual depletion rights are considerably less.

Ak-Chin

The Ak-Chin tribe was awarded up to 85,000 af (less in dry years). The tribe is currently using most of this for Ak-Chin farms and is leasing the remainder to local interests. Prior to the settlement the tribe was able to irrigate only about 5,000 acres; they now irrigate 20,000 acres, using 75,000 af. This is a net increase in water usage of about 50,000 af. Thus, this tribe is very much a wet water user.[13]

Tohono O'odham (Papago)

The Tohono O'odham Nation won a total quantified water right of 66,000 af of surface water but agreed to a 10,000 af limit on groundwater pumping. The majority of the surface water—37,800 af—was to come from the CAP; the remainder was to be "reclaimed" water (treated effluent) traded by the secretary of the interior for other water supplies for the tribe. The surface water was to be divided between two districts—San Xavier and Schuk Toak—to be used primarily in farm operations. The farm at San Xavier had been in operation for many years, but had been dewatered by off-reservation uses; the farm at Schuk Toak was a new construction project.

More than $50 million has been spent on this settlement, but very little wet water is currently available for use on the reservation. Construction on the Schuk Toak farm is proceeding and currently delivers water to 1,200 acres.[14] The Schuk Toak farm is entitled to 10,800 af under the settlement. San Xavier, the other major project under the settlement, celebrated the arrival of CAP water in March 2001. When that component is completed, the San Xavier farms will be entitled to 27,000 af under the settlement. For several years the nation leased water to Tucson, but that contract was canceled due to differences in pricing.[15]

Fort Peck–Montana Compact

The Assiniboine and Sioux tribes of Fort Peck were awarded a diversion right to the lesser of 1.05 million af or the water necessary to supply a consumptive rate of 525,236 af from the Missouri River and certain tributaries, and groundwater. Currently the tribes make no water diversions as a result of the settlement, but they have established instream flows for 58,000 af in a number of tributaries.

San Luis Rey (the Mission tribes)

The five Mission tribes were awarded 16,000 af in the settlement. Negotiators searched long and hard for a source for that water and finally returned to an idea that was proposed at the time of the settlement: line the All-American Canal and use part of the saved water to meet the requirements of the settlement. No water has been diverted to the reservations yet.[16]

Colorado Ute (Animas–La Plata)

The Ute Mountain Utes won a total of 92,000 af from three sources: the Dolores Project, which will provide 1,000 af for municipal and industrial use, 23,300 af for irrigation, and another 800 af for fish and wildlife. The municipal water is being delivered via the Highline-Towaoc Canal. The farm project is currently irrigating 6,300 acres and will grow to 7,800 acres in the next two to three years, so this project is using approximately 81 percent of their portion of the Dolores Project irrigation allocation (about 18,500 af). The second source consists of streams flowing across the reservation; the tribe is entitled to 27,400 af, but currently uses only a nominal amount from these sources. The third source is the ALP; the tribe is entitled to a total of 33,200 af if this project is ever completed.[17]

The Southern Ute tribe was awarded a total of 29,900 af from the ALP, 10,000 af from a variety of streams on the east side of the reservation, and all existing rights to reservation watercourses. Thus far the tribe has not increased its use of water from these sources, but anticipates some municipal and industrial use in the future.[18]

Salt River Pima-Maricopa

This settlement provides 122,400 af to the reservation, relying upon a score of sources.[19] The Indian community currently uses about 60,000 af for the on-reservation irrigation project and small industrial uses. That is about the same water use level as before the settlement; thus the settlement did not result in an appreciable increase in water use, but it did change the sources of that water and create a clear title to it. The settlement also arranged for the Indian community to lease 13,300 af to local municipalities for 99 years.

The problem with this settlement concerns the on-reservation irrigation project, which consumes nearly all of the settlement water. All of the farmers on this project are non-Indians who lease the land at very low rates. The leased lands produce a small amount of income for allottees, but the project as a whole is a money-losing proposition for the community. The project is a classic BIA project—dilapidated, underfunded, and poorly managed, with water leased at below-market prices.[20] To remedy this poor management, the community has demanded control of the project; a bill has been introduced in Congress to establish that control.[21] Thus it is problematic to characterize water going to an all-Anglo project that loses money for the Indian community as an example of wet water for Indian people.[22]

Fort Hall

This settlement utilized a variety of creative sources to give the Shoshone and Bannock tribes a right to 581,031 af of water. New uses of water on the reservation must await the completion of a reservation-wide water inventory, which is in progress. The tribal government is also developing a water code. The tribes agreed to lease 38,000 af to the Bureau of Reclamation for instream flow.[23]

Fort McDowell

The Yavapai Indian community water rights were quantified at 35,233 af, which includes the 7,058 af awarded by the Kent Decree in 1910. The settlement also provides storage space behind Salt River Project dams in order to shift Kent Decree water to late summer usage. The community's new 2,000-acre citrus and pecan orchard is operational and consuming approximately 3,500 af; this amount will increase as the trees mature. The existing farm uses about 3,000 af. The community also plans to lease water to local municipalities. In sum, this settlement diverts wet water to a profitable farm operation for the direct benefit of tribal members. The net increase in water diversion and use as a result of the settlement is currently 3,500 af.[24]

Fallon Paiute-Shoshone/Truckee-Carson–Pyramid Lake

This complicated settlement concerns water for two different reservations with conflicting interests in regard to wet water.

The essence of the settlement for the Fallon Paiute-Shoshones was to reduce their wet water use by funding significant improvements to their irrigation system and solidifying their water rights. The tribes can continue to use 10,587 af of water. They were awarded $43 million, which was the estimated cost of finishing their irrigation project—something the federal government had promised but never delivered. However, the tribes may spend this money as they see fit—they do not have to invest it in their irrigation project. Thus far the tribes have chosen to spend that money elsewhere. The greatest water gain in this region as a result of the settlement has been the purchase of 8,000 af for the Stillwater Wildlife Refuge; this is wet water for birds, not Indians.

The settlement for the Pyramid Lake Paiutes was designed to gradually reduce diversions from the Truckee River and direct more water to the lake to save indigenous fish species (more on this in the vignette in chapter 7). The level of water in Pyramid Lake has indeed risen—33 feet since 1967—but it is due to a series of wet years since 1992 and changes in the Operating Criteria and Principles (OCAP) for the Newlands Project.[25] Internal analyses estimate that 12.5 feet of the lake's increase is due to OCAP adjustments, and 20.5 feet is due to above-average rainfall; none is attributed to the settlement itself. The greatest impact thus far on increased flows in the Truckee River is a result of a water quality agreement signed in 1996, which authorized $24 million for water rights acquisition, the cost to be divided equally between the state of Nevada and the federal government. This program has begun very slowly, but will eventually increase clean-water flows into Pyramid Lake.[26]

Jicarilla Apache

This settlement gave the tribe a "federal project water right" that consists of storage space in two federal reservoirs—one in the Colorado River basin and the other in the Rio Grande basin.[27] This right is for future use and is not based on Winters doctrine claims; rather, the rights are held by the Secretary of the Interior. The tribe was awarded a total allowable diversion of 33,500 af from Navajo Reservoir (on the San Juan River) and 6,500 af from the San Juan-Chama Project (water allocated to the Rio Grande).[28] But both of these rivers are tied up due to problems with endangered species, and this has prevented the tribe from utilizing its settlement water. The tribe is currently developing plans to use its San Juan River allocation in the near future; flow recommendations for the river were adopted in January 1999.[29]

Northern Cheyenne

The compact with the State of Montana quantifies the tribe's water right at 91,330 af. The tribe is not using any of its settlement water now, but discussions are under way to develop an instream flow leasing agreement with the Montana Fish and Wildlife Department. In the long-term there is a potential for downstream hydropower development for the tribe's water stored behind Tongue River Dam and Yellowtail Dam on the Bighorn River. Another possibility is a lease agreement with the power plant at Coalstrip, Montana.[30]

Northern Ute (Utah)

The 1990 Ute Water Compact quantified the tribe's water rights at 470,594 af. However, this compact has not been ratified. No additional water use is occurring as a direct result of the settlement.

San Carlos Apache

The tribe was awarded a total of 154,570 af of water from new and existing sources. This settlement awaits final agreement on the numerous issues outlined in the previous chapter. In the meantime, the tribe is not using wet water as a result of this settlement.

Yavapai/Prescott

This settlement was basically an exchange of CAP water for local sources. It serves to "assist in firming up" the city of Prescott's water supply, which in turn is used to supply the reservation.[31] The tribe will receive 1,000 af in stream flow rights and 550 af of Prescott municipal water.

Do these data indicate that the settlements have been successful in deliv-

Table 5.1   Wet Water in Indian Settlements (acre-feet/year)

Settlement	Total Award	New Diversions
Ak-Chin	85,000	50,000
Papago	66,000	0
Fort Peck	1,100,000	0
San Luis Rey	16,000	0
Ute Mountain	92,000	18,500
Southern Ute	39,900	0
Salt River	122,400	0
Fort Hall	581,031	0
Fort McDowell	35,233	3,500
Fallon	10,587	0
Pyramid Lake	na	na
Jicarilla Apache	40,000	0
Northern Ute	470,594	0
San Carlos	154,570	0
Yavapai	1,550	0
Total	2,814,865	72,000

ering wet water to Indian people? It depends on how you define "wet water." Table 5.1 helps answer this question by presenting data regarding two interpretations of "wet water," one very inclusive, the other its opposite. The column labeled "Total Award" provides the amount of water quantified for each tribe; this is the most expansive definition of "wet water" possible.

The total water allocation to Indians via the fourteen settlements is about 2.8 million af. Compare this figure to some related statistics:

— Although estimates vary widely, the amount of land irrigated on Indian reservations at the beginning of the settlement era was somewhere around 500,000 acres. If we assume a water service of 4 af per acre, then approximately 2 million af were being used on Indian reservations.

— In 1984 the Western Governors' Association calculated that Indian claims to water based on the PIA standard could total 46 million af.[32]

— The Mni-Sose Intertribal Water Rights Coalition claims that Indian tribes in the Missouri River basin have reserved water rights to 75 percent of the total flows of the river.[33]

— The Navajo Nation may have claims totaling five million af in the Colorado River basin.[34]

These comparisons indicate that, while the amount of water gained via settlements is only a tiny fraction of possible PIA claims, settlement water has approximately doubled the amount of water legally allocated to Indian reservations.

Of course, these comparisons are based on the *potential* wet water of the settlements. The right-hand column in table 5.1, labeled "New Diversions," presents a very restrictive interpretation of wet water; this column counts only water that was not diverted prior to the settlement and is currently being diverted and used by tribal members as a direct result of the settlements. This column totals only 72,000 af. The stark difference between these two columns makes it obvious that the settlements have, thus far, produced a great deal more paper water than wet water; the promise of new water flowing across Indian lands is largely unfulfilled at this time. If the linchpin of the settlement strategy is the delivery of wet water to Indian people, then the success of the settlement policy is yet to be demonstrated. There is still a significant *potential* for wet water if the settlements are fully implemented, but, as chapter 4 indicated, this could be problematic. Indian people are still getting lots of ink, but not much water to divert. Of course, not all preferred Indian water uses require diversion; instream uses, ceremonial use, and habitat preservation may be valued to a greater extent. These uses are difficult to quantify and tie directly to the outcome of a negotiation, but they have played a part in some negotiations.

Part of the problem can be attributed to the government's policy of avoiding appreciable water losses to non-Indian water users. "Rivers and groundwater in many parts of the West already are over-allocated," Elizabeth Checchio and Bonnie Colby note in *Indian Water Rights: Negotiating the Future*, "so if settlement agreements are to protect existing non-Indian uses, innovative approaches are required to find 'wet water' for tribes."[35] The widely accepted decision rule in Congress is that all settlements must not "adversely affect people who are using water now."[36] Chambers and Echohawk note that settlements "encourage Indian water resource and other economic development *without* usually cutting off existing non-Indian water uses."[37] This "no-harm" rule limits tribes to acquiring water only through additional construction, efficiency measures, or improved water management. However, resistance to new construction and the practical limits of water conservation seriously constrain tribes in their search for settlement water.

Of course, the no-harm standard was never applied to non-Indian water development. Indeed, western water policy has always taken a position in contrast to a no-harm standard in two ways. First, the prior appropriation doc-trine is based on the assumption that those first in time can freely do harm to subsequent irrigators; in a call on the river, those with junior rights can lose their entire water allotment as senior water users demand their full share. Prior appropriation is very much a "late-comers be damned" concept. A second ele-ment of harm in western water policy is the way in which federal reclamation policy proceeded without regard to the harm it did to Indian water rights. It is worth quoting a famous passage from the 1973 National Water Commission, which makes this point: "This [federal reclamation] policy was pursued with little or no regard for Indian water rights and the Winters doctrine. With the encouragement, or at least the cooperation, of the Secretary of the Interior — the very office entrusted with protection of all Indian rights — many large irri-gation projects were constructed on streams that flowed through or bordered Indian Reservations, sometimes above and more often below the Reservations. With few exceptions the projects were planned and built by the Federal Gov-ernment without an attempt to define, let alone protect, prior rights that Indian tribes might have had in the waters used for the projects."[38] As a result of the no-harm rule, there has been no wholesale transfer of water to Indians during the second treaty era. This raises the question of whether wet water for Indians is a principal goal of the settlement process.

Another way of looking at the wet water provided by settlements is in eco-nomic terms; has it been a good investment? If we compare the amount of money spent on settlements thus far to the total potential allocation of settle-ment water (2,814,865 af), it will provide a rough idea of the relative cost of settlement water. The data in chapter 3 revealed that the settlements have cost about $1 billion in direct expenditures; it is probably safe to assume that the in-direct costs (benefits awarded to non-Indians and federal project costs) would, at the very least, double that amount to $2 billion. Including such costs yields a per acre-foot cost of $5.60. That is a good deal; western irrigation water is occasionally this cheap, but urban water supplies can easily exceed $1,000/af in some parts of the West. However, a calculation based on the amount of Indian water currently diverted and used by Indians as a result of settlements yields a per-acre-foot price that compares favorably to gold. Of course, both of these figures are based on the extremes; the eventual cost of settlement water will fall somewhere in between. These data do, however, suggest that in some cases the most economically rational way to solve Indian water problems is to simply purchase private irrigation rights and reallocate them to tribes (more on this in chapter 8).

Conclusion

It is apparent that a lot more money than water has changed hands as a result of the settlements. Peter Sly notes, "The adage that water settlements can be accomplished with either money or water remains."[39] Thus, it may be more appropriate to characterize the settlement policy as primarily a money-for-water program, where tribes are given development funds and other forms of financial incentives rather than significant amounts of water. There are notable exceptions, described above, but the overall trend in the settlement process has been to award money rather than new water diversions to aggrieved tribes. In this respect the second treaty era resembles the first one; when tribes began making claims for land losses before the Indian Claims Commission, the official policy of the government was to award monetary damages rather than return purloined lands. In water settlements this policy is not the official doctrine of the government, but the practical impact has been similar, at least thus far.

Even though the settlement policy has had limited success in providing water for tribes, it has been more successful in another respect; part of the rationale for the settlement policy is to compensate for past injustices — to cover the government's liability for failure to protect Indian water resources in the past. This is certainly a noble cause and well worth the price paid if it helps the nation recoup its integrity. But this goal is retrospective rather than future oriented. It is inevitable that the value of water in the New West will continue to increase; at what point will settlement money begin to look like a poor trade-off for wet water? How many tribes that received a monetary payment from the Claims Commission for land losses would now prefer to have the land rather than the money? The value of a permanent source of water is virtually infinite; it can be used forever. But funding for settlements is a function of political bargaining and constraints on the federal budget. Money for water may provide a short-term benefit to tribes, but the long-term costs are incalculable. The settlements that result in the actual possession of water, either diverted or instream, offer the best hope for long-term tribal security; settlements that deliver money but little water will exact a high price in the future.

Vignette: Dr. Montezuma's Revenge

In 1872 a Yavapai boy named Wassaja was stolen from his tribe and sold to a Mexican-American family living nearby. The boy was given a new name—

Carlos Montezuma — and treated kindly by his new family. He proved to be a brilliant student and eventually was sent to Chicago to study medicine. After becoming a doctor, Carlos developed a concern for his original people, the Yavapais, and other tribes that had suffered so much at the hands of settlers. He became "one of the first known advocates of human rights."[40]

Dr. Montezuma was concerned that the Yavapais would be forced from their land by encroaching white settlement. He also understood that the small Yavapai Reservation in arid central Arizona could not support the tribe without access to the Verde River, which flows through the reservation. In 1921, the last year of his life, Dr. Montezuma was still struggling to protect the tribe's water rights. In a letter to a friend he expressed his concern: "When I was there [at Fort McDowell] last fall, engineers were sounding the Verde River east of the McDowell Mountain. Do you know what that means? Some day a dam will be built and the McDowell land will be flooded and the water will be used for drinking water for the Salt River Valley people. No wonder the McDowell Indians are hoodwinked and urged to move to the Salt River Reservation. White people's heads are long — they can see many years ahead."[41] Dr. Montezuma's fears were well founded. There has been an almost continuous effort by nearby Anglos to gain title to all the water of the Verde River: "As one goes through the early documents and down to the present time, one is astounded at the frequent attempts of different factions to remove the Yavapai from the McDowell Reservation. These attempts are for one reason only — the water rights to the Verde. It is the only precious thing the Yavapai really have left, and certain people outside the reservation want to take this away."[42]

The greatest threat to the reservation and its water supply occurred in the 1970s when the Bureau of Reclamation wanted to build Orme Dam, which would have flooded nearly the entire reservation. Stewart Udall, the secretary of the interior when the dam was first proposed, argued that the flooded reservation would actually be good for the tribe: "I propose . . . to make the small but fine little reservoir we are creating here into an Indian recreational development."[43] It took an extraordinary effort by the Yavapai people and their allies to stop the dam; a ten-year battle with the Bureau of Reclamation and powerful Arizona water interests finally paid off when plans for the dam were canceled.[44]

In the past, the 25,000-acre reservation was quite far from the Phoenix metropolitan area, but the suburbs have crawled out across the Sonoran Desert until they are at the very doorstep of the reservation. The view to the west of the reservation is a sea of new homes, but the view east, toward the Superstition and Mazatzal Mountains, still offers a broad expanse of undulating desert cut by ephemeral arroyos. Palo verde and the stately saguaro cactus dot the landscape. The Verde River today is a shallow stream that meanders through gravel bars and sand. For many years the tribe has diverted a modest amount of water from the river for their BIA irrigation project.[45]

Bob Farrer, tribal engineer for the Fort McDowell Indian community, gets excited when he talks about the new farm. "Things are really happening here. We've already planted twelve thousand pecan trees. Pecans are among the highest returns in agriculture; the gross per acre is around $3,500. Phase 2 will develop another 1,100 acres; funding for that is already in place. We don't have to worry that Congress will fail to appropriate it."[46]

Mr. Farrer worked for Arizona water agencies for decades, then came to Fort McDowell in 1994 to help manage the new farm and a loan project financed by the Bureau of Reclamation—the same agency that wanted to inundate the reservation twenty years ago. His enthusiasm for the tribe's water settlement is contagious. The settlement provides both a substantial amount of water— nearly 36,000 af—and the money necessary to develop the new farm. The settlement has literally changed the face of the reservation.

I toured the new farm with Joe Kanovich, the construction engineer for the farm. There was a lot to see. New housing developments just east of the reservation crowd against the boundary fence, yet wild horses still roam this part of the reservation. I saw acre upon acre of two-foot high pecan sprigs. Each tree is watered with two "spray emitters" (sprinklers in layman's terms). Mr. Kanovich explained how it all works.

"The old BIA project took water out of the Verde. We used it for wheat and alfalfa. The new project uses a computerized pumping system to deliver a precise amount of water to each tree to produce high-value crops. The focus of the project is on economic efficiency. It's modern, high-tech, and well designed."

It is also very ambitious. The entire project, when finished, will irrigate 2,400 acres (before the settlement only 700 acres were irrigated). This acreage will consist of 53,800 pecan trees and 26,000 citrus trees.[47] The ultimate goal is to serve the long-term needs of the tribe as a whole: "The proposed project will create additional employment opportunities and provide the Community with a major source of income for meeting future Community needs. Community cohesion and self-sufficiency is expected to increase with the continued successful development of tribal agriculture."[48]

There is a certain amount of irony in the tribe's new farming activities. Everywhere else in central Arizona irrigated agriculture is in trouble; numerous irrigation districts have gone bankrupt and cannot pay their CAP allotments. But here, on the edge of the Phoenix megalopolis, a small Indian tribe with a tragic history is carving out a state-of-the art farm that will turn a profit for many years to come. While other irrigators rely on declining groundwater and expensive CAP water, and grow low-value crops such as alfalfa and cotton, the Yavapai people are relying on their traditional source of water to create an investment in their future. For more than a century the Yavapai struggled to hang on to their land and water, often on the verge of losing everything. Now their persistence is paying off. The settlement awarded them both water and money, and they are using both to maximum advantage. If only Dr. Montezuma could see them now. The Fort McDowell settlement is an excellent illustration of wet water, via a settlement.

6

In the Shadow of the Eagle

Neighbors

There was an occasion a decade or so ago when a white man was walking in his fields, watching the water funnel down the furrows between the green rows of crops. The water instantly turned the brown desert soil to a dark, rich hue. To the farmer, the vision of his healthy, prosperous fields was a wondrous sight — one that usually gave him a sense of contentment and pride. But today he saw only trouble, and his mind wandered over the past few years of intense conflict between the local farmers and an Indian tribe upriver. It had been a bitter, ugly confrontation, lasting for years, and the farmer had begun to wonder if there was a future for him and his irrigated fields. It was the only life he had ever known, and he did not want to give it up, but it seemed as if matters were spiraling out of control.

He looked up from his field, toward the distant horizon, and saw an individual walking directly toward him. At first he could not identify the person, but as the figure came nearer, he realized it was an Indian man from the nearby reservation. The farmer grew tense; on a number of occasions these two individuals had faced each other in the hostile setting of courtrooms and government offices. The farmer was pleasantly surprised when the Indian man greeted him warmly. The Indian was not here for idle chatter — he had some important points he wanted to make regarding the ongoing water conflict — but there would be time for that. First it was best to talk as friends.

Rather than talk about water, the two men began to talk about themselves and their families. As their conversation became more personal, one of the men revealed that he was a devout Christian. The other raised his eyebrows; "I am, too," he said. At that juncture, they agreed to pray about their water problems. They knelt down together, their knees in the soft, damp soil, and prayed that the acrimony and hard feelings of the past would give way to empathy and understanding. When each man went home that evening he took with him a commitment to talk through the water problems and to try to find a solution that everyone could live with. There was still a lot of hard work ahead, but a few years later these two individuals became signatories to a water settlement that held the promise of a brighter future for everyone.[1]

Not all water settlements are blessed with such a propitious beginning, but nearly everyone involved in settlements hopes for such an ending. To a great extent the settlement policy grew out of a realization that Indians and non-Indians could both benefit if they focused on what they had in common rather than on their differences. Their differences are, of course, profound, but in the New West they may have more in common than they did a generation ago. Many established water users are potentially threatened by the demands of newcomers, new development, and new ideas about how water should be used; "There is a fear element," says the director of Arizona's water resources department.[2] They feel the pinch of diminishing federal support for water development, and many water users feel the need to solidify their water rights before the law changes in ways that are not beneficial to them. By coming together in a spirit of cooperation, Indians and Anglos can both find common ground in the face of common threats and opportunities.

The word most often used to describe this aspect of the settlement policy is "comity," the good feeling that comes from resolving problems together through a consensual decision-making process. It is based on the belief that Indians and Anglos must share the limited bounty of the West. The reality of a finite landscape applies to everyone regardless of race. As an elderly Navajo man said to me, "We all have to live in the same land now, sharing the earth. We all live in the shadow of the eagle."

The proponents of settlements have always emphasized the comity that can accrue from consensus-based negotiations: "If they are done correctly, you can have a stable community, and you have the kind of benefit you can't put on a balance sheet. You have harmony in the community. These are intangible benefits that clearly outweigh the costs of a settlement."[3] Settlement advocates often make the point that, regardless of past differences, any procedure that reduces conflict is preferable: "You still have to live with your neighbors, so even if you can get more through litigation, you have to ask; is it worth it to harm your relationship with your neighbors?"[4] The desire for comity is also an acknowledgment — sometimes explicit, sometimes tacit — that the second treaty era needs to be more just than the first treaty era; that we will all benefit if the dominant society and Indian people treat one another as neighbors rather than as enemies, within a government-to-government context.

Comity is particularly important in settlements that were negotiated under especially contentious circumstances. Arguing for passage of the San Carlos settlement, Congressman Kolbe of Arizona talked about these circumstances on the House floor: "Many formerly contentious issues have been resolved. The progress on this bill has been nothing short of miraculous, making clear that parties with varied interests can come together to reach agreement without resorting to litigation."[5] Congressman Rhodes called the Salt River settlement a "spirit of visionary cooperation among Indians and non-Indians."[6] And the chairman of the Southern Ute tribe cited the conflict that was avoided by the Colorado Ute settlement: "We are pleased that, together with our neighbors, we can . . . solve what otherwise will be a long and bitter lawsuit affecting all of southwest Colorado."[7]

The value of building comity rather than enmity extends into the future, and affects many other Indian-Anglo issues beyond water. Christopher Kenney, director of the office of Native American affairs at the Bureau of Reclamation, notes, "The most valuable result of a negotiated settlement is the establishment of commercial and governmental relationships that remain after the negotiations are concluded. In most cases, water rights negotiations are the first substantive opportunity for the local non-Indian community to begin to understand and appreciate the needs and capabilities of their Indian neighbors."[8]

Have the settlements encouraged Indians and Anglos to become neighbors rather than adversaries? Have tensions declined as a result of the negotiation process? This chapter will attempt to answer these questions.

Averting a Water War

When the settlement policy was first announced by the Reagan administration, it was billed, in the words of Interior Secretary James Watt, as part of the government's "cooperative Good Neighbor Policy."[9] According to the literature on conflict resolution, negotiation must be built on mutual consensus; no party can be coerced into a friendly agreement.[10] The Reagan administration stressed that negotiations were completely voluntary, and no tribe would be forced to negotiate. However, several participants at the time felt that tribes were indeed pressured to negotiate rather than litigate. A House staffer told me in 1984 that "There are flat-out pressures to negotiate." A BIA official made a similar statement six years later: "I think tribes have been harassed and coerced into negotiating."[11] Even more telling was an internal memorandum circulated among Reagan appointees in the Interior Department: "Thus, even though we maintain that negotiation is voluntary, the fact that we fund those tribes that are interested in negotiations earlier than those that are not could be viewed as blackmail by those who are not interested in negotiations."[12]

The settlement era was off to a rocky start. Tribes became even more leery of the Reagan administration when it vetoed the Southern Arizona/Papago (now Tohono O'odham) settlement. At about the same time, the Ak-Chin settlement began to unravel when the federal government failed to deliver water on schedule. There was a conspicuous lack of comity in the air when the chairwoman of the Ak-Chin community publicly excoriated the Reagan administration and the entire settlement process: "All we get are lies. If this law is not upheld, I will alert every Indian in the nation to be very cautious in any so-called settlement of water rights by negotiation."[13]

The settlement policy appeared to be doomed at an early stage. At that point a conscious decision was made to save it. The southern Arizona settlement was finally passed, the Ak-Chin settlement was renegotiated and fully funded, and western legislators made sure that successive settlements received adequate funding. Negotiation began to look more attractive to tribes and non-Indians when they realized that western problems were easier to negotiate when greased with a substantial dollop of federal funding. Suddenly tribes were queuing up for negotiation teams. It was no longer necessary for the administration to pressure tribes to negotiate.

This does not necessarily mean that the process was completely voluntary. Rather, it indicates an absence of attractive alternatives. Joe Ely, an articulate and thoughtful participant-observer of the negotiation process, explained the true nature of the choices at hand:

> We negotiate because, at present, it is one of the best options that we have for establishing our water rights. Although negotiations are voluntary, and the tribes can choose not to participate, to do nothing is not an option. I have sat, talked with, and listened to many tribes. And the presumed option of doing nothing always comes up. But it is *not* an option. I wish it were, but it is not. I wish we as tribes could simply sit back and say the water is ours—it was, it is, and it will always be. But we know that in this society that is not true. . . . sometimes we are forced to play the game.[14]

This situation is not entirely conducive to a spirit of effusive comity, but it presents possibilities that never arise in the courtroom. There is a constrained set of choices, but at least the flexibility of the negotiation process and the elixir of federal funds assist Indians and Anglos as they search for common interests. As a report to the National Conference of State Legislatures put it, the states and tribes could begin "building new traditions."[15] This task has not been easy. At the beginning of the settlement era, newspaper headlines reflected the depth of the problem: "Averting a Water Rights War,"[16] "Reserved Rights Issue Rages across West,"[17] and "West Faces a Time Bomb."[18] To overcome these difficulties, two problems had to be resolved. First, all parties had to agree to participate. By the mid-1980s this problem was largely resolved as tribes lined up to negotiate. But the second problem—finding an acceptable procedure—has continued to plague the process. It is difficult to develop comity when the parties cannot even agree on the rules of the game.

Game Rules

Every settlement is unique, and every river basin has its own characteristics. Early settlements tended to be negotiated in an ad hoc, independent fashion. Indeed, each negotiation team did not want to be constrained by the experiences of other negotiation teams, and some of the settlement bills specifically state that they do not establish a precedent for other settlements.[19] Nevertheless, it became apparent early in the settlement era that certain procedures needed to be standardized because of a number of problems. It quickly became obvious that the role of the federal government needed to be clarified; if the feds were going to be the sugar daddy, they wanted a big role in the negotiations. Reagan vetoed the first southern Arizona settlement because the federal government was not officially included in the negotiations.

An even greater problem concerned the three-way conflict between the Office of Management and Budget (OMB), the Justice Department, and the Department of the Interior. Each of these agencies had a different perspective on the settlements. OMB, the president's budgetary guardian, wanted to limit expenditures. The Justice Department thought in terms of legal exposure and compared costs of settlements to the government's liability in a lawsuit. The Department of the Interior, along with its allies in Congress, conceived of settlements in terms of the trust responsibility. In several negotiations one or more of these entities would work out a settlement only to have it nixed by the others.

The first Bush administration[20] attempted to solve these coordination problems by developing a formal process. They assumed a written procedure would enhance coordination and reduce the chances of a settlement being rejected late in the process. In 1990, the *Criteria and Procedures* were published in the *Federal Register* to "provide a framework for negotiating settlements."[21] They identified four broad objectives: "(1) The United States will be able to participate in water settlements consistent with the Federal Government's responsibilities as trustee to Indians; (2) Indians receive equivalent benefits for rights which they, and the United States as trustee, may release as part of a settlement; (3) Indians obtain the ability as part of each settlement to realize value from confirmed water rights resulting from settlement; and (4) The settlement contains appropriate cost-sharing by all parties benefiting from the settlement."[22] This language is quite supportive of the goals generally pursued by tribes in a settlement. But this broad language on objectives was followed by a long list of dos and don'ts (or more exactly, ten "shoulds" and twelve "should-nots") that placed significant limitations on negotiators. Many of these new rules were designed to reduce costs and limit the federal role to "calculable legal exposure." Any additional costs related to the government's general trust responsibility could not be included unless a justification was provided as to why such costs could not be covered through "the normal budget process."[23]

It was, of course, the failures of the "normal budget process" that created so many water problems for tribes in the first place. If the BIA water development program had not been chronically underfunded for a century, and the competing programs for Anglos had not been lavished with pork, there would be no Indian water crisis; there would be no desperate attempt by tribes to recover lost waters—an effort that began at Fort Belknap ninety years ago.

The *Criteria and Procedures* provided some useful procedural safeguards, but they were roundly criticized by Indian advocates because of their restrictive view of federal responsibility:

— The *Criteria and Procedures* "allow the feds to run off without helping to solve the crises they created. . . . [They] were developed without any consultation with Indian tribes." John Echohawk, Executive Director, Native American Rights Fund[24]
— "The new *Criteria and Procedures* build walls against our will." Joe Ely, former chairman of the Pyramid Lake tribe[25]
— "We depart very dramatically from the *Criteria and Procedures* because they do not recognize broken promises or past agreements. They don't put it in their calculus." Staff attorney, Senate Committee on Indian Affairs
— "Tribes were absolutely devastated. . . . They were not consulted." Congressional staffer

Tribes and their allies on the hill dug in their heels and fought against the new criteria. The favored strategy was to just ignore them and take negotiated agreements straight to Congress, with a conspicuous lack of OMB review. In 1990 a Bush appointee in the Interior Department confirmed this: "The tribes just bypass us and go straight to Congress, which is, quite frankly, more receptive, and they go ahead and spend the money." Six years later the pattern had not changed: "Since the *Criteria and Procedures* came out I haven't seen any settlements that actually followed that process."[26]

The *Criteria and Procedures* were not without benefit, however. They standardized an organizing and reporting procedure that streamlined negotiations and made the whole process more manageable and efficient. Negotiation teams began to follow the four phases outlined in the procedures: fact-finding, assessment and recommendations, briefings and negotiating position, and negotiations towards settlement. However, the benefits of the *Criteria and Procedures* were often overshadowed by the controversy they generated.

This process hardly sounds like one designed to maximize comity. Indeed, most of the comity generated by settlements has occurred at the local level where Indian and non-Indian people come together and decide how to solve their problems with the help of federal funding. The biggest conflicts often occur when an agreement and its adherents travel to Washington and encounter vastly different agendas among the principal players. That is where the rope-pushing begins. Despite the problems generated by the *Criteria and Procedures* and conflicting congressional agendas, there are still opportunities to establish closer working relationships.

Comity is most likely when it is part of a larger political and social context that encompasses Indian tribes, the Bureau of Reclamation and the Army Corps of Engineers, as well as non-Indian water users. These agencies and their traditional clientele have a long history of conflict with tribes; has the settlement era significantly improved the way these bureaucracies relate to Indian tribes?

Government to Government

When President Clinton came to office, he declared that Indian policy would henceforth be based on a "government-to-government" relationship between tribes and the national government that would reflect "respect for the rights of self-government due the sovereign tribal governments."[27] The memorandum ordered all agency heads to develop, in consultation with tribes, an assessment of how their agency affects Indian tribes and to make an effort to enhance their communication and cooperation with tribes. At about the same time, the Clinton administration launched its massive "reinventing government" program, which required all agency heads to update and streamline their operations. These two initiatives provided an unprecedented opportunity for federal water agencies to improve their relationship with Indian tribes.

The Bureau of Reclamation was one of the first federal agencies to "reinvent" itself. Under the dynamic leadership of Commissioner Daniel Beard, a new agency mission was identified that embraced American Indians as one of reclamation's "new constituent groups": "The Water Resource needs of Native Americans will be an important new program area for Reclamation. This will include: undertaking water resource management and development activities, working to improve the technical expertise of tribes, and continuing our assistance to the Secretary in resolving Indian water disputes."[28] This new mission fits well into the settlement era; the bureau, having created many of the water problems on Indian reservations, is now in a position to help tribes, via well-funded settlements, to develop new sources of water, enhance the efficiency of existing water development, and provide technical assistance to tribes during the negotiation process.

A second policy change at the Interior Department further enhanced the bureau's relationship with tribes. As part of a department-wide policy, Commissioner Beard signed a new "Indian Trust Asset" (ITA) Policy in 1993: "Reclamation will carry out its activities in a manner which protects ITAs and avoids adverse impacts when possible. When Reclamation cannot avoid adverse impacts, it will provide appropriate mitigation or compensation. Under no circumstances should Reclamation engage in a Fifth Amendment taking of ITAS without statutory authority and adequate compensation."[29] If reclamation had adopted such a policy ninety years ago there would be no need for a second treaty era today.

The potential for real comity between tribes and the bureau is finally a possibility. The transition has not been easy, however. Joe Miller, formerly the Director of Native American Affairs at the bureau, explained: "Before Commissioner Beard came, the ITA policy just wasn't politically possible. Now we are building partnerships. Our first task was to present cultural awareness workshops to Bureau employees. However, we still have pockets of people in the Bureau who don't see tribes as our constituents."[30] In recent years this partnership has been expressed through technical assistance in negotiations and other water-related activities on reservations. One example is a recently completed guidebook prepared by the bureau for tribes, which discusses training opportunities, technical assistance programs, and funding possibilities.[31]

The bureau's recent budgets reflect these commitments. Funding for the various Bureau projects on Indian reservations is listed in table 6.1. It should be noted that some of these expenditures are listed in the budgets of other agencies, which means that some funds are counted twice. This occurs because it is now politically wise for federal agencies to take credit for work done on Indian reservations—a stark contrast to historical tendencies.

Table 6.1 Bureau of Reclamation Funding for Native American Programs (in millions of dollars)

Indian Program	FY1999 (actual)	FY2000 (enacted)	FY2001 (requested)
Ak-Chin	4,733	5,296	6,762
Animas–La Plata	500	303	2,000
Central Arizona Project	29,733	12,678	32,779
Garrison Diversion	7,073	5,218	6,338
Headgate Rock	0	2,425	0
Mni Wiconi Project	25,979	22,930	23,421
Native American Affairs	6,711	7,110	8,500
Rocky Boys settlement	950	500	16,000
SAWRSA	3,450	5,598	5,189
Umatilla Basin Project	725	580	548
Yakima Project	2,493	3,223	3,109
YRBWE*	974	6,504	2,330
Other projects	10,732	12,117	9,365
Total	94,053	84,482	116,341

Source: Native American Affairs Office, U.S. Bureau of Reclamation, 2/2/2000

*Yakima River Basin Water Enhancement

This assistance does not come cheap—some of it must be reimbursed.[32] But the new mission of the bureau, coupled with its recognition of tribal assets, represents a new era in which the bureau has an opportunity to become, in the words of former Commissioner of Reclamation Eliud Martinez, "true partners with Indian tribes."[33] This attitude will inevitably enhance comity between former adversaries in the second treaty era.

The other major federal water agency that has an impact on Indian reservations is the U.S. Army Corps of Engineers. The oldest natural resource agency in the federal government, the corps is also one of the most powerful.[34] Its giant dams on the Missouri and Columbia Rivers wrought havoc on numerous Indian reservations. On the Missouri, main-stem dams built by the corps did so much damage to Indian land and communities that one recent book calls it the "river of sacrifice."[35] Five dams inundated 350,667 acres of Indian lands on five reservations.[36] In the Columbia River basin the corps's dams (and a few built by reclamation) took "a great toll on the river and also on Indian people and societies."[37]

For many decades the corps simply proceeded as though Indian rights and needs did not exist. When the agency encountered resistance from tribes, its natural reaction was to fight rather than listen. In an internal memorandum written in 1976, a colonel in the corps described the corps's mindset with stunning frankness: "The only known Corps policy for dealing with Indian Tribes is 'Advise OCE before taking them to court.' This has caused confrontation with Indians and unnecessary and time consuming court cases initiated by the Indians. The Corps has not been responsive to Indian legal demands. There is inconsistency in the Corps's present dealing with the Indians because of lack of a statement of central policy."[38]

Given a past like that, it would be a daunting challenge indeed to metamorphose the corps into a friend of the Indian. But to its credit, the corps has made a significant effort to do so. Its first task was to admit to past injustices: "Decisions the Corps makes in its regulatory, operations, and land management programs may make the difference in the economic viability and cultural survivability of a tribe. Historically, some of these decisions have had disastrous results for the tribes."[39]

The next step was to get involved with tribal water concerns and respond to tribal needs. The corps has documented such activities: "The Corps interacts with Tribes on a fairly routine level in every major program. The operations and maintenance of forty-four Corps projects can significantly impact the trust assets and well being of 15 percent of the Tribes in the lower 48 states. Within the last 5 years (FY89–FY94) tribes have been our partners either as direct sponsors or through subagreements in 296 projects in various stages of planning, engineering or construction. In the last 2 years, Federally Recognized Tribes have applied for 431 permits and commented on 93 permit applications. The Corps has transferred the use of over 9300 acres through outgrants and transfers in the last five years. Thirty-three Tribes have come to us on 50 occasions requesting Emergency Operations Assistance."[40] In short, the Corps of Engineers now functions in a service capacity to a number of tribes. In 1998 the corps developed a set of "Tribal Policy Principles" that recognize that "Tribes retain their inherent rights to self-government" and require the agency to respect treaty rights.[41]

Much of the effort to increase cooperation and comity among tribes, the corps, and the bureau revolves around the idea of *consultation*, which has become something of a mantra among tribal leaders who grew tired of being excluded from decisions. As the policy of consultation developed, it became obvious that it meant different things to different people. To tribes, it meant being a part of the decision-making process. To many federal agency officials, it meant informing tribes of their activities. There is an important distinction between asking and telling. The tribal position was stated succinctly by the Mni-Sose coalition: "The Corps of Engineers and other federal agencies need to understand that consultation is seeking tribal opinion before the fact, not tribal consent at the conclusion of a process."[42]

Both the bureau and the corps have developed formal consultation procedures in recent years. The Department of the Interior developed a department-wide consultation policy in 1993: "Bureaus and offices are required to consult with the recognized tribal government with jurisdiction over the trust property that the proposal may affect. . . . All consultations with tribal governments are to be open and candid so that all interested parties may evaluate for themselves the potential impact of the proposal on trust resources."[43] The corps recently developed a definition of consultation that appears to encompass both asking and telling. Consultation is defined as "any written correspondence, verbal discussion, or meeting used to notify and explain proposed Corps undertakings or activities to tribal governments that are affected and to seek their views and opinions."[44]

Both the Bureau of Reclamation and the Corps of Engineers have evolved over time in a manner that reflects changing attitudes in American society. A policy of confiscation and removal has given way to policy of assistance, at least when such assistance is politically feasible. Both agencies still answer to powerful bosses, but the settlements have provided a means for the agencies to meet the needs of tribes while providing assistance to Anglo constituencies.

Brother against Brother?

Another aspect of comity concerns the relationship between and among Indian people; has the settlement era increased comity among them? In many cases, negotiations have brought Indians and Anglos to the bargaining table in a process that respects each side's position and attempts to maximize gains for all parties. Old enemies have sometimes been able to forge new partnerships. But negotiating a settlement that determines water rights forever is bound to be contentious. It is a high-stakes gamble that can exacerbate old animosities and heighten tension. Some of the settlements have been bitterly debated on Indian reservations and caused troublesome rifts among tribal members.

There are several examples. The settlement for the Northern Utes provoked a bitter recall election and an ongoing conflict over whether to ratify an accompanying compact. The divisions in the Southern Ute tribe, described in chapter 4, have divided the tribe into warring factions, each with a contingent of allies among Anglo interests. The Pyramid Lake negotiations provoked a series of highly conflictive tribal meetings, resulting in a schism that still affects settlement implementation (see chapter 7). The Tohono O'odham settlement, discussed in the vignette at the end of this chapter, caused a dramatic rift in the tribe that threw a wrench into their settlement.

Other settlements have resulted in conflicts between tribes. The Colorado Ute settlement was initially opposed by the Navajo Nation because it takes water out of the San Juan River, which is also the source for the Navajo Indian Irrigation Project. The Navajo Nation dropped its opposition when a pipeline to Shiprock was added to the amended settlement. The Truckee River settlement caused friction between the Fallon Paiute-Shoshone tribes and the Pyramid Lake Paiute tribe; these tribes were competing for the same scarce water from the Truckee River. The Northern Cheyenne settlement created tension with the Crow tribe over rights to water in the Bighorn River. And in central Arizona, numerous tribes are competing for water from the Gila River basin; grants of water made in earlier settlements became constraints on tribal claims in later settlements.

These settlements did not end conflict, but rather changed the line-up of the contending parties; in some cases they shifted the battle from an Anglo vs. Indian conflict to an Indian vs. Indian conflict. In the meantime, non-Indians may still collect their "Indian blanket" and other benefits resulting from settlements.

Conclusion

There are many ways to achieve comity in a settlement. It would not be an exaggeration to say that comity is usually achieved via a generous contribution by the nation's taxpayers. In some cases the cost is fairly modest and the resulting comity is indeed impressive. In other settlements large expenditures were committed, but the settlement failed to achieve this objective and in some cases intensified conflict between Indian people.

Comity may also be achieved by forming alliances against a common enemy. Old animosities can give way to new partnerships when an external threat pops into the picture. Indian tribes and local Anglos have similar concerns about trusting the federal government, sharing water with newcomers, and accepting changes in water law that do not protect existing users. Farmers and ranchers, whether they are Indian or non-Indian, have common concerns about the New West and its claims on resources. And many traditional parties in the West distrust the court system and its failure to resolve long-standing water conflicts. Ironically, comity may be a by-product of new tensions and a common foe.

The effort to achieve a salutary partnership between Anglos and Indian tribes has significant implications for western water policy in general. Investing Indians in the water status quo can make them allies in the fight against change; if a tribe becomes part of the prevailing water regime, it will be more difficult to fundamentally alter that regime. In this age of environmentalism and budget cuts, traditional westerners are in search of new allies—they need all the help they can get. For decades huge projects such as the CAP, CUP, Garrison diversion, and ALP were anathema to the fortunes of tribes; now all of these projects promise benefits to tribes. The "comity" resulting from settlements may simply be an example of joining in an effort to prolong the traditional western approach to water: big projects, federal money, irrigation, and more benefits. It may be that the result of comity in some situations is increased resistance to a new water ethos.

On the other hand, some settlements embody the vision of a new water reality; they focus on water management rather than water development. In these settlements, "new" water is a result of increased efficiency, conservation, and reallocation of water from noneconomic uses to cost-efficient water applications. Thus, settlements rely on a mix of the old and new to achieve comity.

The comity born of settlements should not cause us to lose sight of the larger reality of Anglo-Indian relations. There is still a great deal of animosity, racism, and conflict, and much of it has to do with water. These sentiments were recently expressed in a bill, introduced by western members of Congress, that would emasculate reserved water rights: "The withdrawal, designation, or other reservation of lands by the United States for any purpose (whether by statute or administrative action) does not give rise by implication to a Federal reserved right to water relating to such purpose."[45] This bill did not pass, but some politicians keep trying to legislatively subvert federal reserved water rights; their latest effort is a bill titled "the State Water Sovereignty Protection Act."[46] Overt anti-Winters sentiment is also found in the courts; an Idaho court recently held that "It is arguable that this [Winters] 'doctrine' sets out no substantive rule of law, but is merely a special rule of construction used to divine original intent with respect to water rights on federal reservations."[47] Such sentiments will surely dissuade anyone from subscribing to the delusion that the West has entered an era of tolerant, enlightened attitudes toward Indians and their water.

Amidst the talk of a new era, historic agreements, and visionary progress, Senator Daniel Inouye provided a more realistic assessment of the settlement era: each settlement "represents an ongoing debate regarding what the law of

Federal reserved water rights and Indian reserved water rights is or should be. These matters remain unresolved."[48] Settlements have given us hope, but past injustices, political realities, and persistent prejudice have tempered once-upbeat assessments. In 1990 I interviewed a Department of the Interior official who expressed considerable enthusiasm for the settlement process. He listed the usual set of claimed advantages. Six years later I interviewed the same individual. By then his endorsement of settlements was more restrained: "Comity is the only advantage of settlements." In those settlements in which a certain level of comity has been achieved, it should be considered a historical occasion.

There may be a tendency among some to dismiss the value of comity, to treat it as a superficial feel-good without substance. That tendency is a mistake. The historical animosities between non-Indians and Indians are so great and so pervasive that any successful effort to achieve comity should be hailed as a significant victory. The real concern is if the price paid for settlements was the creation of new sets of adversaries. If that is the case, then settlements have failed to end the "water war" that has plagued the West for a century.

Vignette: The Dove of the Desert

The Sonoran Desert of southwestern Arizona and northern Sonora is the home of the Tohono O'odham — the desert people. No one knows how long they have lived here. The ancient Hohokam, who irrigated the desert 10,000 years ago, may be an ancestral tribe. The Tohono O'odham were here when the Apaches arrived. They were here when the Spanish arrived in search of gold, converts, and empire. They endured thirty years of Mexican rule, which ended when the United States took much of the O'odham land by force in the Mexican War. Still hungry for more land, the United States took another slice of territory by "imperious necessity" a few years later.[49] This acquisition put the international border right through the middle of the traditional lands of the Tohono O'odham.

The Spanish left their mark on the Tohono O'odham. They gave them a new name, the Papago, brought horses and other livestock, and built a mission church at San Xavier del Bac near the Santa Cruz River.[50] This imposing structure, gleaming white in the desert sun, has a favored nickname: the "Dove of the Desert."

The Americans left their mark, too. They created the reservation system as part of an effort to concentrate Indian peoples in specific locations. The land around the church at San Xavier was withdrawn from the public domain in

1874 and became the first reservation for the Tohono O'odham. This 71,000-acre reservation was only a tiny fraction of the original O'odham lands; many of the Tohono O'odham still lived in the desert west of San Xavier. This land remained in the public domain until 1916, when a presidential order created the Papago Reservation. Throughout the ensuing decades the boundaries of the main reservation were adjusted to meet the political exigencies of the moment. In 1935 the reservation was divided into eleven districts; San Xavier was one of them. Exterior boundary lines were finalized in 1939, creating a 2.8-million-acre reservation that included the original San Xavier Reservation even though it was not contiguous to the rest of the reservation.[51]

In such sparse, arid country, clashes between Indians and Anglos over water were inevitable. The Indian agent for the area wrote of such troubles in 1887: "The country is fast filling up with cattlemen (whites), and now at almost every spring or well some white man has a herd of cattle, and the inevitable result follows, the Indian is ordered to leave, and the 'superior race' usually enforces such an order. The large scope of the country over which they are scattered, and the distance from this agency, renders it practically impossible for the agent to protect them against these wrongs, though I have traveled one hundred miles over a desert to secure an Indian the privilege of taking water from a well he had dug himself."[52] The Tohono O'odham traditionally used surface streams as their principal sources of water. At one time the Santa Cruz River, a short distance from the San Xavier Mission, was a vibrant, permanent watercourse lined with large trees and other riparian vegetation.[53] But the U.S. government encouraged the use of wells, at times digging wells in villages despite opposition from local inhabitants. The Tohono O'odham withdrew modest amounts of groundwater from their wells, but non-Indians living in proximity to the reservation dug hundreds, and then thousands, of wells. As a result, the surface water on the reservation virtually disappeared. The Santa Cruz River became a twisting trough of sand; the San Xavier district went dry.

There were water problems on the main reservation as well. Small villages, scattered throughout 2.8 million acres of desert, became reliant on wells. As the water table dropped, wells had to be dug deeper, especially in the eastern district of Schuk Toak. Pumping costs increased and water quality decreased. Then the Corps of Engineers decided to solve a perceived water problem in the central part of the reservation. Bernard Fontana describes what happened: "The Tat Momolikot Dam, the sixth largest earthen dam in the world, stretches two and half miles over Santa Rosa wash. It was built between 1972 and 1974 by the U.S. Army Corps of Engineers at a cost of $10,000,000. It is designed to check a possible once-in-a-hundred-years flash flood. In the meantime, 'Lake St. Clair' behind the dam is a catchment of blowing tumbleweeds. The promised tourists, water skiers, and fishermen — like the water itself — never materialized."[54] The Tohono O'odham also had problems with the corps in the northern part of the reservation, where a number of Indian homes were displaced by a corps project.[55]

For many years the tribe watched as its scarce water resources disappeared. After years of loss and neglect, the tribe filed suit in 1975, attempting to recover the water resources it had lost due to off-reservation groundwater pumping. There were 1,700 defendants, including the city of Tucson. It promised to be a classic, never-ending all-out water brawl among Indians, Anglos, and the federal government. Then local parties began talking about a negotiated settlement. In 1982, amidst a hail of self-congratulatory speeches, a settlement was signed.

The road To San Xavier is lined with huge cottonwood trees — all of them dead. The fields around the mission are girded with concrete irrigation ditches choked with weeds and in disrepair. An ancient-looking water tower looms beside the road — it holds no water. In several places large sinkholes have appeared, some large enough to swallow a car. Fields that used to be green with crops are now matted with desiccated weeds. Except for a few isolated patches, the whole area is the color of desert dust — a wasted monochromatic landscape.

It wasn't always this way. At one time there was a thousand-acre mesquite forest next to the river. An early Spanish visitor described the area around the mission as "the most fertile spot in the whole valley."[56]

The original San Xavier Reservation was allotted in 1890. The allotment era was over by the time the main Papago Reservation was established, so only San Xavier lands went into individual ownership. The first well at San Xavier was dug in 1912. In the ensuing years more than 2,000 acres at San Xavier were watered by pump irrigation. But groundwater is a finite reservoir.[57] In time, the city of Tucson, copper mines, and ranches and farms near the reservation began to pump prodigious quantities of groundwater. As the water table fell, the San Xavier farms began to dry up. By the 1970s farming in the district had become "virtually impossible."[58] The falling groundwater table caused subsidence of the earth. Lands that had been irrigated for thousands of years, first by surface run-off, then by wells, became a dead zone.

The meeting was scheduled for 9:00 am. I was sitting in the tribal council chambers of the Tohono O'odham Nation, expecting the half-dozen members of the tribal water committee to appear any minute. Finally, two members walked into the room. We made small talk for nearly an hour while waiting for the others.

I expressed some impatience. "I came 500 miles to attend this meeting.

The committee chairman agreed on the phone to arrange this meeting, and he hasn't shown up."

The two water committee members, sitting patiently beside me, could see my disappointment. "Don't feel bad," one said with sensitivity. "It's not you. A couple of months ago a group of important people from reclamation came all the way from Washington to meet with the water committee here in Sells. Most members of the committee didn't come to that meeting either. Those big shots from Washington were really mad, but they didn't understand that the Tohono O'odham have their own way of dealing with conflict, and sometimes that means avoiding a face-to-face showdown."

"I just want to get their perspective. I don't want to argue with anyone," I explained.

"I think people from the outside don't understand how difficult this water conflict is for us. Our culture stresses harmony and sharing; a big fight over water is very hard for us."

I did not meet with the water committee that day, but I still learned something very important. Different cultures have different perceptions about, not only water, but how to argue over water—how to decide who gets how much. In the past, the Tohono O'odham adjusted their lifestyle to the demands of the desert; there was a match between water and culture. But most of that resource has been taken by others, leaving the Tohono people with no choice but to somehow decide how to live on the remnant. That decision was made in the 1982 Southern Arizona Water Rights Settlement Act (SAWRSA). Its purpose was to help the Tohono O'odham obtain as much water as possible, given contemporary political and hydrological constraints.

Those constraints are enormous. The burgeoning city of Tucson is one of the largest cities in the world that depends almost exclusively on groundwater. Mines in the area consume enormous quantities of both land and water—and wield a matching quantity of political clout. Cotton farmers, once a basic element in the regional economy, are gradually becoming scarce, but only after they sucked millions of gallons of water out of the ground. These water users consumed the groundwater much faster than nature's ability to replenish the aquifer. This groundwater mining has virtually sucked the lifeblood from the land. In the race to grab the last sources of water, the impoverished Tohono O'odham were overrun by their politically powerful neighbors. But they had one big stick—the Winters Doctrine. Local Anglos feared the tribe could gain control over the water the cities and mines had come to depend upon and pressed hard for a settlement.

But a resolution of the Tohono O'odham water problem involved more than a split between the tribe and their neighbors. The differences in history and geography between the San Xavier district and the rest of the reservation created a schism within the tribe. The allottees at San Xavier feel that they lost the most water, and thus they should be the recipients of the water in the settlement. In the words of the district chairman, "San Xavier was damaged so the benefits need to go directly to us. We do not appreciate being used to benefit members of the entire Nation—they have not been damaged."[59]

The government of the Tohono O'odham Nation disagrees and maintains that the water won in the settlement belongs to the tribe as a whole. It was the perspective of the nation that prevailed in the settlement. As a result, the allottees of San Xavier have waged a continuous campaign to recognize their suzerainty over the waters of the Santa Cruz valley and to demand compensation for their private property losses. They want Congress to amend the settlement "to protect the vital interests of the Allottees and the San Xavier community in an adequate, permanent supply of water."[60] In 1993 some of the allottees of the San Xavier District filed suit against the city of Tucson, Asarco Mines, and an agribusiness firm—all of which draw enormous amounts of groundwater. The allottees asked for $306 million in compensation and damages.[61]

The solicitor of the Interior Department issued an opinion in 1995 concluding that "neither the text of SAWRSA nor its legislative history resolve the fundamental issue of relative entitlements of the Nation and the allottees to settlement water."[62] In other words, a settlement designed to bring comity and resolution to a vexing water issue has created a troubling rift among the Tohono O'odham. Because of this conflict, the original lawsuit, filed in 1975, has never been dismissed. An attorney working for one of the parties had this to say about SAWRSA: "The term 'water settlement' in this case is an oxymoron."

Joseph Antonio grew up, in his words, "all over southern Arizona." For a time he also lived in northern Sonora, which is part of the traditional homeland of the Tohono O'odham. His father was a farm machine operator who took his family with him as he followed work in the fields. Joe graduated from Sells High School on the reservation, and then attended the University of Arizona, where he cut his political teeth on an effort to stop a massive condominium development proposed for the reservation. He later went to work for the tribe as the director of their CAP office. His task is to oversee the implementation of the 1982 settlement, especially the construction of the irrigation projects authorized to be built at San Xavier and Schuk Toak. But work on these projects has been held up because of the conflict between the tribe and the San Xavier allottees. Joe's job at the tribal CAP office is not an easy one; the tribe went through four directors in four years. The original engineering firm was fired, and contract disputes between the Bureau of Reclamation, the tribe, and San Xavier followed.

Joe is friendly and soft-spoken. He is not given to effusive displays of emotion. But when we talked of the stalled irrigation projects, his frustration clearly showed through his quiet demeanor. "The Nation has a resource that needs to be protected. We need to protect it from the city of Tucson and developers." For Mr. Antonio, the best way to protect the tribe's water resources is to use them, and that means irrigation. But he must first overcome a score of internal problems in the tribe before he can do that.

I met Daniel Preston and Renee Red Dog at the district headquarters at San Xavier. We talked for a few moments, then piled into a van for a tour of the district. Both Daniel and Renee have managed to combine seemingly contradictory qualities; neither is loquacious or aggressive, but both have proven to be forceful, outspoken proponents for the district. Both of them got involved in politics when California developers proposed a massive housing project for San Xavier. A new organization, called the Defenders of O'odham Land Rights, helped give voice to tribal members who opposed the development. Daniel, Renee, and others (including Joe Antonio) were ultimately successful in stopping the planned development.

Daniel entered electoral politics in 1987. He ran for vice-chair of the district, with his friend and fellow activist Austin Nunez running for district chair. They won and still held those offices when I visited in 1996. Renee saw her calling as a planner. She worked for the city of Tucson as a planner for many years, then returned to the district as the director of administrative offices. Both are active in the allottees association, and both fiercely oppose the original water settlement, at least in regard to its treatment of allottees.

The first stop on our tour was near the giant Asarco copper mines at the south end of the reservation. Daniel and Renee made no effort to conceal their disdain for the mines. Daniel explained why: "When the government passed environmental laws, Asarco argued it didn't have to comply because they were here before the laws were enacted. But we have to comply, and we've been here since time immemorial. Some day this land will revert back to us, and we'll be the proud owners of giant mine tailings."

It is difficult to describe the size and visual impact of the tailings. They look like a massive, artificial mountain with the top half removed. The terraced slopes spread out across the desert like a frozen tidal wave. Their impact on the land is glaringly obvious, but it is the mine's impact on groundwater, hidden below, that is even more important.

"The Spaniards called this place 'Punta del Agua' because of all the natural springs around here," Renee said, a touch of bitterness in her voice. "Now there are 1,500 sink holes in the district because of all the groundwater mining."

"There is a cone of depression in the water table where Asarco has mined groundwater," Daniel added.

Our next stop was the west bank of the Santa Cruz River, just north of a road bridge. The word "bank" is hardly appropriate, however. Erosion has eaten away the natural bank of the river and consumed several hundred acres of land that used to be farmed. Now, a crumbling twenty-foot cliff of loose soil separates the dry river channel from the remaining portion of the field. Daniel and Renee explained that the construction of the bridge abutments caused the flood flows of the Santa Cruz to shift to the west, resulting in the erosion of the farmland. The Bureau of Reclamation is now working with the district on a bank stabilization program in an effort to save the remainder of the fields. But without water, these fields remain barren.

Our final stop was the small tract of land in the district that is still farmed. Renee explained the situation: "The cooperative is farming about 40 acres now, mostly alfalfa and chilies. We have to pump water 600 to 800 feet to get water to it. The co-op has another 1,000 acres that belong to allottees, but we have no water and no capital to farm it."

As we viewed this small patch of green, I posed a hypothetical question: "You're probably getting $6 or $8 dollars a bale for this alfalfa. Wouldn't it make more sense to just lease the water to some city, for, let's say $1,000 an acre-foot? I know there are cities in the Colorado River basin that would consider buying water at that price if they could."

Daniel hesitated before answering my question. He looked as if he were carefully measuring his words, trying to make sure that I would understand his answer. His answer was emphatic and profound:

No. The land is our mother. Putting water on it and growing crops is not just for money. We are sustaining our mother—it is all part of our home. That's like asking, "Would you sell part of your home?" Giving life to the land gives life to the Tohono O'odham. We all go together: the water, the land, the people. If you take one away, you hurt the others— you take away the health of the land and the spiritual health of the people. The water is part of the spirit of the land, so it would be wrong to sell that. It is better for the people to work the land and grow their own food to be self-sufficient. Look at white society; the parents go away in the morning and leave their children with strangers. Look at all the problems you have. We think it is better to spend the day working the land with our children there to help us. That is what keeps the spirit alive. When you separate these things—parents and children, land and water—you destroy the basis of our culture. We have been here since time immemorial. We will survive the coming of the white man only by remembering this.

In the meantime, the Tohono O'odham do the best they can. A 1992 technical amendment to the settlement reauthorized the cooperative fund and permitted the tribe to lease its water to Tucson until it has a need for it. Also, SAWRSA applied only to the Santa Cruz basin; the nation has water claims in other parts of the reservation that have yet to be settled. Before I left San Xavier I stopped to take pictures of the dilapidated water tower; it seemed a perfect symbolic image for all that has occurred here.

Some of the settlements have resulted in comity. For the Tohono O'odham, comity did not happen, which is ironic because their culture places a great premium on harmony. Their settlement did not reflect that aspect of their culture. Perhaps future amendments to the settlement can accomplish that.

7

Last Refuge

Beautiful in the Extreme

Today it is difficult to imagine what the American West looked like before it was populated by sixty million Americans. Meriwether Lewis, writing in his diary on May 5, 1805, described the Great Plains as "beatifull in the extreme."[1] George Catlin, the painter who ascended the Missouri River in 1832–33, described that river valley as having a "soul-melting" beauty.[2] Today, the Great Plains have been subdued by farms and ranches, and the upper Missouri River has been inundated by five massive dams built by the Corps of Engineers.[3] The West today is home to some of the fastest growing communities in the nation, and millions of tourists flock to once-pristine locations to enjoy "nature."

The growth and development of the West have had a profound impact upon Indian people and their environment, with the most immediate and dramatic changes occurring in two aspects of nature that played a predominant role in Indian life before the arrival of Europeans: wildlife and rivers.

Descriptions of wildlife in early western America stir the soul and defy imagination. On a bluff next to the upper Missouri River, Meriwether Lewis saw "immence quantities of game in every direction around us as we passed up the river; consisting of herds of Buffaloe, Elk, and Antelopes with some deer and woolves."[4] Some thirty years later a mountain man named Warren Angus Ferris effusively described a herd of buffalo (that is, bison) his party encountered on the Great Plains: "Far as the eye could reach the prairie was literally covered, and not only covered but crowded with them . . . a vast expanse of moving, plunging, rolling, rushing life. . . . I never realized before the majesty and power of the mighty tides of life that heave and surge in all great gatherings of human or brute creation. The scene had here a wild sublimity of aspect, that charmed the eye with a spell of power, while the natural sympathy of life with life made the pulse bound and almost madden with excitement."[5]

Another visitor to the buffalo-laden plains, General Isaac Stevens, could scarcely believe his eyes: "July 10, 1853 . . . For a great distance ahead every square mile seemed to have a herd of buffalo upon it. Their number was variously estimated by the members of the party—some as high as half a million. I do not think it any exaggeration to set it down at 200,000. I had heard of the myriads of these animals inhabiting the plains, but I could not realize the truth of these accounts till today, when they surpassed anything I could have imagined."[6] Once numbering perhaps forty million, the great buffalo herds were hunted to near extinction. By 1900 only a few hundred survived as relics of a bygone era.[7]

In addition to the buffalo, many other species were in spectacular abundance. A fur trapper, Zenas Leonard, described a valley in what is now southeastern Wyoming: "Found the prairies or plains in this direction very extensive—unobstructed with timber or brush—handsomely situated, with here and there a small creek passing through them, and in some places literally covered with game, such as Buffaloe, White and Black tailed Deer, Grizzly, Red, and White Bear, Elk, Prarie Dog, wild Goat, Big horned mountain Sheep, Antelope, &c."[8] George Bird Grinnell, traveling in the same area in 1879, viewed "the largest beaver meadow . . . I have ever seen. I presume that there were 500 dams in sight, most of them kept in good repair."[9] Today this area is traversed by Interstate 80 and is the location of the city of Laramie, Wyoming.

The rivers of the West also played a crucial role in traditional Indian life. In the Northwest they provided abundant habitat for fish and other wildlife, on the Great Plains they provided timber and shelter from the wind, and in the Southwest they provided water in an arid land. Indian population was particularly dense along the Columbia River. The great bounty of salmon and other wildlife had permitted an intensive and varied settlement of Indian peoples: "The lower Columbia River valley was one of the most densely populated areas of aboriginal North America. The names of the people who lived there are, however, hardly familiar even to scholars who study Indian peoples. There were Chinooks and Clatsops and also Kathlamets and Wahkiakums near the mouth of the river. Katskanies and Cowlitzes a little farther upstream. Then come Skillutes, Kalamas, Quthlapottles, Clannarminnamons, Multnomahs, Tillamooks, Shotos, Clanninatas, Cathlahnaquiahs, Cathlacommahtups, and many, many more, before the last of the predominantly Chinookan speakers, the Wascos and Wishrams, yielded to Sahaptin speakers at Celilo Falls."[10] Although there was a great diversity of wildlife in the Columbia River basin, salmon provided the main source of nutrition. An estimated sixteen million salmon made their way up the river each year to spawn, struggling past numerous rapids and falls. At the Dalles, Cascades, and Celilo Falls, as well as at Priest

Rapid and Kettle Falls, Indian fishermen waited for the fish as they leaped into the air. Today, these falls and rapids are drowned under a series of reservoirs.

The story is much the same for the Snake River, the Columbia's largest tributary. A fur trader visiting the valley in 1832 noted that "the river is full of salmon and plenty of them are to be had of the Indians whom we meet every few miles fishing on the banks of the stream."[11] Another explorer described Salmon Falls in the Thousand Springs area on the Snake: "The whole stream pitched in one cascade above forty feet in height, with a thundering sound, casting up a volume of spray that hung in the air like a silver mist. These are called by some the Fishing Falls as the salmon are taken here in immense quantities."[12] Because of over-fishing, dams, clear-cutting, and water pollution, the Snake River salmon are now virtually extinct.[13]

Today there are eighteen mainstem dams on the Columbia and Snake Rivers. More than 250 reservoirs have been built in the basin. There are so many dams and ship locks that Lewiston, Idaho, is considered a seaport. The salmon run has dwindled to 2.5 million, and only about 500,000 of these are naturally spawned.[14]

Many rivers of the West have met a similar fate at the hands of dam builders, and much of the country inhabited by Indians is now under water. Osbourne Russel, another trapper, described the Blackfoot River Gorge: "[The] Blackfoot makes a sweeping curve to the South West then gradually turning to the North enters a narrow gorge of basaltic rock thro. which it rushes with impetuosity."[15] That gorge is now beneath the Blackfoot Reservoir. George Bird Grinnell described the upper reaches of the Green River where the Henry's Fork flows in from the West: "It is a glorious river. The territory through which it passes presents some of the most majestic scenery that our country can afford."[16] Most of that section of the Green River is now under Flaming Gorge Reservoir. The stretch of river below the dam is still fairly pristine, but in recent years it became so clogged with rafters and kayakers that the National Park Service commenced a lottery permit system to prevent overcrowding.

Perhaps the most famous description of a canyon that is now inundated is John Wesley Powell's ebullient description of Glen Canyon: "On the walls, and back many miles into the country, numbers of monument-shaped buttes are observed. So we have a curious ensemble of wonderful features — carved walls, royal arches, glens, alcove gulches, mounds, and monuments. . . . Past these towering monuments, past these mounded billows of orange sandstone, past these oak-set glens, past these fern-decked alcoves, past these mural curves, we glide hour after hour, stopping now and then as our attention is arrested by some new wonder."[17] Powell and his crew also discovered numerous Indian ruins, including one where "Great quantities of flint chips are found on the rocks near by, and many arrowheads, some perfect, others broken; and frag-ments of pottery are strewn about in great profusion."[18] Today all of this beauty and history is hundreds of feet beneath the surface of Lake Powell (which is actually a reservoir, not a lake).

These early observers often attempted to predict what the future might hold for the unique, expansive lands of the western landscape. Osbourne Russel guessed that the mineral springs near the Bear River would "doubtless at no distant day be a resort for thousands of the gay and fashionable world."[19] He was partially right; the small town of Soda Springs, Idaho, does indeed play host to tourists, but some of the springs have been inundated by a dam. Cap-tain J. H. Simpson of the U.S. Army thought he saw clearly the potential of the valley just south of the Great Salt Lake: "The whole scene is that of a somber, dreary waste, where neither man nor beast can live for want of the necessary food and water."[20] Today 800,000 people live in that valley, but the "beasts" are found only in the zoo.

In regard to water in the West, it was the one-armed explorer of the Grand Canyon, John Wesley Powell, who was most prescient in his assessment of the future. In a speech before the International Irrigation Congress, he warned them: "You are piling up a heritage of conflict and litigation over water rights for there is not sufficient water to supply the land."[21] But perhaps the gloomiest prediction came from George Bird Grinnell. Writing about the West in general, he prophesied that "Towns will spring up and flourish, and the pure, thin air of the mountains will be blackened and polluted by the smoke vomited from the chimneys of a thousand smelting furnaces; the game, once so plentiful, will have disappeared with the Indian."[22] Like the others, Grinnell was partially cor-rect in his assessment; skies have been polluted, and the great scenes of wildlife described above no longer exist. But the Indian peoples, so closely associated with the game, the rivers, and the land, have survived.

In this chapter we will examine how the environment, especially contro-versies involving dams, endangered species, and instream flow, have played a role in nearly every Indian water settlement.

New West, Old Problems

The West, now the fastest growing region of the country, is experiencing un-precedented pressures for development. In some areas, urban sprawl is literally at the reservation boundary. In others, new demands for urban water, recre-ation, and new industry are threatening to consume vast quantities of water coveted by Indians and traditional water users. Simultaneously, powerful environmental groups are attempting to prevent the development of the last few remaining wild rivers in the West. Can these various interests find a way to share the "extreme beauty" of this land? Can the New West find a way to coexist with the West's original inhabitants, even though such benign coexistence largely eluded the old West? Will the advent of a new social order that is largely urban, well educated, and environmentally aware overcome age-old animosities and find a way to share the West's abundance with Indian tribes, or will the hordes of newcomers simply exacerbate the water conflicts between Indians and Anglos?

There is a complex relationship between environmentalists and American Indians. The sentimentality of the tearful warrior saddened by pollution and the apocryphal homilies of Chief Seattle have given way to a gritty recognition that environmental groups, often representing the demands of middle- and upper-class Anglos, do not necessarily pursue policy objectives that are in the best interests of contemporary Indian tribes. Nevertheless, Indians and environmentalists sometimes find common ground in attempting to protect land, habitat, and waterways.

In other words, there are two aspects to the relationship between Indians and environmentalists. The first can be called the "natural allies" perspective, which assumes that Indians — "America's first stewards of the land"[23] — and environmental groups possess a common respect for the earth, and thus are destined to be political allies in the struggle to save what remains of the West's environment. Much of the philosophy of modern environmentalism has been derived from traditional indigenous concepts of stewardship and harmony with the land.[24]

A second perspective can be called the "last refuge." In this scenario, environmentalists tend to view Indian reservations as the last great stretches of land that have not been developed or protected. Thus, reservations are not merely tribal homelands but have a larger significance as ecological preserves of wilderness, habitat for wildlife and native flora, open space, and a source of clean air and water. This perspective places Indians and environmentalists in conflict as the former attempt to develop their reservations to improve living standards, while the latter oppose such development in order to maintain reservations as the last refuge of a once-wild West. A Northern Cheyenne expressed this viewpoint: "[W]e often find ourselves fighting environmentalists to protect our ancestral lands and treaty rights."[25] In that statement, "protect" means the right for tribal government to do what they want with their own lands.

The official policy of the federal government is aligned with the first perspective. In recent years federal agencies that implement environmental policies have attempted, on paper at least, to create a sense of partnership with tribes.

For example, the official policy of the Environmental Protection Agency (EPA) is "to realize the long-range objective of including Tribal Governments as partners in decision-making and program management on reservation lands."[26] The U.S. Fish and Wildlife Service "is seeking partnerships with Native American governments" and claims to have a "long history of working with Native American governments in managing fish and wildlife resources."[27] The Corps of Engineers' policy is "to encourage cooperative undertakings and activities with affected tribal governments in the spirit of partnerships."[28] In reality, however, tribes and federal agencies are sometimes in direct conflict over environmental matters. In such situations, environmental groups are heavily involved. This conflict has, on occasion, become a critical part of the debate over Indian water settlements. This chapter will examine that debate.

The Greening of Settlements

One of the arguments in favor of settlements is that litigation cannot accommodate Mother Nature; in contrast, negotiations can fashion solutions that take into account environmental needs. Thus, water settlements can be negotiated in a manner that is sensitive to the impact on the land. To a great extent, the role of environmental considerations in settlements reflects a larger debate in water policy. For many years, water resources policy simply consisted of efforts to enhance supply. This usually meant more diversions, more dams and pipelines, and more environmental degradation. This approach resulted in huge construction projects that involved complex exchanges of water, money, and power. These projects were enormously expensive and proceeded with little regard for either the environment or Indian tribes.

A newer approach to water policy places the emphasis on effective management rather than massive construction. This emphasis often focuses on controlling the demand for water, rather than enlarging the supply, and has potentially less negative impact on fish and wildlife habitat, surrounding land, and rivers and lakes. Therefore, it is favored by environmentalists as a way of resolving water problems. The Clinton administration made the new approach the official policy of the Bureau of Reclamation. In 1992 the bureau revised its mission statement to reflect this approach: "Our mission: To manage, develop, and protect water and related resources in an environmentally and economically sound manner in the interest of the American public."[29] The extent to which water settlements meet an environmental mandate is in large part determined by the extent to which they follow this new mission statement.

Do settlements rely on concrete or creative management? To answer this question, it is helpful to divide environmental water issues into three related topics: dam construction, habitat preservation and the Endangered Species Act, and instream flow. Each of these issues has had a role in the negotiation of Indian water settlements.

Dam Construction

It has become commonplace to hear water managers say that the big dam is dead, that the age of large, federally funded dams has given way to a more enlightened era of wise management and river protection. This statement is not entirely true, however; the federal government has planned several large dams recently, and nearly all of them are associated with Indian water settlements.

A new political calculus helps explain why new dams and Indian settlements are related. The old iron triangle of Anglo water interests has lost much of its clout; at one time this alliance of government bureaucracies, pro-development interest groups, and senior congressmen and senators, chiefly from the South and the West, held virtual carte blanche over water policy. They funneled federal funds to innumerable pet projects in home districts and states. The favored strategy of this iron triangle was log rolling, where widespread support for questionable expenditures was attained by promising a project for nearly everyone; I'll vote for your unnecessary dam if you vote for my wasteful levee. Water authorization bills became known as "Christmas tree bills" because every legislator wanted to hang an ornament on them.[30]

This strategy was effective until a significant backlash against wasteful expenditures and environmentally destructive dams developed in the 1970s. Environmental groups, anti-tax conservatives, and legislators from the East and Midwest began to criticize the traditional approach to water policy. This criticism made it more difficult to engage in log rolling and thereby generate sufficient political support for more dams. Western Anglos needed the "Indian blanket" (explained in chapter 3) to boost political support for dams. The advent of the settlement policy provided an avenue to express this newfound alliance between traditional enemies—western dam builders and Indian tribes.

This alliance has placed tribes in a precarious political position. Just as the government is officially backing away from dam building, some tribes are now demanding their share of the water pork barrel. As one Indian lawyer put it, "We missed the dollar days of federal water development." Their complaint is understandable; in the heyday of concrete solutions, just about everyone in the country received some kind of project—except Indian people. Some Indians are asking to receive only what others have received. But widespread opposition to new dams makes meeting their requests difficult. Thus tribes have had to negotiate settlements within the confines of the new water policy. When settlements have ventured into the highly conflictive world of dam building, political opposition has been fierce, usually led by environmental groups and their allies in the federal bureaucracy.

Without a doubt the best example of this conflict is the Animas–La Plata Project (ALP) and its central role in the Colorado Ute settlement. As described in chapter 4, the ALP and the settlement have bitterly divided the Southern Utes. The anti-dam faction is closely aligned with several environmental groups. Project proponents feel that these groups have ignored the value of the settlement agreement because "it complicates their standard arguments in opposing water conservation through water storage."[31]

Another example of conflict over dams is the 1992 settlement for the Northern Utes of the Uintah and Ouray Reservation in Utah. This settlement was part of a larger political effort to reauthorize the Central Utah Project (CUP). This giant federal project consumed all of its authorized funding by the late 1980s but was still far from complete. When project sponsors went to Congress to ask for more money, reformers saw it as an opportunity to impose new environmental and cost restrictions (the Northern Utes and the CUP are discussed in greater detail in the vignette in chapter 8). After several years of contentious debate, a reauthorization passed in 1992 that included the settlement for the Northern Utes and authorization for a Uintah Basin Replacement Project, which is where the Uintah and Ouray Reservation is located.

After several years of study, the Central Utah Water Conservancy District (the contracting entity) proposed to build two dams in the Uintah basin. The proposed 216-foot-high Lower Uintah Dam and the accompanying reservoir would be built entirely on Indian land; not quite half of its storage space would be allocated to the Ute tribe.[32] Another proposed dam, the 180-foot high Crystal Ranch Dam, and accompanying reservoir would straddle tribal, private, and federal lands. The reservoir's capacity would be 24,000 af, of which 9,230 af would be allocated to tribal water storage.[33]

As soon as the district announced its plans to build these two dams, environmentalists began lobbying against them. The Utah Rivers Council took a lead role, arguing that the district ignored cheaper and more environmentally benign alternatives, and instead preferred to "divert both of these incredible free-flowing ecosystems into sterile canals."[34] American Rivers, the national river preservation group, declared the Uintah River to be one of America's "twenty most endangered rivers."

Initially the Ute tribe was supportive of the dams, but in July 1998 the tribal council surprised many people by announcing they would not support the construction of the dams unless substantial changes were made in their operation. Ron Wopsock, the chairman of the tribal council, explained why: "We're saying, unless it's an Indian project, in the future, we don't want it on the reservation."[35] After nine months of further discussion, the tribal council voted to withdraw its support for the dams, effectively killing them.[36] Although these two dams were not officially part of the Ute settlement, the dams and the settlement were both incorporated into the CUP Completion Act and thus were part of a series of horse trades and log rolls. The tribe's opposition could directly affect the district's cooperation regarding the settlement and its implementation. It should also be noted that the tribe did not object to the dams for environmental reasons; rather, tribal leaders were concerned about tribal control over the stored water and the reservoir sites.[37]

The two dams proposed for the Uintah Basin Replacement Project were not the first time that the Northern Ute tribe had experience with dams built by the Bureau of Reclamation and its successor, the Central Utah Water Conservancy District. In the late 1980s the agency built a dam on Rock Creek, just above the reservation, and began diverting water away from the reservation. While this dam was being built the bureau was busy explaining that the Ute Indian unit—the part of the CUP designed for the tribe—could not be built because it cost too much.[38] The tribal council began to question the wisdom of working with an agency that seemed much more intent on diverting water away from the reservation than providing assistance to the Ute people.[39] Rock Creek Dam was completed on time; the 1992 settlement was in essence the government's liability payment to the tribe for its failure to build the promised Ute Indian unit.

The Colorado Ute and the Northern Ute settlements have clearly demonstrated the political difficulties that are inevitable when new dams are proposed. Other tribes have anticipated these difficulties and designed settlements to depend upon existing water projects. In Arizona, the Central Arizona Project is being tapped to supply water to several settlements, including Ak-Chin, Fort McDowell, Salt River Pima-Maricopa, San Carlos, Yavapai-Prescott, and Tohono O'odham (if it is ever completed as planned). The total amount of CAP water reallocated to Indian use may be as high as 309,828 af.[40] The Fort Hall settlement utilizes water from Palisades Reservoir and Ririe Reservoir. The Salt River Pima-Maricopa settlement relies in part on water from Roosevelt Lake (a reservoir) and the Salt River Project. The Fort McDowell settlement relies in part on water stored behind Bartlett and Horseshoe Dams. And Stampede Reservoir provides water storage for the Pyramid Lake settlement.

The Northern Cheyenne settlement used a unique approach that authorized the enlargement of an existing dam. The enlargement had little environmental consequences, and thus evoked no opposition from environmental groups. The U.S. Fish and Wildlife Service concluded that the dam enlargement would have no long-term impact on fish and wildlife resources.[41] The EPA expressed some concerns over wetlands mitigation, but project sponsors worked with the Montana Riparian and Wetland Association to alleviate those concerns.[42] The Salt River Pima-Maricopa settlement also relies in part on the enlargement of a dam.[43]

In short, settlements have been much more involved with existing dams than new ones, and the San Luis Rey settlement attempted to avoid reliance on any dams. This approach has helped avoid confrontations with environmental groups and tax-conscious conservatives. But it is a significant restraint on negotiators who must operate under the no-harm rule described in previous chapters. The no-harm rule means that wet water for Indians cannot come at the expense of non-Indian water users, even if those water users created the problem in the first place. Without the option of creating new storage behind new dams, negotiators must engage in some fairly complex thinking to find a combination of money and water that satisfies all parties. Thus, future settlements that rely on creative water management will stand a much better chance of successful implementation.

Habitat Preservation and Endangered Species

There is a great irony in the contemporary relationship between Indian tribes and wildlife.[44] Prior to the coming of Europeans, many tribes were wholly dependent on wildlife for their existence. Many tribal rituals and spirituality are often rich in animal totems and obeisance to the spirits of brother animals. But the onslaught of millions of settlers and farmers greatly diminished the habitat for wildlife, and it was not until late in the twentieth century that the U.S. government took steps to prevent the wholesale extinction of plant and animal species.

In passing the 1973 Endangered Species Act, Congress "intended endangered species to be afforded the highest of priorities."[45] Indeed, it may be afforded a priority higher than the preservation of Indian sovereignty. In some cases, enforcement of the Endangered Species Act on Indian lands has illustrated the "last refuge" perspective described earlier. In effect, the government is saying to Indian people, "We Anglos destroyed 99 percent of species X; it is now incumbent upon you Indian people to set aside reservation lands to preserve the last remnant of that species." As a Northern Ute leader put it, "We're being punished because we've taken care of our wildlife in the Indian way."[46] Thus, the wildlife that once sustained tribes has now become a burden on some tribes.

But the picture is more complicated than that. Many traditional Indian people still revere wildlife and express this reverence in both ceremony and politics. And some tribes continue a traditional dependence on wildlife for provender as well as economic sustenance. In these situations, the Endangered Species Act has been of great benefit to Indian people and has allied tribes with wildlife groups in an effort to preserve habitat. In such cases, the "natural allies" perspective holds a great deal of validity.

Both of these scenarios are evident in water settlements. Some tribes have been aided by the Endangered Species Act in their settlement efforts, while others have been hampered. In general, settlements that rely on new structural development have run afoul of the Endangered Species Act, while those that emphasize efficient water management and reallocation of existing sources have avoided endangered species problems.

Much of the conflict between tribes and the Endangered Species Act has occurred in the San Juan River Basin, home to the Southern Ute, Ute Mountain Ute, Jicarilla Apache, and Navajo Reservations. The controversy there is primarily over three native fish species: the Colorado pikeminnow (formerly called the Colorado squawfish), the humpback chub, and the razorback sucker. In decades past, these fish were considered "trash" fish, and fish and game agencies went to great lengths to eliminate them. But with the passage of the Endangered Species Act, the mandate of U.S. Fish and Wildlife Service was fundamentally revised. The law not only prohibits the killing of endangered species; it also gives the agency the power to prevent the destruction of their habitat. This is a powerful tool that has been wielded to great effect by the Fish and Wildlife Service and environmental groups.

The reliance of the Colorado Ute settlement on the Animas–La Plata Project (ALP) placed it squarely on a collision course with the Endangered Species Act. The proposed project would require significant diversions of water from a tributary of the San Juan River, which would greatly diminish the viability of the endangered fish living in the river. Originally authorized by Congress in 1968, ALP grew into a $700 million project with two dams, seven pumping stations, and miles of canals and pipelines.[47] Although ALP has been under fire from environmentalists and concerned local citizens for years, the Endangered Species Act dramatically altered the balance of power between contending parties.

The "final" environmental impact statement on the project was completed in 1980. Rapidly rising costs, however, delayed construction. In 1986 Congress mandated cost-sharing as a response to ALP's expanding price tag. In 1986, federal, local, and tribal officials reached an agreement and signed the Colorado Ute Indian Water Rights Final Settlement Agreement.[48]

The Endangered Species Act entered the picture four years later when the Fish and Wildlife Service issued a jeopardy opinion on the endangered Colorado pikeminnow (formerly squawfish). According to a spokesman for then-Secretary of the Interior Manuel Lujan Jr. ALP was "[o]bviously . . . on indefinite hold."[49] In April of 1991, Fish and Wildlife Service issued a revised draft biological opinion setting out reasonable and prudent alternatives. The one adopted required flows from the existing Navajo Dam on the San Juan River to mimic the natural flows of the river.

The project appeared to be back on schedule in October of 1991 with the signing of a memorandum of understanding by the Colorado Ute tribes, the Jicarilla Apache tribe of northern New Mexico, the Department of the Interior, and the States of Colorado, New Mexico, and Utah. The signatories agreed to develop and implement the Fish and Wildlife Service's reasonable and prudent alternative, which included development of a recovery implementation program for the San Juan River. On October 6, 1991, a groundbreaking ceremony was held.

But just before construction began, environmental groups filed suit in Colorado federal district court challenging the project. Led by the Sierra Club Legal Defense Fund, the groups alleged that the Bureau of Reclamation had failed to comply with the National Environmental Policy Act, the Clean Water Act, and the Endangered Species Act.[50] The groups claimed that ALP would be lethal to the pikeminnow and the razorback sucker because it would increase heavy metals and selenium concentrations in San Juan basin waters. In addition, the groups argued that ALP would destroy wetlands and block recreational use on the Animas River.[51] In April 1992, the bureau agreed to supplement its 1980 final EIS to address the groups' concerns.

Environmentalists won another victory in September of that year, when the district court barred the bureau from excavating for the project at a possible Anasazi burial site until the supplemental EIS was complete.[52] Finally, in December 1992, the court ordered the Department of the Interior to divulge documents containing responses to Office of Management and Budget questions about ALP pursuant to the Freedom of Information Act.[53] Then, in December of that same year, the Environmental Protection Agency announced a number of objections to the project, including concern that ALP would further harm water quality in New Mexico, would increase the amount of toxic substances harmful to the endangered fish, and destroy wetlands.[54]

Despite these setbacks, tribal leaders continued to push for the ALP. In 1995 Judy Knight-Frank, then chairperson of the Ute Mountain Ute tribe, expressed frustration: "Presently our water settlement is not complete because of the environmental issues. . . . We constantly have environmental groups coming in and telling us what is best for us, and we have problems with this because they have not lived our life and they don't understand us."[55] The final supplement to the EIS for the project recommended completing the full project consistent with the results of the seven-year study for the biological opinion.[56] However, flagging political support for the ALP forced the agency to scale back the project in an effort to keep it alive. Senator Ben Nighthorse Campbell has pushed hard for a somewhat scaled-down ALP. In contrast, Southern Ute opponents encouraged Congress to find an alternative solution that "would be kinder to the rivers and lands we hold sacred, and provide more useful benefits to our people."[57] In the meantime, the Bureau of Reclamation finished yet another EIS — this one with the dubious title of "Draft Supplemental EIS to the Final Supplement to the Final Environmental Statement for the Animas–La Plata,"[58] followed by a record of decision in September 2000. A much revised and scaled-down ALP was authorized by Congress later that year. This legislation stated: "In order to meet the requirements of the Endangered Species Act, and in particular the various biological opinions issued by the Fish and Wildlife Service, the amendments made by this title are needed to provide for a significant reduction in the facilities and water supply contemplated under the [original 1988] Agreement."[59]

The Jicarilla Apache tribe's settlement has also been affected by the Endangered Species Act. The tribe's 1992 settlement entitled them to water from two river basins — both of which are mired in endangered species problems.[60] However, the Endangered Species Act has blocked the tribe's ability to use the water guaranteed to it in the settlement act.[61] Although the tribe retains the legal right to the water quantified in its settlement, it must leave most of it in the San Juan River until the fish species are no longer considered threatened. Of the 40,000 af provided in the settlement, only 6,500 af are included in the environmental baseline established for the biological assessment.

The Navajo Nation has also encountered Endangered Species Act difficulties in the San Juan basin. Unlike the other tribes discussed in this chapter, the Navajo Nation has not completed a water settlement. In regard to the water of the San Juan River, the nation is still trying to complete the Navajo Indian Irrigation Project (NIIP), originally authorized in 1962. The NIIP was not a settlement but merely an agreement with the Bureau of Reclamation to build a project on tribal land in return for a clear title to water for the San Juan–Chama Project.[62] Any settlement of the nation's claims to the San Juan River will be extremely difficult until the endangered fish are sufficiently recovered.

Navajo water claims are not limited to the San Juan River. The nation has been negotiating for several years with non-Indian water users and the Hopi tribe to settle competing claims in the Little Colorado River basin. However, the parties encountered Endangered Species Act problems. The Navajo Nation had hoped to build a reservoir at Tucker Flats, near a tributary of the Little Colorado called Chevelon Creek. However, Chevelon Creek, for the eight miles above its confluence with the Little Colorado, is critical habitat for the Little Colorado spinedace, an endangered fish.

According to Stanley Pollack, the Navajo Nation's water rights attorney, Tucker Flats Reservoir was the centerpiece of the Nation's original settlement proposal. In Pollack's view, the Tucker Flats Project was critical to the settlement process and the spinedace problem threatened the entire negotiation.[63] Leslie Fitzpatrick, the U.S. Fish and Wildlife Service's representative in the Little Colorado basin, provides a different view of the situation. She claims the Fish and Wildlife Service never held the position that the Navajo Nation may not use the water of Chevelon Creek, but only that they must design the project so that it provides sufficient flows to protect the endangered spinedace (1994).[64] The Navajo Nation downsized the proposed Tucker Flats Project and eliminated the irrigation component, which eliminated the need to divert water from Chevelon Creek. The nation's reformulation of the project was in direct response to the U.S. Fish and Wildlife Service's concern for the endangered spinedace. After negotiations stalled in 1994 and 1995 over this problem and others, the Navajo Nation agreed to abandon the Tucker Flats proposal altogether and instead focus on a small project called the Blue Ridge alternative.[65] Negotiations have now moved on to other alternatives (more on this in chapter 9).

Mr. Pollack feels that the spinedace problem is typical of the hurdles the Navajo Nation faces in trying to develop its water resources: "We have [Endangered Species Act] problems everywhere we go. Pick your river."[66] In addition to endangered fish, the tribe's water development efforts are also hampered by endangered plant species. Parrish's alkali grass, which grows only near Tuba City, Arizona, has been proposed for endangered status; the Fish and Wildlife Service claims it is harmed by groundwater pumping.[67]

Clearly the Endangered Species Act has greatly complicated the search for settlements in the San Juan River basin. The two Colorado Ute tribes, the Jicarilla Apache, and the Navajo Nation have experienced difficulties developing their water supplies because of endangered species. In an act of frustration, a Navajo man attending a water conference succinctly voiced an opinion on this matter: "We Indian people are the endangered species. The fish can wait."[68]

On the other hand, some tribes have benefited greatly by using the clout of the Endangered Species Act in their efforts to protect fish and wildlife that play a crucial role in their continued existence. For example, the listing of salmon in the Columbia/Snake River basin has been of assistance to tribes in that area that want to bring back the great salmon runs.[69] The significance of the salmon is clear in the mission statement of the Columbia River Intertribal Fish Commission: "The Sacred Salmon runs are in decline. It is the moral duty, therefore, of the Indian People of the Columbia River Valley to see them restored. We have to take care of them so that they can take care of us. Entwined together inextricably, no less now than ever before, are the fates of both the Salmon and the Indian People. The quest for Salmon recovery is about restoring what is sacred to its sacred place."[70] In regard to settlements, the power of the Endangered Species Act to assist tribal claims was most evident in the Pyramid Lake negotiations, which is the subject of the vignette at the end of this chapter. The controversies involving the Endangered Species Act and tribes are but one facet of the larger conflict that exists in both the Anglo and Indian communities: At what point is the trade-off between economic gain and habitat loss worth it? At what point does development simply become too destructive?

The Endangered Species Act has proven to be either a boost or a stumbling block for the tribes discussed above. For tribes that seek to restore fisheries or habitat, the Endangered Species Act has proved to be a powerful ally in the negotiation process. On the other hand, the presence of listed species can block settlements that depend upon further water and land development. These different experiences with the Endangered Species Act clearly illustrate both the "natural allies" and the "last refuge" perspectives.

Instream Flow

The New Eden was premised on one simple fact: diverting water onto fields will grow a whole new society, and thus water flowing to the sea is water wasted. This simple philosophy remained unchanged through a hundred years of western expansion and growth. It permitted giant new swaths of crops to flourish in the deserts, but it wreaked havoc on river ecosystems. Only in the last twenty years have western states begun to recognize the value of water left in its natural watercourse. As a result, the notion of beneficial use has been expanded to include the preservation of riverine and riparian habitats, fishing and other forms of river recreation, aesthetics, water quality, and cultural uses.[71]

Instream flow played an important role in three of the settlements: Fort Hall, Northern Utes, and Pyramid Lake.[72] The Fort Hall Reservation of the Shoshone and Bannock tribes is in the Snake River valley of southern Idaho. The site of the old Fort Hall trading post is beside the river on the south bank in an area known as the Fort Hall bottoms. This riparian area is rich in both plant and animal life and is valued by tribal members as a natural area. The Shoshones and Bannocks have a long history of fishing in the Snake River and its tributaries. Early trappers in the area west of Fort Hall observed them taking great catches of salmon along the river: "[The Shoshones] absolutely thronged its banks to profit by the abundance of salmon, and lay up a stock for winter provisions. Scaffolds were everywhere erected, and immense quantities of fish drying upon them."[73]

The tribe's desire to protect the bottomlands and attempt to restore the salmon runs played a role in their water settlement. Rather than attempt to gain dramatic new diversions, the tribe opted for a water-marketing proviso that permits the tribes to lease their federal storage water within the state of Idaho. This option was chosen as a way for the tribe to provide instream flow and "protect and enhance anadromous fish runs, as well as provide benefits for resident fish and wildlife."[74] Leasing the water downstream keeps the water in the river, at least until it passes the reservation. Although environmental groups were not involved in the negotiations, they have subsequently expressed support for the instream flow provisions of the settlement.[75]

Instream flow was also a major issue in the Northern Ute settlement in Utah. At one time the Bureau of Reclamation planned to build two dams on Rock Creek, one of the premier "blue-ribbon" trout fisheries on the reservation. Eventually only one dam was built, Upper Stillwater Dam. The purpose of this dam was to divert nearly the entire stream into a series of pipelines and siphons for use by Anglo farmers hundreds of miles away.[76] To make matters worse, the bureau made the mistake of dumping mineral-laden soils into the reservoir site. When the reservoir filled, the soil went into suspension, creating what looked like a giant lake of tomato soup. Tribal attorneys filed suit for damages.[77]

The Northern Ute tribe consistently opposed the destruction of Rock Creek's fish habitat and forced the bureau and other CUP participants to sign an instream flow agreement in 1980.[78] By the time of the 1992 settlement, the tribe's concern for instream flows had broadened to include other reservation streams. The settlement provided a total of 44,000 af "to the preservation of minimum stream flows in the Uintah Basin," including a specific amount of water for Rock Creek.[79]

Tribal concerns over instream flows in the Fort Hall and Northern Ute settlements clearly indicate that these tribal governments are concerned with preserving riverine habitat; that concern is expressed in their water settlements. But the most protracted conflict over instream flows occurred in western

Nevada, where the Pyramid Lake tribe has fought for decades to preserve the unique fish life in the lake that gives the tribe its name. The vignette at the end of this chapter describes that struggle.

Conclusion

For two centuries American Indian policy was burdened with the oppressive weight of paternalism. A government of Anglos continually made decisions it deemed were in the best interest of American Indians. In reality, many of these policies were formulated with only the Anglos' best interests in mind; other policies were well-meaning but created perverse consequences for Indians because they were formulated without Indian input. The Indian Reorganization Act of 1934 and the Indian Self-Determination Act of 1975 were efforts to restore at least a semblance of tribal self-government—within the confines of Anglo institutions. The basic premise of those laws is that Indian tribes should be able to decide for themselves how to govern their reservations. Implementation of these laws has been fraught with failures and conflicts, but at least there was a recognition that Indian peoples should have some form of control over their own destiny.

But an important exception to that policy has developed; environmental regulations have often been applied unilaterally to Indian tribes. Some environmental statutes have been amended to give tribes the same administrative role as states or other governing entities, including the "Superfund" law, the Safe Drinking Water Act, and the Clean Water Act.[80]

It is commendable that tribes have received the same recognition as states in the administration of some federal environmental mandates, but this is not the same thing as sovereignty. The unilateral application of the Endangered Species Act on some reservations makes this lack of sovereignty evident.

It is probably true that most American Indians generally favor environmentally conscious regulation, but whether they want it imposed upon them is another question. For their part, environmental groups are in a difficult position. Many environmentalists are undoubtedly sympathetic to the needs and interests of American Indians. But when forced to make a choice, environmental groups have consistently given priority to environmental protection over tribal sovereignty, a stand that is much in evidence in the conflicts and negotiations over Indian water settlements.

Perhaps the most pernicious result of this is that government agencies sometimes perceive tribes as just another interest group. For example, a supervisor with the U.S. Fish and Wildlife Service stated that Indians were not being treated unfairly under the Endangered Species Act because they are "treated just like any other water developer." This policy is not the official position of the Department of the Interior; in a 1993 secretarial order Secretary Babbitt stated that "It is the intent of this Order that each bureau and office will operate within a government-to-government relationship with federally recognized Indian tribes."[81] But in practice the federal government has applied the Endangered Species Act on Indian reservations without due consideration of tribal sovereignty.

In regard to Indian water settlements, environmentalists and Indian tribes have a mixed relationship; they are sometimes allies, sometimes adversaries. It is clear that, in many negotiations, there are numerous parties at the table that have a compelling interest in diminishing tribal sovereignty in order to impose their own environmental objectives. And there is ample evidence that the Department of the Interior continues to play its traditional schizophrenic role of supporting and representing both Indian tribes and their adversaries.

Many environmentalists are undoubtedly more comfortable with the "natural allies" perspective alluded to earlier. But in some situations the value preferences of Anglo environmentalists will be at odds with the needs of American Indian tribes. Most federal resource management agencies are now adopting the concept of ecosystem management, which emphasizes the preservation of diversity in life-forms and habitat.[82] Perhaps that approach needs to be expanded to include cultural diversity as well.

The complex relationship between Indian tribes, environmentalists, and water has played a major role in shaping water settlements. In many ways the effort to bring harmony to this conflict reflects the lesson of the "parable of Navajo Mountain" at the beginning of this book: water, land, and culture are inextricably related, and changing just one of these elements changes all of them. Billy Frank, chairman of the Northwest Indian Fisheries Commission, provided a stark example of this ecological maxim when discussing the destruction of the Columbia River salmon runs: "They took all of our way of life away from us. They took our food, and they gave us surplus food. When they gave us surplus food, they gave us sugar diabetes. When they took our water away, they gave us sugar diabetes. When they took our culture away and our way of doing what we do, they gave us sugar diabetes."[83]

At one level, there is an obvious simplicity to this issue. Gerald Peabody, a member of the Ute Mountain Ute tribe, succinctly identified this: "We call water the water of life. We have this connection with water; without it there is no life, and we give thanks to the Creator that we are blessed with it. All people, not just Ute people, have a common bond, a common goal, to have enough water."[84]

In stark contrast to this simple truth, the politics of water is Byzantine—a convoluted exercise in pressure group politics. This political reality is perhaps inevitable when there are so many diverse water users, ranging from endangered fish to embattled tribes to the burgeoning megacities of the New West. The environmental issues that have emerged in the settlements are diverse, but there is a common thread of fear—fear of losing control, fear of not having enough of nature's bounty to sustain a people. A new water ethic, based on a more holistic view of water as an integral part of a larger natural and cultural environment, may be the best response to this well-founded fear. Such an ethic would move beyond the narrow view of water as solely a commodity to be diverted—the heart of the New Eden philosophy. This approach might help negotiators find common ground on environmental issues and prevent settlements from becoming yet another threat to the western ecosystem.[85]

Vignette: The Tears of Stone Mother

Nevada state highway 445 runs north out of Reno through a broad desert valley. The hills are covered with brown grass and sage. Black volcanic rock forms outcrops along the hillsides. It is an austere, forbidding landscape, seemingly devoid of appreciable amounts of water. But after many miles, highway 445 comes up over a rise and suddenly, splayed out from mountainside to mountainside, is a giant lake.

Pyramid Lake lies in a natural depression at the foot of the Sierra Nevada Mountains. Its beauty is startling. It is easy to see how the lake got its Anglo name; a pyramid-shaped rock protrudes from the water on the far side of the lake. It is not so easy to see how the lake got its Indian name, which derives from the unique fish species that used to inhabit the lake in great numbers. In the Paiute creation story, the lake was formed from the tears of Stone Mother.[86]

For many years, the challenge to Indian economic development was isolation; there were no markets or suppliers close by. Today many tribes face a different problem—being overrun by the explosive population growth in the New West.

Reno, Nevada, is in many ways a microcosm of this new era. It is experiencing rapid growth in a fragile desert environment. West of Reno, housing developments carpet the hillsides. These new subdivisions consist of neat little box houses arranged in undulating rows that roughly follow the contours of the Sierra Nevada foothills. A little further west is a new development appropriately named Boomtown. Next to the truck stop at Boomtown, a patch of grazing land along the interstate still supports a herd of longhorn cattle; the old West and New West can be seen in one glance. A little further up the highway is the monument to the Donner party—a reminder that the new Westerners were preceded by people who knew hardship that we cannot even imagine today.

East of Reno, new development tends to follow the Truckee River valley. The Truckee River, after it leaves Reno, passes through Sparks and a score of smaller communities that have sprung up along this narrow river corridor. The river creates a course of green life amidst barren hillsides. One of these communities, called Rainbow Bend, seems a surprising candidate for rapid growth; it is sandwiched between the hills, the river, and the interstate highway. The focus of intense real estate development, Rainbow Bend has sprung up right next to the river. A giant sign announces that it is a "planned community," and phase 2 is now open. It consists of prefabricated manufactured homes tightly arrayed in a line on the south bank of the Truckee. The streets all have fancy French names, such as Rue de La Rouge and Avenue de Coulours. When I visited this place, the river was roaring, but at other times it is bone dry. The river has an unpleasant odor here, reflecting the fact that the Truckee meadows municipalities have an inadequate sewage treatment plant.

Downstream from Rainbow Bend is Derby Dam. It looks old and haggard, as though the nearly one hundred years of bitter conflict over it have aged it prematurely. The rutted dirt road to the dam passes through a narrow underpass below a railroad; bright orange graffiti on the bridgehead warns all comers: "Avoid grief: do not enter."

The nature of the Truckee River changes below Derby Dam. Because of the river's low flows and lack of late summer water, the banks are sparsely vegetated. At one time this riparian area supported innumerable cottonwood trees and a complete ecosystem. Today it looks more like a meandering canal than a living river. The river turns north and heads toward Pyramid Lake. Along the way it cuts a gentle-sided canyon. This canyon was the scene of a military conflict in 1860 between the Pyramid Lake Paiutes, local militia and the U.S. Army. Back then they were fighting over land; today the same parties are arrayed against each other in a fight over water.

The history of the Pyramid Lake Paiutes' struggle to save their namesake lake is long and agonizing. It is one of the most extreme examples of the federal government's failure as a trustee for American Indian interests.

In 1844, when Colonel John C. Fremont came upon a group of Indian people living around a large, high-desert lake, the Indians shared a meal of fish with him. Fremont decided to name this unique and impressive body of water Pyramid Lake. Of course, it already had a name, *cui-ui pah*, a name that it shared with a unique kind of fish that could be found in great abundance in the lake's deep, cold waters. Also found in the lake was another large game fish, the lahonton cutthroat trout. Together, these fish provided the Paiute people with a healthy, plentiful diet.[87]

In the ensuing decades many changes came to the Pyramid Lake Paiutes and their lake. The federal government chose the Truckee River—the source of water that keeps Pyramid Lake alive—as the water source for its first reclamation project, the Newlands Project. The lake and the fish that lived there began to die slowly as the water that formerly went to the lake was now diverted to the Newlands Project. The lake level dropped forty feet in just eighteen years, blocking the spawning beds of the fish. By 1940 the lahonton cutthroat trout was extinct in the lake; a minute number of cui-ui managed to survive.

One hundred years after Fremont's fish dinner with the Paiutes, the federal government sent an emissary of a different order. A federal court issued a decree that settled a water rights case that had been in litigation since 1913.[88] This Orr Ditch Decree was a disaster for the Pyramid Lake Paiutes. The federal government, acting as legal trustee for the tribe, claimed only water for irrigation; Justice Department attorneys completely ignored the tribe's long history of fishing and their relationship to the lake.

There are many possible explanations for this conspicuous failure to act in the best interests of the tribe. One reason may be that the U.S. government also represented the other party in the litigation, the Newlands Project. In the decree the tribe was awarded sufficient water to irrigate 5,800 acres; the Newlands Project was given water for 232,800 acres. No water for Pyramid Lake fish was awarded.[89] Indeed, any water use beyond those specified in the decree was "declared to be wasteful, and all wasteful or excessive use of water is hereby prohibited."[90]

Thirty years later the tribe hired its own lawyers and sued the government, pointing out that their interests were not fairly represented by a trustee with an obvious conflict of interest—something that would get a private attorney disbarred. A successor case went to the Supreme Court, which concluded that the conflict of interest existed, but allowed the Orr Decree to stand without modification.[91]

In short, the tribe had played its Winters hand and lost, thanks to the divided loyalties of the federal government. But by the time the Supreme Court delivered its blow to the tribe in 1983, other legal and political imperatives were beginning to play a role. In 1967, relying on a predecessor of the Endangered Species Act, the U.S. Fish and Wildlife Service declared the cui-ui to be a threatened species. With the passage of the 1973 act, the tribe had an even better weapon at its disposal. Back in 1902, Congressman Newlands had declared that any water reaching Pyramid Lake was "running to waste."[92] Eighty years later, that kind of thinking had been replaced by a widespread concern for the lake's ecosystem. When Congressman Newlands spoke in 1902, all the powers of the New Eden stood with him. By the 1980s, the political fulcrum had shifted much closer to the dream of restoring the lake and its fishery. All parties were ready to attempt to negotiate.

It was not easy. The negotiations over the Truckee River involved two states (California and Nevada), the city of Reno and several other municipalities, Washoe County, a power company, several water user associations including the powerful Truckee-Carson Irrigation District, another Indian tribe (the Fallon Paiutes), the Stillwater National Wildlife Refuge, several dams and water projects, and another important lake, Tahoe. Most of these interests, including those of the Fallon Paiutes, the national wildlife refuge, and the irrigation district, benefited from continued diversions from the Truckee River. Negotiations in one form or another dragged on for years.

Within the Pyramid Lake tribe, there was no clear consensus on a negotiation stance. An initial settlement was developed and presented to Congress, but a significant portion of the tribe opposed it. These opponents organized an ad hoc committee and circulated a petition to hold a referendum on the proposed settlement. Several contentious tribal meetings were held in an effort to reach agreement among tribal members. When congressional hearings were held on the settlement, both factions testified. In the meantime, tribal elections were held, and the results changed the make-up of the council.

The new council was chaired by Joe Ely, a man with considerable leadership and negotiation skills. The council held a series of information meetings prior to the referendum vote. The referendum ballot offered tribal members several alternatives, ranging from a complete rejection of the current settlement to a list of parameters or goals to be achieved in a subsequent settlement. This last option proved to be the most popular. With this mandate the council developed a new settlement. However, a core of opposition still existed among tribal members, and another petition was filed to oppose the settlement. This petition, if successful, would have killed the settlement. Initially the petition garnered enough signatures to succeed, but during a council meeting several members were convinced to remove their names from the petition. At that point the petition lacked sufficient signatures to pass. This meeting occurred just two days before congressional hearings on the settlement began. By then the Truckee-Carson Irrigation District had dropped out of the negotiations.[93]

Despite these tribulations, a settlement was eventually passed in 1990. However, it left many issues unsettled and is more accurately described as an endangered fish settlement rather than a water settlement. And calling it a "settlement" is something of an act of bravado; it offers only to "encourage settlement of litigation and claims."[94] It was a milestone along the way to a true settlement, but many critical issues were left unresolved. A Truckee River operating agreement had to be negotiated, operating criteria (OCAP) for the river were being continually revised, a final EIS had to be produced, the Tahoe-Truckee Restoration-Recovery Implementation Plan had to be developed, and conflicts with the Truckee-Carson Irrigation District, which did not sign the settlement, loomed as a continuing threat. In addition, there were related unresolved issues concerning the Fallon Reservation and the wetlands. There were even unresolved problems with the U.S. Navy.

The conditional, unresolved character of the settlement makes more sense when viewed in the larger legal and political context. The Pyramid Lake Paiutes' losses in court necessitated a unique and imaginative legal strategy for regaining water for the lake; the settlement became just one part of this strategy. In addition to the settlement, the tribe and the federal government have pursued numerous other efforts to secure water for the lake, including a recoupment lawsuit against the Truckee-Carson Irrigation District, litigation based on state water law use requirements, federal reclamation requirements, changes in the operation of Derby Dam, reclassifying irrigation lands to conserve water, and a water quality agreement. All of these efforts are designed to produce, as one federal manager put it, "death by a thousand cuts" to the water use regime that was destroying the lake. Leading the tribe through these multiple hurdles has required an uncommon degree of tenacity and creativity.

Mervin Wright Jr., chairman of the Pyramid Lake Paiute tribe, was 32 years old when I interviewed him in 1997, but he looked considerably younger. When he was born the conflict over Pyramid Lake water rights was already over a half-century old. On the wall over his desk, next to family snapshots, was a picture of Derby Dam with a red circle-and-slash symbol on it. His goal as chairman was to advance the unrelenting effort to undo ninety years of reclamation policy, mitigate the damage done to his tribe, and win back a river for his people. Chairman Wright continued throughout his tenure in office to struggle with the negotiations over a Truckee River operating agreement, which he says should be called a disagreement rather than an agreement.[95]

Despite all the challenges, there have been victories. An aggressive fish recovery program (funded via the settlement) has dramatically increased the number of fish in the lake.[96] The water rights acquisition program has begun. The water releases from Stampede Reservoir are now timed to aid in fish recovery. And a ruling by the state engineer in 1998 awarded the tribe the right to the unappropriated waters of the Truckee River.[97]

In sum, the settlement left many difficult decisions to the future; in the words of the tribe's water resources director, "it allowed the parties to come together."[98] The basic thrust was to initiate a process that would ultimately protect the fishery resource in Pyramid Lake; the settlement forbade the secretary of the interior to sign any Truckee River operating agreement that might be "likely to jeopardize the continued existence of any endangered or threatened species or result in the destruction or adverse modification of any designated critical habitat of such species."[99] In other words, the future of Pyramid Lake hinges on endangered species.

The Pyramid Lake settlement, for all its limitations, holds a promise—a promise that some day the sacred cui-ui will once again thrive in the waters of Pyramid Lake. The settlement is a superb illustration of how conflicts over environmental issues play a role in negotiating the water rights of American Indian tribes.

8

Another Kind of Green

A Tale of Two Meetings

In late 1922, after nearly a year of fruitless negotiations, a contentious group of elite water policy makers gathered in the bridal suite at Bishop's Lodge, a posh resort near Santa Fe. The chair of the meeting, Herbert Hoover, was an unfortunate choice to lead such a momentous group; history reveals him as having a limited vision when responding to unprecedented problems. And this was no time to lack vision. The objective of the meeting was daunting: divide the waters of the Colorado River, the most important water source in the American Southwest. There was a sense of urgency. The politics of the Colorado River had degenerated into a greedy grabfest. Like hungry villagers butchering the last cow from the commons, each basin state wanted to snatch the biggest piece. California had attempted to bully its way to the front of the line, but the other states ganged up on it. It was obvious some sort of agreement had to be worked out to allow for the continued development of the river.

The aging white men at Bishop's Lodge were desperate for an agreement. They gave up on the idea of allocating a specific amount to each state, and instead arbitrarily divided the river into upper and lower basins, awarding 7.5 million af of water to each basin. The total allocation, 15 million af, was considerably more than the river could actually deliver, but it looked good on paper.[1] Amidst much fanfare, the negotiators reconvened at the Palace of the Governors to sign the Colorado River Compact on November 24, 1922.[2]

The compact divvied up the river, not according to demand, supply, basin hydrology, or the needs of the environment, but in response to the political imperatives of the day. The intricate problems of the Colorado River demanded a judicious and delicate hand, but instead the compact offered an arbitrary solution that set the stage for a half-century of conflict and an irrational, wasteful race to develop the river regardless of cost or ecology.

Significantly, the compact ignored Indian water rights, which were "passed off as inconsequential."[3] In the waning moments of the negotiations, Chairman Hoover worried that some legislators might object to the way Indians were ignored and try to scuttle the compact: "You always find some congressmen who will bob up and say, 'What is going to happen to the poor Indian?'"[4] Hoover then proposed what he called his "wild Indian article," which was unanimously approved: "Nothing in this compact shall be construed as affecting the obligations of the United States of America to Indian tribes."[5] Hoover later explained that the Indian provision had been added as "merely a declaration that the States, in entering into the agreement, disclaim any intention of affecting the performance of any obligations owing by the United States to Indians. It is presumed that the States have no power to disturb these relations and it was thought wise to declare that no such result was intended."[6] The omission of any consideration of Indian rights left unresolved one of the most important problems in the basin.

Another critical question that was not adequately resolved in the compact concerned the rights to surplus waters. If the upper basin does not use its full allocation, and the water flows to the lower basin, who has title to it? And just as important, can states or tribes sell or lease their unused water in other states?

Seventy years later, at a meeting in Albuquerque, New Mexico, a cautious, tentative step was taken to end the era established at Bishop's Lodge. Representatives from seven Colorado River basin states and ten tribes from the basin crammed into a small, windowless hotel meeting room to discuss a volatile topic: water marketing. These states and tribes had been in conflict for most of the twentieth century over water; the very fact that they were willing to come together and talk was a milestone. There was considerable tension in the air. It was obvious that this meeting was an important precedent that could possibly lead to dramatic changes in western water policy. As more people crowded in, the room grew hot and stuffy. Someone made a reference to "this historic meeting."[7]

Dan Israel, an attorney for several tribes, began the meeting with a simple idea: "Let's see if we can make a deal." He suggested that the states and tribes attempt to develop a general memorandum of understanding as a beginning. The basic idea was to create an open, basinwide market for water between the tribes and the states, including transfers from the upper basin to the lower basin. In an open capitalist economy, it would seem such an idea would be commonplace, without a need for much debate. But in fact, it was revolutionary and could possibly free the Colorado River from the shackles of the Colorado River Compact.

Elisabeth Rieke, then director of the Arizona Department of Water Resources, forcefully articulated her state's position; she was willing to listen and participate, but expressed concern over how marketing could affect Arizona. A spokesman for Nevada stated bluntly that they desperately needed more water, and they were quite willing to consider leasing water from Indian tribes in the upper basin. In contrast, California, long the 500-pound gorilla in western water politics, expressed "grave concerns" about the whole idea.

The memorandum of understanding envisioned by attorney Israel and the tribes never materialized. But the tribes took the initiative and formed a partnership, called the Colorado River Tribal Partnership.[8] But as trade barriers throughout the world fall to global markets, western water policy remains mired in the delusion that government restraint of trade is the best public policy. It is certainly ironic that Indian tribes, once called "examples of socialism" by Secretary of the Interior James Watt, are leading the way to a new era of interstate water marketing.

The effort to lease tribal water has played an important and often controversial role in water settlements; proponents of interstate water marketing have run headlong into the defenders of the water status quo. In the long run, the water marketing provisions in settlements may have a greater impact on reservations than all other elements combined; it may be the most significant long-term legacy of the second treaty era. At stake are hundreds of millions of dollars in potential profits — figures that dwarf the money awarded in settlements for tribal development funds. This chapter examines how the controversy over water marketing has affected the negotiation of Indian water settlements.

Money for Something

The Colorado River compact and a series of statutes and court cases form what is known as the "Law of the River," making the Colorado the most regulated river in the West, if not the world. Despite all the regulations, many questions regarding the use of Colorado River water remain unanswered. These unanswered questions and the importance of the river as the only major source of surface water in the region have given rise to nearly continuous conflict: "The Colorado River is not only one of the most physically developed and controlled rivers in the nation, it is also one of the most institutionally encompassed rivers in the country. There is no other river in the Western Hemisphere that has been the subject of as many disputes of such wide scope during the last half century as the Colorado River. These controversies have permeated the political, social, economic, and legal facets of the seven Colorado Basin States."[9]

One of the greatest controversies is over water marketing. Because so many Indian water settlements have involved the Colorado River system, the Law of the River has had a direct impact on most of them. However, this issue is certainly not limited to that river basin. Water marketing is an issue in the Columbia River basin, especially in regard to salmon restoration efforts. It is also at the heart of a long-standing conflict over the Fort Peck water settlement in the Missouri River basin.

Water marketing is a complex issue that requires an understanding of geography, the economics of water use, case law, and the seemingly intractable politics of western water. Mix these together in the bowl of volatile change, and you have a sense of how important water marketing is in the New West, and why it has been such a contentious issue in water settlements.

The potential for marketing is in large part an artifact of geography and human settlement patterns. There are two geographical factors that shape the current debate over Indian water marketing. First, early inhabitants of the American West tended to locate close to water sources. This was certainly true of American Indians; their villages and traditional territories tended to cluster around rivers and springs. But later immigrants, especially those arriving in the twentieth century, located according to a number of other variables, including employment prospects, quality of life, and social amenities. Thus, many western cities burgeoned far beyond the natural supply of water in the area: Los Angeles, San Diego, Phoenix, Tucson, Salt Lake City, Reno, Las Vegas, and Denver. In other words, instead of people moving to where the water was, the water had to be moved to where the people were.

A second geographic factor concerns basin settlement patterns. Most western cities are relatively low (down river) in their respective river basins. Settlements clustered around ports, navigable stretches of river, or broad, fertile valleys. Thus, many cities are at or near the mouths of rivers on the coast: Los Angeles, San Francisco, San Diego, Portland, Seattle. Others are situated in valleys far from the headwaters of the local river: Phoenix, Tucson, Denver, and Albuquerque. This location pattern is also true for a score of smaller cities: Boise, Spokane, Billings, Saint George, Cheyenne, Pocatello, Grand Junction. In contrast, prime land was rarely left in Indian hands; many Indian reservations are located upstream, often in barren deserts and highlands that are traversed or bordered by watercourses.

A third factor has to do with water pricing and politics. In an effort to protect and support the earliest Anglo water users, the federal government and the western states set up an elaborate set of laws and policies designed to deliver large amounts of water at rock-bottom prices to western farmers. This practice has resulted in two dramatic economic phenomena. First, agriculture in the American West consumes more than 80 percent of the water, even though it is just a small fraction of the modern western economy. Second, there are astounding price differentials between agricultural water and other uses. For example, water from the Boysen and Glendo Reservoirs in Wyoming is sold to farmers for $5 per acre-foot; the same water is sold to municipal users for $75 per acre-foot.[10] In Arizona, irrigation water from the CAP ranges in price from $17 per acre-foot to $41 per acre-foot, but Tucson residents pay $462 per acre-foot.[11] In 1994 the city of Albuquerque paid $1,200 per acre-foot for Rio Grande water while downstream irrigators were paying between $10 and $20 per acre-foot.[12] The disparity in pricing is common throughout the West, and existing laws create roadblocks to change. This disparity is especially true in the Colorado River basin: "The Colorado River Compact . . . pays no attention whatever to this disparity in water values. It simply imposes a rigid allocation to the upper and lower basins. In the process, society, as a whole, foregoes the difference in the net benefits between the highest valued prospective use and the lower valued actual use. Economists call this 'misallocation' or 'economic inefficiency.' "[13] Other people just call it foolish. Removing impediments to marketing would create incentives to transfer water to uses that have greater overall benefit to society.

Put all these factors together and the stark potential of Indian water marketing becomes clear: Indian tribes hold significant amounts of water *upstream* from millions of western residents. Picture for a moment a tribal member on, say, the Uintah and Ouray Reservation in northeastern Utah (the subject of this chapter's vignette). He could divert water from a nearby stream and send it flooding across a field of hay. It would be a good, rich field that would provide abundant fodder for his livestock. In the meantime, the city of Los Angeles desperately searches for more water and is willing to pay hundreds, perhaps thousands, of dollars an acre-foot for new sources.

What is the connection between these two seemingly isolated occurrences? The connection is, quite simply, the marketplace. Suppose Los Angeles paid the Ute farmer a very handsome sum *not* to divert his water, which would then remain in the stream. From there it would flow into the Uintah River, then the Green River, then the Colorado River, and through the Colorado aqueduct to the city of Los Angeles. With this new source of water, the city would not have to build new dams and diversions; the water would remain in the river for the benefit of fish, riparian habitat, and recreation; and the Ute farmer would yield a profit that is far beyond the value of a crop of hay.

But of course, western water is never that simple. Throughout the history of the West, economic rationality has given way to politics. So it is with water marketing. Let's return to the Colorado River compact to get a sense of how politics has intruded upon the marketplace. As explained above, the compact failed to clarify rights to surplus waters in the river; it merely split the river between the upper and lower basins and awarded each an absolute amount of flow. This omission, along with the compact's failure to allocate water among the states within each basin, immediately led to conflict. A race began to see who could divert the most water. In this drama, Arizona, acting like an angry mongrel dog, was constantly nipping at the heels of the California gorilla. Arizona refused to ratify the Colorado River compact. At one point in the 1920s the governor of Arizona sent a steamer laden with Arizona national guardsmen into the river to stop construction of Parker Dam; the press quickly dubbed the steamer the "Arizona Navy."[14]

But before the Arizona Navy could deliver a broadside, the federal government stepped in with the Boulder Canyon Project Act of 1928, which authorized Hoover Dam. The states continued to feud, which ultimately led to the landmark case of *Arizona v. California*, which split the surplus flow evenly between the two states.[15] In the meantime the upper basin states, having apparently learned an important lesson, agreed to divide their share of the river on a percentage basis rather than an absolute amount. Other legislation followed, authorizing the Central Arizona Project, the Central Utah Project, Glen Canyon Dam, and five projects in southwestern Colorado (the "Aspinall projects"). This great welter of acts, compacts, and court cases became the Law of the River. But despite all this activity, the legality of cross-basin water marketing, especially involving Indian water, was never clarified.

If the upper and lower basins had developed and diverted their full allocation of water, the marketing question would be less relevant. But full development occurred only in the lower basin. Indeed, California regularly exceeds its allocation.[16] But the upper basin consumes only about 4 million af out of its allocation of 7.5 million.[17] The remainder is left in the river and eventually ends up as diversions in the lower basin. This situation creates a bizarre set of incentives. The lower basin states oppose an open water market because it would force them to pay for upper basin surpluses that they now use for free. This is especially true for California; situated near the end of the Colorado River, unused water in the river is currently siphoned over the mountains to the southern part of the state. It is not surprising, then, that the lower basin states claim that inter-basin water marketing violates the Law of the River.[18]

This places the upper basin states in an odd predicament. The only way they can force the lower basin to yield on this issue is to develop sufficient water project capacity to divert their entire allocation out of the river basin, leaving no surplus to flow past Lee's Ferry—the dividing point between the basins. In essence, the more money and water that the upper basin can waste on unnecessary water projects, the stronger their water marketing bargaining position vis-a-vis the lower basin. But it is essentially too late for the upper basin to develop ways to use all the allocated water; the days of giant dams and wasteful projects are gradually going the way of the drive-in movie. It makes no economic sense to divert enormous amounts of water from the upper stretches of the river, and it would be enormously harmful to the riverine environment and endangered species.

This possibility does not mean, however, that policy leaders in the upper basin favor water marketing, even though it could be enormously lucrative. In their minds, selling or leasing water to the lower basin violates the guarantees established in the compact that allocated water for the sole use of the upper basin. In 1984, when the Galloway Group proposed to lease river water from the state of Colorado to San Diego, the Upper Colorado River Commission denounced it: "[The Commission] finds from its review of the Galloway Group's proposal that there are serious legal and institutional problems which do not appear to be amenable to resolution and which threaten comity among the States."[19]

Many stalwarts from the upper basin still proclaim a strange gospel: "Don't let California get it." This mind-set has led to an irrational set of priorities; many upper basin water users would gladly flood-irrigate alfalfa and then sell the alfalfa to California, but they would rather waltz naked through a bonfire than see the water go directly to that state, even if such direct marketing generated significantly more income. In Utah, where southern California is viewed as a kind of undeserving Sodom that wants to pilfer water from yeoman farmers in Zion's hinterland, the feelings are especially strong.[20] Thus, these leaders, like many in the lower basin, also have an aversion to water marketing. It should not be surprising, then, that the very mention of interstate marketing of tribal water provokes an intense response.

This discussion does not mean that water marketing does not have disadvantages; there are good reasons to limit or control marketing—under some conditions, for some people. Water does not behave like other commodities; its fickleness and unique character, combined with its necessity for life, provide good reason for public controls. Markets are an effective means of allocating private economic goods, but they completely lack any sensitivity to nonmarket values. A market has no respect for culture, no long-term understanding of the public good, no sense of justice. Also, there is a score of well-known market failures: monopoly, inadequate consumer information, imperfect competition, and externalities, to name a few. Proponents of markets often overlook these limitations to marketing, which leads some of the more zealous proponents of marketing to make absurd assumptions: "What about the noneconomic, non-market values that are affected by transfer negotiations? . . . There may be circumstances where public goods are significant, but in most cases in water allocation my sense is that they are not very important."[21] Water, necessary for all life; could anything be more important to our collective welfare?

The myopia of some market proponents creates a blind spot in their discussion of marketing; they talk of "higher valued" uses of water, meaning that people who want the water the most will be willing to pay the most for it. Thus they focus exclusively on *willingness* to pay. But an equally important dimension is *ability* to pay. There is nothing democratic about markets; we do not all have an equal vote. In a hypothetical scenario, a wealthy homeowner wanting to fill a swimming pool could outbid a poor reservation in need of drinking water; is this an example of water going to a "higher valued use"? Indian people may value water to an extraordinary degree but lack the financial resources to compete in an open market. Water marketing can provide valuable assets to Indians when they are in the position of seller; if they have to buy water on the open market, their poverty would put them at a distinct disadvantage. Once Indian water rights are quantified, any additional water would have to be purchased; in the New West it may come at a dear price.

Thus, water marketing must take place within a legal context that protects third parties, the environment, and the economically disadvantaged. Current policy is a roadblock to marketing; future policy should encourage marketing while protecting the public interest. Unfortunately, many current laws protect special interests rather than the public interest. This protection in turn has created a powerful incentive for these special interests to oppose an open market in water where they would have to compete with other users for water. This attitude is quite evident in the discussions of water leasing in the settlement negotiations.

Opening Pandora's Box

When a water marketing provision was included in an early version of the Colorado Ute bill, a group of legislators from the lower basin were furious: "[We] strongly oppose the off-reservation, out-of-state water sale or lease provisions in the settlement agreement . . . it would upset the present legal stability [and] . . . open up a Pandora's box. . . . The legal controversy that such a transaction would precipitate boggles the mind."[22] The negative response was not limited to lower basin legislators. Senator McClure of Idaho, apparently one of those with a boggled mind, vociferously opposed Indian water marketing in the Senate, declaring it was "unconscionable" to violate the Law of the River by allowing interbasin transfers of water.[23] Their assumption was clear: "Any inter-basin or interstate transfer of the water rights of the two Ute Indian reservations would be impermissible under the Law of the River."[24]

In fact, it is not at all clear that Indian water marketing is a direct viola-tion of the Law of the River. Article III of the Colorado River compact specifies that "The states of the Upper Division shall not withhold water . . . which can-not reasonably be applied to domestic and agricultural use." Also, the Supreme Court, in *Arizona v. California*, ruled that those two states are entitled to an equal division of surplus flows.[25] That decision also held that any Indian water diversions must be counted against the allocation of the state where the reser-vation is located.

Proponents of Indian marketing make two points in regard to Indian water marketing and the Law of the River. First, they point out that the upper basin is entitled to 7.5 million af for "exclusive beneficial consumptive use" (article III of the compact). Leasing water for profit could certainly be considered a beneficial use, especially if leasing is the most profitable use of the water.[26] Furthermore, this water could be "reasonably applied to domestic and agricultural use" only if large diversion projects were built in the upper basin, as they were in the lower basin — an unlikely scenario. Arguably the leasing of Indian water would not violate these provisos.

A second argument pertains specifically to Indians. No Indian people and no BIA officials were present at the compact negotiations. No tribes are signa-tories to the compact. No tribe has ever approved of, or recognized, the com-pact. And except for Hoover's condescending reference to his "wild Indian" proviso, Indians are not even mentioned in the compact. No tribal water rights are identified in the compact. The applicability of the compact to Indian tribes has never been tested in court; it remains an open question. All of this is also true for the 1948 Upper Basin Compact; it too ignores Indians, except for its own "wild Indian" clause: "Nothing in the Compact shall be construed as . . . affecting the obligations of the United States of America to Indian tribes."[27] Indian proponents argue that tribes have no obligation whatsoever to abide by these compacts.

The meaning and application of the Law of the River are only part of the unknown legal questions. Another legal problem concerns Indian water law and the acceptable uses of reserved water rights. The Supreme Court has neither proscribed nor condoned the marketing of reserved water rights to off-reservation buyers.[28] This did not stop the Reagan administration from advocating Indian water marketing as a way to enhance tribal self-sufficiency (and thus allow the federal government to reduce its budgetary support for tribes).[29] But attempts to market reserved water have met with vitriolic opposition. As a result, all of the marketing provisions that have been approved in settlement acts involve water delivered from federal projects and not reserved water. As one Indian negotiator put it, "any discussion of marketing reserved water is a deal killer."

However, there is a growing consensus that tribes may be able to market water that they are currently using and for which they have a clear title, which avoids the situation in which a tribe attempts to market its implied Winters water that is already being consumed for free by downstream water users.[30] The "current use" proviso obviously puts tribes at a great disadvantage in the marketplace. Historically, tribes have received the least assistance in developing their water resources, and consequently they have little water in their "current use" portfolio. These legal questions may be resolved, one way or another, by the courts, or they may be resolved piecemeal in future negotiations.

Thus, the legality of Indian marketing is not clear, but the politics are: upper and lower basin states have an incentive to resist the development of Indian water resources. The lower basin receives by default any unused Indian water.[31] The upper basin must count Indian water diversions and leases as part of their Colorado River allocation.

This issue is not limited to the Colorado River basin; attorneys for the Fort Peck Reservation in the Missouri basin have repeatedly attempted to amend the Fort Peck settlement of 1985 to permit off-reservation marketing of tribal water, but they ran into "huge problems" from downstream states that do not want to pay for surplus Indian water that flows down the river to them.[32] Water marketing is also becoming an issue in the Columbia River basin. Increased use of marketing (such as the current leasing of Fort Hall's stored water) could contribute to the salmon restoration efforts by allowing water to remain in the river.

Beyond the legal and political questions is a larger concern that involves numerous parties in the marketing debate. Water transfers often affect people who are neither buyers nor sellers. Many western states prohibit water transfers when they affect the rights of other local water users. Western water law calls these "third-party effects."[33] But marketing also has the potential to produce widespread social benefits, such as environmental protection. Leaving water in streams and avoiding the construction of more costly and environmentally destructive water diversion projects are common arguments for marketing. This benefit is why some environmental groups, such as the Environmental Defense Fund, have endorsed Indian water marketing.[34]

In short, external impacts must be included in the costs of the transaction. A marketing arrangement that yields widespread dividends for society may be deserving of some form of subsidy; conversely, a transfer that imposes costs on third parties, or society as a whole, should perhaps be taxed in order to provide compensation for those bearing the costs. The possibility of external impacts, of course, greatly complicates any market transaction.

This discussion of legal concepts and economic efficiency helps explain much of the debate over Indian water marketing. But western water politics is a gut-level, seat-of-the-pants exercise that owes more to emotion than to logic, and one of the greatest emotional factors in this debate is fear.

States fear that Indian tribes may become a kind of water cartel, selling water at inflated prices to cities that are desperately bidding for new supplies. Perhaps states are worried that Indians may try to use water to get even for past injustices; perhaps the greatest fear of all is that water-rich tribes might treat western states the same way the states have treated them. Some of this debate clearly reflects racial stereotypes. The image of Indian tribes becoming powerful, wealthy water brokers is simply too much for some traditional westerners. The thought that Indians could become the beneficiaries of fortuitous geography and economics strikes some as somehow unfair because Indians didn't "earn" this money, because reservations were never intended to create great wealth. Never mind that being in the right place at the right time has been a critical part of this country's economy since its inception. This sentiment is evident in current negotiations involving tribes in the Colorado River basin: "Other users worry that the Indians . . . will become lucrative power brokers in doling out their unused water to cities, farmers, and industrial users."[35] It also played a role in the Big Horn cases, where the State of Wyoming feared that the Wind River tribes might receive a "windfall" and try to "convert their water rights to money."[36] Throughout the West it is common for water owners to "convert their water rights to money," but the same notion applied to Indians appears to be objectionable to some people.

States and cities also fear a bidding war. In an open market, a tribe could put a specific amount of water up for bid and potential purchasers would have to compete against each other. Indian lessors would get top dollar for their water, but Anglo purchasers obviously prefer a market where competition is constrained or eliminated by government fiat, especially if prices are also controlled by the government. For example, if the Southern Utes could openly market their water, the cities of Tucson, Phoenix, Los Angeles, San Diego, and Las Vegas are all potential downstream customers. But as long as the tribe is restricted to local marketing, the only viable customers would be Durango or a local irrigation company—hardly the setting for a vast water cartel.

Tribes have also voiced a number of fears. First and foremost is a concern that water marketing is contrary to many traditional Indian cultures and thus will diminish tribal identity in the long run. A man from Acoma Pueblo expressed this feeling at a symposium on Indian water settlements: "You can't sell water. How would you like to sell your mother? Non-Indian people only think in terms of profits. But water is priceless; you cannot put a price on water."[37] Luke Duncan, former chairman of the Northern Ute tribe in Utah, made a similar point: "Water is not something we can give away. It was put here by the creator, and you can't have land without water."[38] Vine Deloria Jr. argues that the whole concept of water as private property—a necessary prerequisite to a market—is flawed: "It completely eliminates the intuitive sense of life and emotional content that makes water important as an element of universal life and reduces it to a quantifiable income-producing entity."[39]

These fears are palpable in any discussion of western water rights: fear of change, fear of a loss of power or identity, fear of economic dislocation. But perhaps the greatest fear of all is shared by both Indians and non-Indians; just two words—Owens Valley—can cause heart palpitations in anyone thinking about water markets. This is the fear that, once water is leased, it can never be retrieved regardless of the legal safeguards built into the deal. No matter that the taking of Owens Valley water was accomplished within the limits of the law; no matter that it did not involve interstate marketing or Indian water. The image is there: a big city with lots of political clout gets its hands on a water source and never lets go. This sentiment is pervasive among water users who are upstream from a megalopolis. The fear is particularly acute among some Indians, who see water marketing as a devious way for Anglos to take Indian water in the second treaty era the way they took land in the first treaty era.

In sum, if tribal governments want to lease a certain portion of their water rights, they have to face a diverse set of opponents. In negotiations it has proven impossible to reach an agreement on open, unfettered marketing; rather, tribes have settled for a tightly constrained marketing regime that favors local in-state water users. The text below briefly summarizes the marketing provisions in the settlements.

Ak-Chin

The 1978 and 1984 settlement acts provided no authority for the tribe to market water. Technical amendments passed in 1992 permitted the tribe to lease water temporarily to specific local areas within Arizona (sec. 10(b)). A lease with Del Webb Corporation is now in place, which generates about $11 million for the Indian community.

Tohono O'odham (Papago)

The 1982 settlement act gave the tribe the right to lease water temporarily in the local area of southern Arizona (the Tucson Active Management Area and adjacent lands). Tucson leased water from the tribe from 1992 to 1994. Then the leasing agreement fell victim to the lower prices offered by the Central Arizona Water Conservancy District and was canceled.[40]

Fort Peck–Montana Compact

The 1985 compact permits the use of limited amounts of water outside the reservation, but all uses must comply with applicable state water laws. The export of tribal water outside the state of Montana must be in compliance with "all valid provisions of state law in effect at the time of the proposed transfer that prohibit, regulate, condition, or permit the transportation of water outside the State."[41] Furthermore, the compact adds "eight basic limitations" on marketing. All water transfers must not permanently alienate the tribal water right.[42] As a practical matter, the tribe has not been able to market water downstream in the face of bitter opposition from downstream states. Efforts to pass federal legislation to authorize such marketing have failed.

San Luis Rey (the Mission tribes)

The 1988 settlement contains no marketing provision.

Colorado Ute (Animas–La Plata)

Marketing was a contentious issue in the negotiation of this settlement. The settlement went through several significant changes in the marketing language, each more restrictive than the previous version. The final 1988 act contained two significant tribal concessions to the state of Colorado and the lower basin states. First, any tribal water leased off-reservation must be treated as a state water right, meaning it is subject to all relevant provisions of "State laws, Federal laws, interstate compacts, and international treaties applicable to the Colorado River." The leased water again becomes tribal water when it reverts back to on-reservation use.[43] Second, no water can be leased to the lower basin unless "water within the Colorado River Basin held by non-Federal, non-Indian holders of that water pursuant to any water rights could be so sold, exchanged, leased, used, or otherwise disposed of under State law, Federal law, interstate compacts, or international treaty pursuant to a final, nonappealable order of a

Federal court or pursuant to an agreement of the seven States signatory to the Colorado River Compact."[44] In other words, the Utes cannot lease their water to the lower basin without first getting permission to do so from the very entities that currently use that water for free. During the debate over ALP opponents wanted to make water leasing a major part of the alternative to building the project. However, the settlements amendment act that passed in 2000 did not change any of the leasing provisions found in the original 1988 settlement.

Salt River Pima-Maricopa

The 1988 settlement authorizes the tribe to lease 13,300 af of its CAP water to local municipalities, starting in the year 2000 and ending in 2098. The tribe received $15.9 million ($1,200 per acre-foot for the lease period) for this water. All other water marketing is prohibited.

Fort Hall

The 1990 settlement permits the tribes to rent their federal storage space, as defined in earlier legislation, but it must do so in accordance with specific sections of the Idaho water code. All other water marketing is prohibited.

Fort McDowell

The 1990 settlement authorizes a 99-year lease of tribal CAP water to Phoenix (4,300 af). The Yavapai Indian community may also lease the water provided by section 406 of the settlement, but only to local counties; water marketing beyond this three-county area is forbidden.

Fallon Paiute-Shoshone/Truckee-Carson–Pyramid Lake

This 1990 settlement involved two tribes. The Fallon Paiute-Shoshone settlement provided no explicit marketing rights, and it included a disclaimer that nothing in the act "is intended to affect the jurisdiction of the Tribes or the State of Nevada, if any, over the use and transfer of water rights within the Reservation or off the Reservation."[45] Marketing was not an issue in the Pyramid Lake settlement. However, part of the plan to increase flows to Pyramid Lake involves purchasing water from willing sellers, primarily farmers.

Jicarilla Apache

The 1992 settlement authorized the tribe to contract with third parties to use its water outside reservation boundaries, provided that such use is consistent with all applicable federal, state, and international laws and interstate compacts. The act also included a disclaimer: "Nothing in this Act shall be construed to establish, address, prejudice, or prevent any party from litigating, whether or to what extent any of the aforementioned laws do or do not permit, govern, or apply to the use of the Tribe's water outside the State." The inclusion of such language clearly indicates that the parties consider interstate water marketing to be a delicate, potentially explosive issue.

Northern Cheyenne

The 1992 settlement authorized off-reservation leasing according to the conditions set forth in the compact between the tribe and the state of Montana. That compact stipulates that all off-reservation uses of tribal water must comply with "all permits, certificates, variances and other authorizations required by state laws." The compact identifies five specific conditions that must be met before the state will grant permission for an off-reservation transfer.[46] The Montana Department of Fish and Wildlife has expressed an interest in leasing Tongue River water from the tribe for instream flows.[47] In regard to interstate water marketing, the tribe faces the same opposition as the Fort Peck Reservation.

Northern Ute (Utah)

The 1992 settlement contains a lengthy proviso that clearly indicates the power of lower basin states to circumscribe Indian water marketing. It is worth quoting at length:

> (c) RESTRICTION ON DISPOSAL OF WATERS INTO THE LOWER COLORADO RIVER BASIN. — None of the waters secured to the Tribe in the Revised Ute Compact of 1990 may be sold, exchanged, leased, used, or otherwise disposed of into or in the Lower Colorado River Basin, below Lees Ferry, unless water rights within the Upper Colorado River Basin in the State of Utah held by non-Federal, non-Indian users could be so sold, exchanged, leased, used or otherwise disposed of under Utah State law, Federal law, interstate compacts, or international treaty pursuant to a final, nonappealable order of a Federal court or pursuant to an agreement of the seven States signatory to the Colorado River Compact.[48]

The 1990 compact, which was authorized by the settlement act,[49] contains the same paragraph, just in case someone missed the point in the settlement act. The compact also contains an extensive disclaimer clause:

> Nothing in this Compact shall:
> (1) constitute specific authority for the sale, exchange, lease, use or other disposition of any federal reserved water right off the reservation;
> (2) constitute specific authority for the sale, exchange, lease, use, or other disposition of any tribal water rights outside the State of Utah;
> (3) be deemed or construed a congressional determination that any holders of water rights do or do not have authority under existing law to sell, exchange, lease, use, or otherwise dispose of such water or water rights outside the State of Utah;
> or,
> (4) be deemed or construed to establish, address, or prejudice whether, or the extent to which, or to prevent any party from litigating whether, or the extent to which, any of the aforementioned laws do or do not permit, govern or apply to the use of the Tribe's water outside the State of Utah.[50]

This clause has paranoia written all over it. The opponents of Indian water marketing in both the lower and upper basins wanted to make sure that no one could possibly view the Ute compact as offering the slightest hint that Ute water could be leased in an open, competitive market. When the executive director of the Utah Department of Natural Resources was asked how he would respond to an effort by the Utes to lease their water to Las Vegas, he responded with a threat: "We could tie it up in court for at least twenty years."[51] The marketing language in the settlement and compact virtually ensures that the tribe would lose such a legal contest *if* the compact is ever approved by a tribal referendum.

The compact also contains a clause that is unique in water settlements; if the tribe somehow manages to overcome all the marketing obstacles thrown up by the settlement and compact and leases its Green River water, the State of Utah gets 20 percent of the income (Article 3). So much for "Indian" water.

In contrast to the obviously hostile approach to interstate marketing, the Ute settlement supports a limited marketing agreement—at a set price—that provides income from tribal waters that are diverted for use in the Central Utah Project (the Ute settlement is the subject of this chapter's vignette).

San Carlos Apache

The 1992 settlement permits the marketing of the tribe's CAP water only to local counties and cities, and expressly prohibits any other use of water off-reservation.

Yavapai/Prescott

There are no marketing provisions in this settlement.

Observing the settlements as a whole, a number of trends are evident. First, secretarial approval is required for all transfers of Indian water, which gives the federal government a great deal of control over Indian water and allows a political appointee to squelch any deal that generates too much political baggage. Second, all of the marketing provisions are limited to local areas. These tribes are thus effectively eliminated from participation in an open West-wide water market. If tribes are ever given a clear right to market their water, by either Congress or the Supreme Court, the tribes that have signed settlements with state-level marketing limitations will be at a severe disadvantage. Third, the settlements have been used to force tribes to abide by state law when and if they choose to lease their water. Thus, the "Indian" water–the wet water of the settlements—is not totally "Indian" in terms of applicable laws and controls. In effect, the marketing restrictions in settlements have reduced tribes to just another water rights holder, like an irrigation district or a farmer; lost is their special semi-sovereign status and the government-to-government relationship so coveted by tribes. And finally, even though tribes may not be legally subject to the Colorado River compact or the upper basin compact (remember they were not signatories and were not represented), the settlements have imposed the compacts on the tribes in the basin.

In sum, a clear trend is evident; the water quantified and labeled as "Indian water" in the settlements is subject to significant constraints if it is marketed off-reservation. It is "Indian water" only to a certain extent; it must abide by non-Indian water laws and must not impair non-Indian water use of tribes' surplus waters. Tribes have sacrificed their open marketing potential in the settlements, which will cost them dearly in the future but permit non-Indians to continue using "Indian water" that cannot be diverted at the reservation boundary. In the long run, it would probably be better for tribes to negotiate for a smaller quantification of water that is free of constraints, rather than a larger allocation that cannot be leased in an open and fair water market. The loss of interstate marketing rights may well be the greatest tribal "give" in the give-and-take process of negotiation.

Conclusion

A report sponsored by the Western States Water Council and the Native American Rights Fund concisely outlined the hopes and fears surrounding the concept of an open market for tribal water: "Tribal water marketing can contribute to the resolution of a host of economic and resource constraints in the arid West. Tribal water marketing agreements can allow existing water uses to continue, while also providing tribes with financial resources and infrastructure development needed to develop their communities. Tribal water marketing can thereby promote tribal self-reliance and productivity and further the federal goal of promoting tribal self-determination. . . . However, tribal water marketing is not a panacea. Many tribes oppose water marketing in principle. States also oppose tribal water marketing outside state regulatory controls."[52]

The negotiation of Indian water settlements has taken place within a larger context of political and economic change in the West. The Law of the River, the prior appropriation doctrine, and restrictions on water transfers all reflect the priorities of the first treaty era, when irrigated farming was expected to be the West's salvation. That vision of an irrigated empire and the mind-set that goes with it are now under enormous pressure. A comprehensive attempt to introduce reforms in the lower Colorado River basin, including water banking and market transfers, is reflective of this new approach.[53] The old adage that water flows uphill to money is gradually edging out the New Eden and replacing it with the New West. As surely as the Soviet Union fell to economic imperatives, the obsolete roadblocks against marketing set up under the Colorado River Compact and other western water laws are doomed to fall to the economic forces that are now transforming the West. Western water law has become, metaphorically, a dam itself, holding back a great reservoir of water transfers. The metaphoric New Eden of yesterday increasingly looks more like an effete weed patch, incapable of providing for the extended family of contemporary westerners.

But still, many people resist marketing. Beginning nearly a century ago, the reclamation movement held out the promise of economic stability. To encourage this stability, traditional western water policy built a wall of protection around the West's earliest water users, mainly alfalfa farmers. In contrast, water marketing places a premium on change; it responds to forces that leap the walls of the old regime. Marketing is perhaps the gravest threat to the water status quo since the high court handed down a decision in *Winters*. In essence, a water allocation system based on government fiat, tradition, and rigidity is being challenged by an allocation system based on market pricing, new needs, and flexibility. It is easy to see why many traditional westerners would find this new regime so disturbing.

Water marketing offers tantalizing new opportunities to Indian tribes — if they have not given away such opportunities in settlements. The dangers of the marketplace can be mitigated by wise public policy. Markets have the potential to dramatically increase the efficiency of water use and to enhance access to water resources. Still, there is an important role to be played by our democratic institutions. A West-wide market of fair competition for water resources that accounts for environmental, social, and economic externalities, and is congruent with the Indian trust obligations of the federal government, would be an important step in bringing western water policy into the modern era.

Vignette: The Blue Sky People

In October 1861, President Abraham Lincoln had his hands full. The South was in full rebellion and the northern army had already been dealt its first ignominious defeat at Bull Run. But the besieged president still found the time to respond to a letter from his Secretary of the Interior recommending that the entire valley of the Uintah River be set aside as a Ute Indian reservation. "Let the reservation be established," the President replied in an executive order.[54] The new reservation encompassed more than two million acres. Twenty years later, when the Uncompahgre and White River Utes were forced off their lands on the west slope of the Rockies, another reservation was established. Contiguous with the Uintah Reservation, it added another two million acres. Thus, the Utes, sometimes called the Blue Sky People by other tribes, were promised a home in Utah.[55]

The loss of millions of acres of traditional use lands in Colorado had dealt a severe blow to the Utes, but at least they had a substantial reservation in northeastern Utah. Most of the land was barren desert scrub, but two areas of the reservation held great promise; the northern section of the reservation encompassed a great swath of forest in the Uintah Mountains, and the central section consisted of the flat, verdant lands along the Duschesne and Uintah Rivers. The Utes faced a future that was not of their making, but if they had to be farmers and live in wooden houses, at least this reservation offered arable land, good water in the bottomlands, and timber.[56]

In 1905 the Indian agent at Fort Duschesne, Utah, became aware of a serious water problem. He was informed that white settlers in the Heber Valley, just west of the Ute Reservation, were diverting water from the reservation "with-out the consent or authorization of the Indian agent or of the Department of the Interior."[57] The settlers had surreptitiously built a diversion tunnel thir-teen years earlier and were using water from the Duschesne River drainage—the heart of the reservation—to water their crops.[58] After much hemming and hawing, the agent decided to use some of the soldiers that were quartered at Fort Duschesne to destroy the illegal diversion tunnels. But before the troops could accomplish their task, the settlers used their political connections with Senator Reed Smoot to apply pressure on the Interior Department. It worked; the agent backed down, and the farmers continued diverting water through the tunnel for another ninety years.[59]

The loss of this water was unfortunate but paled in significance to the land losses suffered by the Northern Utes at that time; their reservation was whittled down to a shell. The government took "1,010,000 acres of the reservation as a forest reserve; 2,100 acres in townsites, 1,004,285 acres opened to homestead entry, 2,140 acres in mining claims, and 60,160 acres under reclamations."[60] Reservation trust land shrank from 4 million acres to 366,000 acres.[61] A local newspaper warned direfully that such losses could incite "the wanton ferocity of the [Ute] race."[62] The timberlands were gone, the western portion of the reser-vation taken for Strawberry Reservoir, and the fecund bottomlands had been sold to settlers as "surplus" under the allotment act. But at least the North-ern Utes still had water; the streams of the Uintah Mountains, fed by generous snowfall, ran through the remainder of the reservation.[63]

I traveled to the Uintah and Ouray Reservation in the summer of 1990 to talk with Curtis Cesspooch, the new vice chairman of the tribe. I planned to inter-view him; instead, he interviewed me. Splayed out on his desk were numerous books and articles on water policy, some of which I had written. He shot ques-tions at me about the Winters doctrine, the tribe's water litigation, historical use, and the Central Utah Project (CUP). It was clear he had done his home-work; he knew all about western water law and the enormous power wielded by the water establishment. Yet he was prepared to confront them head on.

The Goliath in this battle was the Central Utah Water Conservancy Dis-trict, the local sponsors of the CUP, a massively expensive scheme to take water out of the Uintah Valley and siphon it over the mountains to farms and cities in the Bonneville basin. The whole project depended on Ute water, and it was clear that nothing could be built until the district and the federal government got permission from the tribe to use their water. An early planning document warned of this: "An agreement between CUP and the Ute Indians limiting the total acreage of Indian-owned and Indian water rights land is a must for successful operation."[64] In order to obtain that permission, the government promised the Utes a "Ute Indian Project," which would "in good faith be diligently pursued" in return for the Utes' promise to defer their use of water until after the CUP was completed.[65] This "deferral agreement" was signed in 1965 at the urging of the tribe's attorney, John Boyden, who explained that the Utes agreed to sign because they were "good neighbors to the non-Indians so the CUP can proceed in an orderly way."[66] It was a bad idea. It should have been obvious by then that the federal government was not to be trusted, especially when a powerful western water district wanted Indian water.

Decades before, BIA officials had been more insightful; when the reservation's water resources were surveyed at the turn of the century, the acting Indian commissioner made what was essentially a statement about wet water versus paper water: "If canals belonging to Indians and white persons both take water from the same stream the experience of the past has shown that while the rights of the Indians may be theoretically superior, practical enforcement through white officials is extremely difficult."[67] This statement was telling; the Ute Indian Project was never built, but the rest of the CUP proceeded with plans to divert water from the reservation for use by cities and farmers in central Utah.[68]

Throughout the succeeding decades there were various efforts to negotiate another deal with the tribe, but to no avail. In the meantime, most of the CUP was constructed and began diverting water from the reservation. The Utes demanded a resolution to the problem, but the water district and Utah's entrenched congressional delegation fiercely protected the CUP and continued construction without regard to Ute claims. It looked like a replay of the situation in 1905 when Heber was taking water from the reservation.

By 1989 the Utes had had enough. A recall of tribal council members placed Curtis Cesspooch and Luke Duncan on the council; they were named vice chairman and chairman, respectively. A Salt Lake newspaper dubbed them the "dissident Ute leaders" and warned they would be "tough taskmasters in future negotiations."[69] One of their first acts was to declare the deferral agreement null and void: "The Ute Indian Tribe and its members are suffering from poverty and a loss of hope in part because of the transfer of water and other economic development opportunities out of the Uintah Basin into the Wasatch Front. . . . Water is the lifeblood of the Ute Tribe and represents a resource which can sustain the Tribe for future generations. . . . Because the non-Indian parties breached their obligations to the Ute Indian Tribe, the Tribe declares the 1965 Deferral Agreement no longer valid."[70] Utah's congressional delegation tried to downplay the importance of this startling challenge to the water status quo. Two weeks after the Utes revolted against the deferral agreement and the CUP,

Utah Congressman Howard Nielson blithely told his colleagues in the House that "Relations between the Indians and non-Indians in Utah's Uintah Basin and the State have never been better."[71]

Suddenly the CUP, which had already consumed more than a billion dollars in construction funding, was without a legal title to the water it was diverting. The tribe had thrown in a big wrench, and this time they got people's attention. All of this occurred at an opportune time; the CUP was out of money and the Utah congressional delegation had gone to Washington asking for another billion dollars. It was clear they would not get it until they resolved the problem with the Northern Utes, and the tribe was in no mood to make any more sacrifices. Luke Duncan, the new chairman of the tribal council, put it bluntly: "People have to understand that since 1965 we've been a part of the CUP, but we really haven't been included in the benefits. Now we're asking for compensation."[72] They got it; in 1992 Congress reauthorized the CUP and in the same law provided a water settlement for the Northern Utes.

The 1992 Ute Water Settlement is unique among the settlements; it is basically a liability payment. Its $198 million price tag is far larger than any other settlement.[73] It occurred not because Congress was feeling unusually beneficent toward the Utes, but because it recognized the government's enormous legal exposure for its failure to honor the 1965 deferral agreement. One purpose of the act was to "put the Tribe in the same economic position it would have enjoyed had the features contemplated by the September 20, 1965, Agreement been constructed."[74]

The unique purpose of the settlement made it necessary to negotiate a separate agreement that included the actual quantification of the tribe's water rights — the 1990 Revised Ute Indian Compact, which was ratified in the settlement act "subject to re-ratification by the State and the Tribe."[75] Article 5 of the compact defines tribal approval as a "referendum of the Tribe's membership." After the settlement was passed, the tribe held several "informational" meetings about the settlement and the compact. But conflicts between bands, individuals, and families became part of the debate over the compact. After so many broken promises, tribal members simply did not trust anyone. At one informational meeting, an elderly Ute woman listened patiently to a presentation about the settlement from a group of attorneys and engineers, then rose to give her opinion: "You're like a rattlesnake on a hot rock. You've got the forked tongue." Another member of the tribe said, "Until you keep some of your promises, we don't want the compact."[76]

The atmosphere was further poisoned when the State of Utah filed a court case against the tribe in an effort to gain jurisdiction over all the parts of the reservation that had been withdrawn from tribal trust lands. This case infuriated the Ute leadership and made them extremely reluctant to deal with state officials.[77] Relations were further strained when the tribe withdrew its approval of two CUP dams in April 1999.[78]

Initially there was a concern that, if the tribe refused to ratify the compact, Congress would, at the behest of Utah's congressional delegation, withhold funding authorized in the settlement. But this did not happen; the feds were anxious to have a settlement of the deferral agreement fiasco, and the state wanted to continue building the CUP.[79] These desires put the Northern Ute tribe in a unique situation; they are currently getting the money from their settlement—most of it has been appropriated—but have yet to quantify their water rights. It also puts the $3 billion CUP in grave danger; the project has no clear legal title to the water it is diverting from above the reservation.

If the tribe chooses to go to court rather than approve the compact, what could they gain? The compact allocates to the tribe a depletion right of 248,943 af, an amount that is based on an early study of the tribe's irrigable acreage (the Decker report). If the tribe went to court, it could probably win a similar amount. But the real question concerns a clause in the settlement act that gives the tribe a portion of the money generated by the sale of CUP water for municipal water supply. The amount received by the tribe is a percentage for the first fifty years; after that it floats to 7 percent of fair market value.[80] What if the tribe had the ability to market that water to the highest bidder rather than being forced to sell it through the CUP?

If an open market in western water develops, the Northern Ute tribe is in an advantageous position to market its water, for two reasons; it is upstream from numerous big cities, and, thanks to the CUP, it has the ability to divert water away from downstream users who refuse to pay. In other words, the tribe can turn off the water supply if downstream lessees do not want to pay for the water they are using. It is also worth noting that the provisions in the settlement act that severely constrain Ute water marketing apply only to water secured via the compact. Would they apply to water won in court? This question is typical of the many unanswered questions regarding Indian water marketing.

Water marketing will also have an impact on the determination of fair market value. The urban Wasatch front is beginning to use water from the CUP (at least the part referenced in the settlement). A competitive market could dramatically increase the price of the "fair market value" that is promised to the tribe in the settlement. Besides, how can you have a "fair" market when there is only one customer?

There is one final reason the Ute tribe is a prime candidate for water marketing. The best agricultural lands on the reservation were lost to homesteaders after the turn of the century; it just does not make a lot of sense for the tribe to attempt to scratch out a living irrigating the remainder. In addition, the Utes have never been farmers; the agricultural program on the reservation has been a notable failure.[81] In contrast, the Utes have been wily traders since before the coming of the white man. For centuries they roamed throughout the inter-mountain west, trading, buying, and selling. In the nineteenth century it was horses; in the twenty-first century it may be water.[82]

The Northern Ute tribe and the city of Las Vegas have held several meetings to discuss the possible lease of Ute water. Although such a lease faces formidable legal and political obstacles, the day may come when Ute water bubbles up out of the "volcano" on the strip—and a hefty check goes to the tribe to pay for schools, college education, housing, job training, and cultural preservation. How ironic that the gauche tourist mecca of southern Nevada may end up paying for programs to preserve the culture of the people who were once described as "practicing communists."[83]

The situation on the Uintah and Ouray Reservation clearly illustrates the convoluted politics and law, and the promise and perils, of water marketing. The settlement for the Northern Utes places enormous restrictions on water marketing at a time when the potential benefits of marketing are becoming apparent. This settlement is quite typical of those negotiated thus far. Only time will tell whether Ute water goes to local users at a lower price, or to distant cities at a higher price.

9

"Come On, Big Village. Be Quick"

Shoot Every Male Indian

In the days of the pioneers, the California Trail wound its way along the Snake River in what is today southern Idaho. There were periodic clashes between immigrant wagon trains and Indians. Rumors of these conflicts circulated widely, and the story often grew more sensational as it was repeated. A San Francisco paper claimed some of the attacks were committed by Shoshones with a "penchant for murdering white men and ravishing emigrant girls."[1] Another paper, caught up in the hysteria over the Civil War in 1862, claimed some of the Indian war parties included confederate sympathizers dressed as Indians.[2] Newspapers and politicians demanded retribution. In response, Colonel Patrick Conner (the perpetrator of the Bear River massacre described in chapter 2) issued an order to "shoot every male Indian in the region of the late murders."[3]

On one fateful day in 1861 an entire wagon train was attacked and besieged by Indians near the present-day town of Almo, Idaho. After four days, the immigrants ran out of water. They tried digging wells, but to no avail. Then five members of the party escaped by crawling through the grass at night, including a woman who carried her infant in a blanket held in her teeth. The next day, when the remaining immigrants ran out of ammunition, they were murdered by the Indians in "a scene too wild and awful to contemplate."[4] The few whites who escaped told their story, and soon newspapers all over the West were calling for revenge. Years later a respected western historian referred to this massacre at Almo as "perhaps the most horrible and wanton slaughter of all," concluding the pioneers were "victims of red barbarity."[5]

Today, the white people of southern Idaho regard the Almo massacre as a dark day in history when many innocent people met a violent death. A stone monument in the little town of Almo commemorates the event with these words: "Dedicated to the memory of those who lost their lives in a horrible

Indian massacre, 1861. Three hundred immigrants west bound, only five escaped. Erected by S&D [Sons and Daughters] of Idaho Pioneers, 1938." There is just one problem with the Almo massacre: it never happened. Relying upon wild rumors and imagination, and with a hope to increase tourism, a reporter concocted the whole thing in the early 1930s.[6] The fictitious massacre at Almo worked a disservice to both history and the Shoshone people. It does, however, offer a telling lesson; if something is repeated often enough, it becomes reality in the minds of those who hear it, especially if they wish it to be true.

This book is an effort to assess whether water settlements live up to the oft-repeated claims for them; do the results actually match these claims? Have settlements achieved a level of justice and resolution that warrants a continuation of this policy? The litany of advantages are stated often, but it is necessary to take a close look to make sure these advantages actually accrue, or, like the Almo massacre, are merely the stuff of fertile minds and repeated incantations. There is no simple answer to this question; the record is mixed. But if the negotiation era continues, we must gain insights from past settlements that permit an improvement in both the way settlements are negotiated and the results achieved from them. This chapter first considers the *process* of negotiation and ways it might be improved, followed by a discussion of the overall *substantive* impact of settlements. A final vignette takes us to the Navajo Reservation to examine a negotiation in progress and the way it is perceived by local people.

We Talk, We Listen

When the settlement era first began, negotiators had to make up the process as they went along. It was a creative, innovative effort, and the negotiators deserve to be commended for their pioneering efforts; they initiated the second treaty era. But, like all governing processes, there is room for continued innovation and improvement. There are a number of factors to be considered as the negotiation process undergoes further refinement.

First, it is important to view negotiated water settlements as just one type of collaborative problem solving. States, counties, special districts, regional coalitions, and nongovernmental entities are using negotiation and creative problem-solving in an effort to improve understanding, provide a means of nonconfrontational communication, and resolve a score of difficult issues. Everything from anti-gang task forces to regional environmental cooperatives is using innovative institutional arrangements to get people to work together in a way that benefits all jurisdictions. A review of these cooperative arrangements reveals a number of labels and concepts that are quite telling: intercommunity partnerships,[7] intergovernmental management,[8] multiple partnership configurations,[9] and collaborative alliances.[10] Most Indian water negotiations have used previous settlements as models, despite the disclaimers attached to many settlements stating they have no precedential value. In future settlements it may be useful to move beyond the traditional model of negotiation/settlement/implementation and explore these other venues of cooperative policy making. There is much that can be learned from other governing entities that are working through a collaborative, conflict-resolution process to solve long-term problems.

It is also important to realize that many issues in Indian country other than water are currently the subject of government-to-government negotiation and collaboration. In addition to the water settlements, there have been twenty-one land settlements.[11] Other issues are also the subject of tribal-state cooperation, including tourism,[12] economic issues,[13] law enforcement, gaming, and some environmental problems.[14] This is reflective of the widespread acceptance of cooperative negotiation as a preferred alternative to confrontation, competition, and litigation. It also reflects increasing acceptance of tribes as legitimate quasi-sovereign governments.

State, local, and federal governments are more likely to engage in cooperative agreements with tribal governments if they view tribes as professional, independent entities that are quite capable of handling their own affairs. Thus tribes can increase their effectiveness in water negotiations by developing their own water-related expertise and institutions. An important element in this process is the development of tribal water codes. For decades tribes were hamstrung in this area by a secretarial order, dating from 1975, that forbade those tribes with governments set up according to the Indian Reorganization Act from writing their own water codes. The intent was to create a planning vacuum that could be filled only by paternalistic federal bureaucrats or encroaching state water authorities. Bruce Babbitt finally lifted the secretarial order in 1996, thus giving tribes the autonomy they need to plan their own water future. The Navajo Nation, which was not subject to the ban, had already developed a comprehensive and sophisticated water code designed to "provide for a permanent homeland . . . ; to protect the health, the welfare and the economic security . . . ; [and] to develop, manage and preserve the water resources of the Navajo Nation."[15] The Mni-Sose Intertribal Water Rights Coalition has developed a model water code to assist tribes in their planning efforts.[16]

However, it takes more than a well-designed water code and an understanding of water problems to succeed in the negotiation process; tribes must also develop their own independent legal and political expertise. History clearly shows that the Justice Department and the Interior Department are often compromised in their ability to assist tribes. When tribes depend on individuals whose first loyalty is to their agency or department, or to personal remuneration, serious problems arise. A case in point concerns U.S. attorney Herbert Becker and water negotiations at the Zuni Reservation. Mr. Becker told negotiators for the Zuni tribe that he had filed the necessary papers to close the Zuni River basin and thus establish a moratorium on water development by non-Indians while negotiations were in progress. Mr. Becker repeatedly assured the tribe that the basin had been closed, and the tribe proceeded in negotiations under that assumption. But in August 1993, it was revealed that Mr. Becker had failed to file the necessary notifications; the basin was finally closed in 1994—ten years after the tribe had received assurances that this action had been completed. This caused serious problems in the continuing negotiations.[17] In 1997, Mr. Becker encountered further problems; he pleaded guilty to felony charges of conflict of interest and filing false claims in another matter not related to the Zuni case.[18] Although this kind of malfeasance is rare, it points out the advantages of tribes' hiring their own experts.

While tribes develop their water and legal expertise, they must simultaneously fight efforts to emasculate tribal autonomy. A prolonged effort has been made by some parties to diminish the legitimacy and significance of treaty rights. This effort is as old as Columbus, but a recent manifestation was led by the Wisconsin Counties Association, which proposed to "modernize" treaties, or in other words, render them ineffectual.[19] Such talk polarizes people involved in the discussion and creates a tense, distrustful relationship. It is difficult to encourage a second treaty era while some parties still refuse to honor the first one.

In the battle to honor treaty rights, tribes have been fortunate to have a few stalwart defenders in Congress, including Senator Daniel Inouye, Democrat from Hawaii; Senator John McCain, Republican from Arizona; and Colorado's Senator Ben Nighthorse Campbell, currently a Republican. In contrast, former Senator Slade Gorton, Republican of Washington state, led several attacks on tribal sovereignty, including efforts to cut funding for Indian programs in an effort to force tribes to accept restrictions on their water use.[20] His defeat in 2000 was in part due to his anti-Indian activities. These anti-Indian efforts poison the atmosphere and make cooperation difficult. The lesson is clear; future negotiations need to take place in a larger political context of trust rather than confrontation. To attack Indian sovereignty on one level, and then plead for cooperation and collaboration in regard to water, is not conducive to successful settlements.

In future negotiations, water issues will become enmeshed in other issues affecting Indian country. As cooperative mechanisms become more common, the numerous issues on the table will become more integrated. Negotiations over water rights, land rights, gaming, provision of local services, BIA funding, and scores of related issues may all appear on the same table. A limit on water rights may be traded for the return of a parcel of land. A deal over the administration of a water project may include a commitment for more funding for economic development, and so on. Issues left over from the first treaty era will become part of the negotiations of the second treaty era. Water rights can no longer be isolated from the general welfare of Indian tribes. Water negotiations will be more successful if conducted within a larger framework of cooperation and good will across all issues. Slashing BIA budgets and attacking Indian independence is certain to create strains that inhibit negotiations over water.

Sovereignty issues are not, however, limited to relations between tribes and non-Indian governments. Sub-tribal sovereignty may well become the sticking point in many future negotiations. One dimension of such sovereignty is the conflict between allottees and tribal governments, which continues to be an issue in both the Tohono O'odham and the Northern Ute settlements. Another aspect concerns tribal sub-divisions. For example, the Navajo Reservation is divided into 110 chapters; can one of them negotiate its own water settlement? Other reservations are home to more than one tribe; for example, the Shoshones and Bannocks share the Fort Hall Reservation, and the Eastern Shoshones and Arapahos share the Wind River Reservation. Can one of these tribes negotiate a water settlement independent of the other? The Northern Utes are divided into three distinct bands, each with a separate history; can any one of them conclude an independent negotiation? If Indians are sovereign, a relevant question is sovereign from whom? Many traditional tribal governments were very decentralized; a return to this traditional model of Indian governance could strengthen sub-tribal claims for autonomy. Just as Indian and non-Indian jurisdictions must learn to cooperate, so too must elements within tribes. Otherwise the entire fabric of cooperation may break down.

In sum, the process of negotiation is much more likely to succeed if it takes place within a larger context of cooperative relations. The best way to improve water settlements is to improve the overall climate of Indian policy and government-to-government cooperation.

Show Me the Water

The most enlightened cooperative process in the world is of little utility if it fails to bring results. The ultimate test of a good settlement is whether it actually delivers the goods. Well-meaning people have, on occasion, come together in a spirit of cooperation and written bad water settlements. In a sense, then, the best way to evaluate the negotiation process is to look at the product. A brief summary of what the settlements have delivered will help us gain a clearer sense of the results of the second treaty era so far.

Clearly the biggest question revolves around water; did the tribes finally get a just and equitable amount of water, or have paper settlements led only to more paper water? There are two perspectives from which to view this issue. The first perspective, described in chapter 5, compares the water allocated under the settlements to historical water allocations. Without a doubt the settlements have dramatically increased the amount of water to which tribes can claim title. There are, of course, significant limitations to their use of that water, but nevertheless, the historic tradition of giving lip service to Indian water claims while ignoring them in substance may be coming to an end.

A second perspective offers a less sanguine view. It could be argued that the water, and even the associated funding, that has accrued to Indians via the settlements is a hollow victory because they won only what was already due them. In effect, the "win/win" calculus claimed by adherents of negotiation only provided tribes with some of the benefits promised in the first treaty era. If the government had consistently honored its trust responsibility, it would have developed Indian water resources with the same zeal with which it showered them on non-Indians. If the federal trust responsibility created by the first treaty era had created viable homelands for Indian people, the second treaty era would not be necessary. According to this perspective, the settlements are an admission that the nation has failed to honor its treaty commitments from the first era; the government is basically saying to tribes, "We'll give you part of what we promised if you agree to give up the rest of it." This is a cynical view of the process, but not without some merit. The realpolitik response suggests it does not matter what has been promised, it only matters what can be delivered.

A second substantive concern involves time. If settlements bring justice to the present generation but not future generations, then we have, in essence, negotiated a temporary justice. The well-known indigenous belief that decisions should be made with the next seven generations in mind is one criterion that could be applied. Again there are two perspectives. A more benign interpretation points to quantification of water rights as the best method of guaranteeing future generations that tribes will forever hold title to a legally defensible amount of water. The funding for water settlements also represents an investment in tribal infrastructure, economic development, and cultural preservation that will yield dividends for all future generations. The unprecedented government spending on water settlements has created new opportunities for tribes that simply would not have occurred otherwise.

But again, there is an alternative view that considers the money in settlements as a sell-out similar to the sale of aboriginal lands in the first treaty era. After the money is spent, what will subsequent generations think of their settlement? Without a doubt the most shortsighted aspect of the settlements is the limitations on water marketing. In the long run, these limits will cost future generations many opportunities to use their tribal water in the manner that is most beneficial to them; it robs them of critical choices. Of course, it is easier to give up something that does not exist yet, but within seven generations it is quite likely that water markets will open a whole new era in the allocation of western water. The tribes that have agreed to severe marketing constraints will be left out of the gold rush.

Another consideration in regard to the substantive results of water settlements concerns the way in which water is used. Settlements that focus on large-scale irrigation are tying tribes to an economic era that is rapidly disappearing. For some tribes, a settlement may be viewed as a way to keep things from getting worse, but preserving the status quo will poorly serve tribes in a time of rapid change. Future water settlements must attempt the difficult combination of fitting Indian water uses into the New West while helping to preserve tribal traditions. This combination could, for example, mean emphasizing tourism rather than alfalfa; it could mean providing water for tourist facilities rather than mechanized farming. The issue of tourism in Indian country is a delicate one, but if properly managed it need not occur at the expense of traditional culture. Indeed, it is the preservation of Indian culture and Indian lands that will bring visitors.

Combining these goals — preserving Indian culture while adapting to the New West — will require an unprecedented level of creativity. For example, the Navajos have expressed an interest in creating their own rafting operation on the San Juan River. But the Bureau of Land Management claims it has sole control over rafting permits and recreation on the river, even though the San Juan flows through the reservation and forms its northern border. A claim for instream flows for a rafting operation might bring more benefits to the tribe than, say, a claim for more water for the corporate farming operations upstream at the Navajo Indian Irrigation Project, which has yet to turn a profit and employs few tribal members.[21] The potential for recreation on the San Juan is significant (more than 11,000 people float the Utah portion annually), but the Navajo people derive no economic benefits from all this recreational activity.[22]

The point is simply this: the greatest economic asset on Indian reservations may be the uniqueness of the land and its people. Non-Indian communities throughout the West are realizing that irrigated farming and extractive industries such as timber and mining no longer offer economic security; the future is in the amenity values of land and culture.[23] Preserving the landscape and culture of Indian people will require a different vision of the future; instream flow, marketing, cultural preservation, and recreation may replace large-scale farming and water for extractive industry as the preferred uses of water claimed in a settlement.[24] This vision will be true for both Indian and non-Indian parties in future negotiations.

A final point in regard to the substantive results of water settlements concerns the competition for water. The easiest water settlements have probably already been negotiated; future settlements will severely test our government's commitment to being "good neighbors" engaged in good-faith negotiations. As water grows more scarce, non-Indian parties may be less willing to concede any appreciable amounts of water to Indian reservations. But it is important to keep this water "scarcity" in perspective. The reason most water in the West is already allocated is that irrigated agriculture consumes more than 80 percent of it. In effect, we do not have a water shortage in the West; we have an oversupply of underpriced, subsidized water to irrigated farmland. In many western states, alfalfa, a low-value, high water–use crop, consumes much of the irrigation supply. On lands watered by Bureau of Reclamation projects, 23 percent of the acreage is planted in hay.[25]

Much of this farming is possible only because of an elaborate system of multiple subsidies provided by the federal government; interest-free loans, below-cost water sales, extremely generous payback schedules, and subsidies to both grow — and not grow — certain crops have inflated western farming operations far beyond what is economically rational.[26] In a very real sense these subsidies are at the heart of the water "scarcity" issue that will severely limit future Indian water negotiations, especially if the government continues its no-harm-to-whites policy.

These subsidies are so gratuitous they defy belief, but they are the result of decades of special-interest lobbying and an archaic policy that has been deftly transformed from a social program for the New Eden into a massive transfer of public wealth to a small group of private businesses. The principal beneficiaries are corporate agribusinesses, and the amount of water consumed is staggering; Bureau of Reclamation projects delivered 29.8 million af of water in 1998, nearly all of it to agriculture.[27] This figure reveals an important truth about the water that is potentially available to Indian tribes in future negotiations; one way to make sufficient water available to Indian tribes is to bring some economic sanity to the federal water development program. A significant reduction in water subsidies would mean that only cost-effective farming operations would remain in business.[28] The many irrigation operations that currently lose money — if subsidies are figured into their costs — could not survive a dose of economic realism. Thus, rational market pricing of irrigation water would free up enormous amounts of water, which would then be available for urban water users, recreational and environmental purposes, profitable farming operations, and yes, Indian tribes. Perhaps the no-harm-to-whites rule should be modified to a no-harm-to-taxpayers rule.

This approach fits well into the prevailing political climate. Smaller government and a reduction in government waste would create new opportunities for future water rights negotiators. Indian tribes could be awarded wet water rather than large monetary settlements; the water could then be used to generate income or to preserve traditional culture, or in whatever ways tribal members chose to use it. In addition, the no-harm rule would no longer serve as a stricture on future settlements because new water supplies would be available for allocation. The goal of such a policy is not to harm Anglo water users; most Anglos, especially taxpayers, would benefit. Rather, the goal is to bring water policy into the twenty-first century while honoring the government's historic trust responsibility to Indian tribes.

In the nineteenth and twentieth centuries the United States displayed a marked inability to keep the promises it made in the first treaty era. Perhaps in this century we will do better with the treaties of the second treaty era.

Conclusion

Water settlements have promised a great deal: certainty, finality, wet water, secure rights to a specific amount of water, federal funding, and peace and harmony brought about by "good faith" bargaining. That is a tall order, yet it is clear that, in some cases, some of these goals have been realized. What may look like an opportunity, however, may also offer hidden dangers. Just before riding off to eternity, Lt. Colonel George Custer penned a brief note to Captain Benteen, who was a few miles to the south: "Come on, big village. Be quick." Benteen, who apparently had a better eye for death traps than Custer, declined the invitation. There was indeed an opportunity at hand, but not the one that Custer envisioned. The lesson of the Little Bighorn is directly applicable to negotiated water settlements: Plan carefully, try to consider all possible ramifications, and walk away from those who promise much but speak little of the dangers.

This important juncture in time — the beginning of the new millennium — offers an opportunity to reassess the way our society relates to both water and Indian people. The idea of a permanent, viable homeland is at the heart of Indian policy today; perhaps the nation as a whole needs to consider such a concept. One way to realize this goal may be to examine traditional American Indian metaphysics to see if there is a lesson that is relevant in the next millennium. In indigenous cosmology, there is no dividing line between the land and the people that inhabit it. It is this geographic orientation to space that differentiates the aboriginal worldview from the Anglo-European fixation on time. Indian people tend to organize their cognitive processes through spatial relationships, while Anglos think linearly. In the dominant society, the basic elements of existence are separate, each with its own time line—religion, humanity, life, death, earth, water. Each exists in its own separate dimension. But in the Indian construct of life, these elements are inseparable; the prosaic and the divine deftly coexist as different dimensions of the same thing. Perhaps such a holistic view would enable us to secure an Anglo water future while providing for a vision of sharing the land and the water with Indian people.

The ultimate goal is to avoid extinction. This threat may seem distant to the dominant culture, but for Indian people it has been a part of their existence since Christopher Columbus first arrived and declared that the peaceable Indians would make excellent slaves. Extinction was assumed to be the fate of Indian people until fairly recently. A western newspaper in 1874 editorialized about the fate of Indian people: "Humanitarians may weep for poor Lo, [the poor Indian,] and tell the wrongs he has suffered, but he is passing away. Their prayers, their entreaties, can not change the law of nature; can not arrest the causes which are carrying them on to their ultimate destiny—extinction."[29] A new approach to water policy in general, and particularly in regard to Indian tribes, will go a long way toward ensuring that both the dominant culture and the Indian people who live within it, will not disappear from this Earth. In such a context, future water settlements may well exceed past settlements in their quest to bring justice to a long-troubled area of policy.

Vignette: Pipe Dreams

We are sitting under a veranda built of scrap lumber and willow fronds, next to the home of the Canyon family. Their house, a simple concrete block structure, is a mile east of Cameron, Arizona, on the western edge of the Navajo Reservation. An austere, barren desert is splayed out before us. The remnants of abandoned uranium mines are visible in the distance. An enormous high-voltage power line runs within a hundred yards of their house, yet they have no electricity. The shallow canyon of the Little Colorado River is just south of their house, yet they have no running water. In the distance, a series of mesas form the horizon in the east, traversed by more high-voltage power lines. The blue outline of the San Francisco Peaks, one of the Navajos' four sacred mountains, is visible seventy miles to the southwest. Everything shimmers with heat, and the high-pitched buzz of cicadas drifts intermittently across the landscape.

Jean and Edward Canyon are in their eighties; they do not speak English. Their daughter Elise and their son Daniel interpret for them. I have come here to talk with them about the future of the Little Colorado River, which has been the subject of a long and troubled negotiation. They have heard that many people are talking about what to do with the river. They have heard that promises have been made.

But before we delve deeply into that subject, Jean Canyon says she wants me to look at some papers that don't quite make sense to her. Daniel retrieves some papers from the house. "There's this man that says he wants to write a history about our family," he explains.

I am puzzled. "Is he an anthropologist?" I ask. I begin to examine the papers. Across the top of the first page it declares in bold print: "The WORLD BOOK OF THE CANYONS IS ABOUT TO BE PUBLISHED." Below that the letter promises that, for a large fee, this book would explain how the Canyon family "immigrated to these shores and why they left their European birthplace." Furthermore, the book promises to trace the Canyons' origins "back to your homeland."

"They send this stuff to everyone, it's meaningless," I explain, laughing at the absurdity of the whole thing. "It's just an advertising gimmick."

"You mean it isn't true? This book is not really about us?" Mrs. Canyon asks.

"No, it's just a sales pitch. I got one too, promising to tell me my Scottish plaid—you know, the criss-cross pattern on those little skirts that Scotsmen wear."

Elise can see the humor in it, particularly the part about the little skirt. She translates my reply for her mother, then translates her mother's response: "So, they can't keep that promise—writing a book about us." Mrs. Canyon looks disappointed.

"No. This company has no idea who you are."

"See, we can't trust white people; they will say *anything* to get what they want," Daniel adds with anger in his voice.

What follows is a long silence. In Anglo circles such a prolonged interval would be awkward, but it is clear that they need some time to pass before we can talk about the Little Colorado River.

Daniel Canyon is the first to bring up the subject of the river. He is a devout follower of Lyndon LaRouche, the right-wing extremist, who has been proselytizing heavily on Indian reservations in recent years. Pointing out the obvious injustices to American Indians, the LaRouche organization has had some success in recruiting Indian people.

"The river is being sold to people back east by the federal government," Daniel opines, noting that nothing ever seems to change under the current regime. "There's gonna be a revolution against the federal government," he says grimly.

Daniel's parents do not dwell on such things. For Edward Canyon, the issue is the death of a river. He is a hand trembler — a kind of diagnostician in Navajo culture — and he laments the loss of the river, not just the water in it. For him, the only just solution is to bring the river back to life; otherwise his home is not complete.

Elise Canyon explains that the river used to flow in great quantities. "When I was a little girl, I would ride my horse across the river, even when it was fast and deep. Now it's mostly just sand."

Jean Canyon focuses on the practical. She wants to know how they could get water piped to their house so they don't have to haul it in large plastic barrels from Cameron. "We should just make our own negotiation for water. Forget Window Rock," she says defiantly.

The next day we attend a chapter house meeting at Cameron. On the way we walk across the highway bridge over the Little Colorado. The canyon is not deep at this point, perhaps a hundred feet from rim to bottom. The sandstone walls of the canyon vary in hue from a chocolate brown to a slight beige. On this day the river is bone dry; a wide, meandering swath of damp sand marks where it passed in wetter times.

Upon entering the chapter house, I am introduced to the chapter president, Semour Tso, who recently retired from the Navajo Nation Tribal Council. I ask him if he knows of the Little Colorado River negotiations.

"Yeh, I've heard about the talks over the Little Colorado. They should build that pipeline, all the way down highway 89 to here, with turnouts every five miles for homes and fields."

He is referring to a proposal, put on the table by the Hopis as part of the Little Colorado negotiations, to build a pipeline from Lake Powell to the Hopi towns. The idea soon expanded to include other communities as well. Mr. Tso's proposal for the pipeline is the most expansive one I have heard. He strikes me as a wily politician with an eye for confrontational politics. He describes his frustration with the lack of progress on a local sewage problem: "If we don't get some money soon to expand the Cameron sewage lagoon, we're just gonna let it overflow; we're gonna let this thing explode. That will get their attention. We tried that a few years ago up at Tuba City and it worked then."

Mr. Tso is particularly vocal about the Bennett Freeze, an order issued thirty-five years ago by the Secretary of the Interior that forbids all Navajos in the area from making any improvements to their homes or building any new structures. It was part of the conflict in this area between the Hopis and the Navajos.[30] "The freeze put us thirty years behind. It's the government's fault. The only way we will catch up is if the government builds that pipeline. That's what we need out of this negotiation." Mr. Tso is emphatic. For him and the other Navajo people of Cameron, the Little Colorado settlement is an opportunity to settle old grievances and make amends for past injustices.

After the chapter meeting we drive to Tuba City, twenty-five miles north of Cameron. Tuba City is on the far western edge of the Navajo Reservation but consists of both a Hopi and a Navajo community. We stop to visit Dan Akee, a relative of the Canyons and a former member of the Tuba City farm board. He and his wife seem to expect us, even though we have not called ahead. Mr. Akee was a Navajo code-talker with the U.S. Marines during World War II. I am here to talk about water, but I cannot resist asking about his code-talking days. At my urging, he shows me his yellow code-talker shirt, bedecked with medals and ribbons. I am very pleased when he agrees to allow Elise Canyon to take our picture together.

Mr. Akee is quite knowledgeable about the area's water problems and knows of the proposal to build a pipeline from Lake Powell south to the reservations. "We used to grow a lot of crops in this area down at Curly's [a broad valley just west of town]. But we had to stop most of that because we didn't have enough water."

His view of the pipeline revolves around the idea of a fair share: "If Peabody [Coal Company] can get water for their slurry line, and the Hopi villages can get water, why not extend the pipeline so we can get water too? If we got that water, it would change everything. We could raise cabbage, carrots, alfalfa, and dairy products. We could provide our own food to the schools here, like we used to do."

For Mr. Akee, the Canyons, and the people at the Cameron chapter house, the pipeline idea holds great promise. It might not bring back the river, but it would be the first opportunity in decades to receive assistance with their water problems and help mitigate the losses of the past.[31]

Stan Pollack has been the water lawyer for the Navajo Nation for the past fourteen years. He is a mixture of thoughtful contemplation and impatient dynamism, and he gets excited when he talks water. He can barely stay in his seat when he describes his Odyssean journey through the shoals and whirlpools of water negotiations for the Little Colorado River.

The Little Colorado River negotiations began in 1986 but did not really become serious until the early 1990s. In addition to the Navajo Nation, the Hopi tribe, numerous non-Indian water users, Phelps-Dodge Mining Company, the state of Arizona, the U.S. Fish and Wildlife Service, and all the usual players from the Interior Department are all involved in the negotiations. An early version of the settlement concerned the construction of a new dam and reservoir at Tucker Flats, but that idea ran into a wall of opposition due to antidam sentiment, cost, endangered species problems, and water supply. The next proposal was to purchase the Blue Ridge Reservoir from Phelps Dodge, transfer it to the Navajo Nation, and use it to supply water to the Leupp area on the reservation. However, none of that water would be slated for irrigation.

Then the Hopis proposed building a 50,000-af pipeline from Lake Powell to Red Lake, then farther south to the Tuba City area. Currently the Hopi villages use about 350 af per year. In 1994 Secretary of the Interior Babbitt indicated he would support a pipeline for 10,000 af, which would supply 4,000 af to the Peabody coal slurry and 6,000 af to Tuba City and the Hopi Reservation.[32] This proposal led to numerous counterproposals and continued disagreement among the parties. An official price tag for the pipeline has not been released, but one official described recent internal cost estimates as "pretty scary." The cost began to escalate as non-Indian communities started requesting that the pipeline be extended to them: "Arizona said maybe they could get in on it and help things along by sending the pipeline water to Grand Canyon. Then everyone started lining up: Williams, Flagstaff, etcetera."[33] The director of the Arizona Department of Water Resources recently alluded to this expansion of benefits, arguing that it made both political and economic sense to increase the list of beneficiaries.[34] But the pipeline is caught up in the budget woes of the U.S. government and faces a broad array of critics ranging from budget hawks to environmentalists and downstream water users. The prognosis for the pipe dream is not good. In the meantime, the Canyon family continues to haul water in plastic barrels, hoping beyond all reason that the Little Colorado River will once again come to life.[35] Perhaps, one day, a settlement will accomplish that.

Notes

Preface

1. This book reflects the considerable inadequacy of our language in regard to Indians and Anglos. In recent years a number of Indian people have expressed a preference for the term "American Indian" or just "Indian," despite its historical baggage, so I usually use that term, but occasionally use "Native American" or "indigenous people." In effect, I have tried to use the words that I hear Indian people apply to themselves. In addition, there is no truly acceptable word for those who are not Indian. Three terms are in common usage: "Anglo" or "white," even though they apply to many Americans who are neither, and "non-Indian," which is technically more accurate but is expressed in the negative, as though we can be defined only by something we are not. In true Anglo fashion, perhaps we need to invent an acronym for ourselves, such as people of non-indigenous culture (PONICs).

2. This research was funded in part by the U.S. Geological Survey, Department of the Interior, award number 1434-92-G2255. The views and conclusions contained in this article are those of the author and should not be interpreted as necessarily representing the official policies, either expressed or implied, of the U.S. Geological Survey.

3. Berkeley: University of California Press, 1987; reprint, Tucson: University of Arizona Press, 1994.

4. The Western European mode of decision making, with its emphasis on hierarchy, formal rules of authority, jurisdictional parameters, empirical justification, and time constraints, is fundamentally different from traditional indigenous modes of decision making. See LaDonna Harris, Stephen Sachs, and Benjamin Broome, "Harmony through Wisdom of the People: Recreating Traditional Ways of Building Consensus among Comanches" (revision of paper prepared for the 1994 American Political Science Association Meeting); Sharon O'Brien, *American Indian Tribal Governments* (Norman: University of Oklahoma Press, 1989), chap. 2; Vine Deloria Jr., *The Metaphysics of Modern Existence* (New York: Harper & Row, 1979).

5. Andrew Othole, former councilman, Zuni Tribe, interview by author, Zuni Reservation, New Mexico, March 22, 1996.

Chapter 1. Rivers of Ink

1. Mr. Whitehat completed his MPA degree and became the financial administrator for the new Navajo Mountain School.

2. This study does not include the last three water settlements. The Las Vegas Paiute settlement

was a small settlement concerning a state groundwater adjudication that did not require federal funding or congressional approval; the Rocky Boys and Shivwits settlements became law after the fieldwork for this study was completed. For an analysis of the Rocky Boys settlement, see Barbara Cosens, "The 1997 Water Rights Settlement between the State of Montana and the Chippewa Cree Tribe of the Rocky Boy's Reservation: The Role of Community and of the Trustee," *UCLA Journal of Environmental Law and Policy* 16, no. 2 (1997–98): 255–95. This study also excludes the Seminole settlement and a dozen other settlements that are primarily land, not water, settlements.

3. S. 421 (Feb. 11, 1999).

4. The reservations are Nambe, Pojoaque, San Ildelfonso, Tesuque, Zia, Jemez, Santa Ana, Blackfeet, Crow, Duck Valley, Flathead, Fort Belknap, Gila River, Acoma, Laguna, Klamath, Lummi, Navajo, Hopi, Nez Perce, Zuni, Ramah Navajo, Shivwits, Soboba, and Taos.

5. Prucha counts 367 treaties ratified by Congress, 6 more that are "questionable," and perhaps as many as 150 unratified treaties. See Francis Paul Prucha, *American Indian Treaties: The History of a Political Anomaly* (Berkeley: University of California Press, 1994), 1, 517. The Institute for the Development of Indian Law counted 800 treaties signed between "Indians and non-Indians." See Kirk Kickingbird et al., "Indian Treaties" (in-house document, Washington, D.C.: Institute for the Development of Indian Law, 1980), 2. The most comprehensive account of all types of Indian-Anglo agreements is Vine Deloria Jr. and Raymond J. DeMallie, comps., *Documents of American Indian Diplomacy: Treaties, Agreements, and Conventions, 1775–1979* (Austin: University of Texas Press, 1999).

6. Wallace Stegner, *Beyond the Hundredth Meridian: John Wesley Powell and the Second Opening of the West* (New York: Penguin, 1992), 2.

7. *U.S. v. Mose Anderson et al.*, Memorandum Order 1 (1905).

8. Ibid., 2.

9. Cyrus Babb, District Engineer, Chinook, Montana, to H. M. Savage, Supervising Engineer, Reclamation Service, Billings, Montana, April 19, 1906, p. 1, National Archives, RG 115, General Administrative and Project Records, 1902–19, Milk River, 548.

10. Ibid., p. 3. The Fort Belknap Project actually won a reserved water right to twice that amount, but the Indian agent, in an apparent attempt to smooth tensions, agreed to claim only half the reserved right that year.

11. *Henry Winters et al. v. The United States of America*, 1243 (9th Ct., 1906).

12. H. N. Savage, Supervising Engineer, Reclamation Service, Billings, Montana, to Morris Bien, Chief Engineer, U.S. Reclamation Service, Washington, D.C., March 22, 1906, pp. 2–3, National Archives, RG 115, General Administrative and Project Records, 1902–19, Milk River, 548.

13. This phrase has been used in numerous treaties, statutes, and court cases, sometimes with less than sterling sincerity. In *Lone Wolf v. Hitchcock*, 187 U.S. 553–68, the Supreme Court presumed that "Congress acted in perfect good faith in the dealings with the Indians." The Court then gave Congress the power to act in bad faith by unilaterally abrogating treaty rights without regard to Indian preferences.

14. *Henry Winters, John W. Acker, Chris. Cruse, Agnes Downs et al. v. The United States of America*, 499 Sup. Ct. 125 (1906).

15. *Henry Winters et al. v. The United States of America*, 158 Sup. Ct. 36 (1907; supplemental brief for the United States).

16. W. B. Hill, U.S. Indian Inspector, Fort Belknap Agency, Montana, to W. H. Code, Chief Engineer, Indian Service, Los Angeles, California, Aug. 29, 1907, p. 20, National Archives, RG 75, Fort Belknap file.

17. *U.S. v. Winters*, 207 U.S. 568 (1908).

18. Ibid., 569.

19. W. S. Hanna, Superintendent of Irrigation, U.S. Indian Service, Billings, Montana, to W. M. Reed, Chief Engineer, U.S. Indian Irrigation Service, Washington, D.C., March 31, 1916, p. 2, National Archives, RG 75, Fort Belknap file.

20. For an excellent review of these cases see Shelly C. Dudley, "Pima Indians, Water Rights, and the Federal Government: *U.S. v. Gila Valley Irrigation District*" (M.A. thesis, Arizona State University, 1996), ch. 3.

21. *Conrad Investment Co. v. U.S.*, 161 F 829 (9th Cir., 1908). This case was actually filed before the Fort Belknap case; see John Lytle Shurts, "The Winters Doctrine: Origin and Development of the Indian Reserved Water Rights Doctrine in Its Social and Legal Context, 1880s–1930s" (Ph.D. dissertation, University of Oregon, 1997), 220. See also Shurts, *Indian Reserved Water Rights: The Winters Doctrine in Its Social and Legal Context, 1880s-1930s* (Norman: University of Oklahoma Press, 2000).

22. *U.S. v. Walker River Irrigation District*, 104 F 2d 334 (9th Cir., 1939).

23. *Skeem v. U.S.*, 273 F. 93 (9th Cir., 1921).

24. *U.S. v. Powers*, 305 U.S. 527 (1939).

25. *U.S. v. Ahtanum Irrigation District*, 236 F. 2d 321 (9th Cir., 1956).

26. *Arizona v. California*, 373 U.S. 546 (1963).

27. *Cappaert v. U.S.*, 426 U.S. 128 (1977). Also see Interlocutory Review of Sept. 30, 1988, Order, Superior Court in Maricopa County, Judge Noel A. Fidel, on behalf of the Arizona Supreme Court, answering two questions: "Do federal reserved water rights extend to groundwater (underground water) that is not subject to prior appropriation under Arizona law?" and "Are federal reserved water rights holders entitled to greater protection from groundwater pumping than are water users who hold only state law rights?"

28. For a more detailed discussion of the development of the reserved rights doctrine, see David Getches, "Indian Water Rights Conflicts in Perspective," in *Indian Water in the New West*, ed. Thomas McGuire, William Lord, and Mary Wallace (Tucson: University of Arizona Press, 1993), 7–26; Daniel McCool, *Command of the Waters: Iron Triangles, Federal Water Development, and Indian Water* (Berkeley: University of California Press, 1987; reprint, Tucson: University of Arizona Press, 1994); Jana Walker and Susan Williams, "Indian Reserved Water Rights," *Natural Resources and the Environment* 5, no. 4 (1992): 50; Lloyd Burton, *American Indian Water Rights and the Limits of Law* (Lawrence: University Press of Kansas, 1991).

29. Comments of Honorable Bruce Babbitt, Secretary of the Interior, "Indian Water—1997: Trends and Directions in Federal Water Policy," Western Water Policy Advisory Commission, Oct. 1997 (final report, on compact disc).

30. *U.S. v. New Mexico*, 438 U.S. 697 (1978).

31. *Colorado River Water Conservation District v. U.S.*, 424 U.S. 800 (1976). For a full discussion of the impact of the McCarran Amendment cases, see Mary Wallace, "The Supreme Court and Indian Water Rights," in *American Indian Policy in the Twentieth Century*, ed. Vine Deloria Jr. (Norman: University of Oklahoma Press, 1985), 197–220.

32. *Nevada v. U.S.*, 103 Sup. Ct. 2906 (1983).

33. *Arizona v. California*, 103 Sup. Ct. 1382 (1983).

34. *Arizona v. San Carlos Apache Tribe of Arizona et al.*, 103 Sup. Ct. 1382 (1983). The protection of *res judicata* was also an issue in the other two cases.

35. Western States Water Council, "Indian Water Rights in the West" (study prepared for the Western Governors' Association, May 1984).

36. 15 Stat. 673 (1868).

37. Teno Roncalio, "The Big Horns of a Dilemma," in *Indian Water in the New West*, ed. Thomas McGuire, William Lord, and Mary Wallace (Tucson: University of Arizona Press, 1993), 211. Joseph Membrino demonstrates that the state of Wyoming spent $8,586,860 just to litigate the water rights to 6,290 acres of Indian land. That is $1,365 per acre in attorney fees—for just one side of the litigants. See Joseph Membrino, "Indian Reserved Water Rights, Federalism and the Trust Responsibility," *Land and Water Law Review* 27, no. 1 (1992): 7.

38. Remarks by Susan Williams, attorney, at the Sixth Symposium on the Settlement of Indian Reserved Water Rights Claims, Missoula, Mont., Sept. 8–10, 1999, sponsored by the Native American Rights Fund and the Western States Water Council.

39. For more extensive discussion of the Big Horn cases, see Walter Rusinek, "A Preview of Coming Attractions? *Wyoming v. United States* and the Reserved Rights Doctrine," *Ecology Law Quarterly* 17, no. 2 (1990): 355–413; Wes Williams, "Changing Water Use for Federally Reserved Indian Water Rights: Wind River Indian Reservation," *University of California Law Review* 27 (1994): 501–32.

40. The court appointed Teno Roncalio as special master. Roncalio was a former congressman who, as chair of the House Subcommittee on Indian Affairs and Public Lands from 1978 to 1980, was not especially known as a friend of the Indians. He later became more sensitive to the Indian point of view. See Roncalio, "The Big Horns of a Dilemma."

41. This decision was later amended, but the usage limitation remained.

42. *In Re The General Adjudication of All Rights to Use Water in the Big Horn River System and All Other Sources*, 753 P. Wyo. 2d 61 (1988). See Peggy Sue Kirk, "Cowboys, Indians, and Reserved Rights: May a State Court Limit How Indian Tribes Use Their Water?" *Land and Water Law Review* 28 (1993): 467–88.

43. An acre-foot is the amount necessary to cover one acre to a depth of one foot. It is equivalent to 325,851 gallons.

44. Brief for the Petitioner on Writ of Certiorari, *Wyoming v. U.S.*, 31–32.

45. See Sylvia F. Liu, "American Indian Reserved Water Rights: The Federal Obligation to Protect Tribal Water Resources and Tribal Autonomy," *Environmental Law* 25 (Spring 1995): note 34.

46. *Wyoming v. U.S.*, 492 U.S. 406 (1989).

47. *Wyoming v. U.S. et al.*, Oral Argument, 88-309, Official Transcript (1989).

48. Quoted in *U.S. Water News*, Oct. 19, 1989, 19.

49. *Big Horn III*, 835 P. 2d 273 (1991).

50. Ibid.

51. Eric Hannum, "Administration of Reserved and Non-Reserved Water Rights on an Indian Reservation: Postadjudication Questions on the Big Horn River," *Natural Resources Journal* 32 (Summer 1992): 682–704.

52. *Big Horn III*, 835 P. 2d 303 (1991); dissenting opinion, Justice Michael Golden.

53. This estimate was made by Secretary of the Interior William Clark, quoted in the *Denver Post*, June 3, 1984, sec. B, p. 6.

54. Jay Hair, President, National Wildlife Federation, "State Court Trims Water Right," *Rock Springs (WY) Daily Rocket-Miner*, September 29, 1992.

55. Carl Rasch, U.S. Attorney, Helena, Montana, to W. R. Logan, Superintendent, Fort Belknap Reservation, April 26, 1906, National Archives, RG 115, General Administrative and Project Records, 1902–19, Milk River, 548.

56. W. M. Reed, Chief Engineer, Indian Service, to W. S. Hanna, Supervising Engineer, Billings, Montana, Nov. 13, 1923, National Archives, RG 115, General Administrative and Project Records, 1917–23, Milk River, 548.

57. Inspector General, U.S. Department of the Interior, "Rehabilitation and Completion of the Fort Belknap Irrigation Project" (draft memorandum audit report, Aug. 1985).

58. Senate Committee on Indian Affairs, "BIA Management and Operation of Indian Irrigation Projects," 101st Cong., 1st. sess. July 12, 1990, p. 92; Testimony of Donovan Archambault, Chairman, Fort Belknap Community Council.

59. Chief Engineer, U.S. Indian Irrigation Service Annual Reports, to the Commissioner of Indian Affairs, 1920, U.S. Department of the Interior, National Archives, RG 75, BIA Irrigation Service, entry 654, box 67.

60. Porter Preston and Charles Engle, *Report of Advisers on Irrigation on Indian Reservations* (June 8, 1928). Printed in Hearings before a Subcommittee of the Committee on Indian Affairs. U.S. Senate, 71 Cong., 2d sess., Part 6 (January 21, 1930).

61. House Committee on Appropriations, Subcommittee on the Department of the Interior and Related Agencies, "Appropriations for 1977," 94th Cong., 1st sess., 1976, 106.

62. Western States Water Council, "Indian Water Rights in the West" (study prepared for the Western Governors' Association, May 1984). See also McCool, *Command of the Waters*, 122–27; Reid Peyton Chambers and John Echohawk, "Implementing the Winters Doctrine of Indian Reserved Water Rights: Producing Indian Water Development and Economic Development without Injuring Non-Indian Water Users?" *Gonzaga Law Review* 27, no. 3 (1991–92): 447–48.

63. Remarks by Sam Miller, Chief of Division of Land and Water Resources, Bureau of Indian Affairs, at "The Mni-Sose Intertribal Water Rights Coalition Symposium on Reserved Water Rights and Water Related Issues, Albuquerque, 1994.

64. The estimated claim of 46 million acre-feet is from the 1984 report by the Western States Water Council cited above. In 1996 the BIA officially claimed that over a million acres of Indian land was being irrigated, but these statistics are notoriously unreliable. Recently the BIA put together a Power and Irrigation Reconciliation Team in an attempt to reconcile their bad record keeping. There have been five audits of the BIA's record keeping since 1988, and they have uncovered numerous deficiencies.

65. Bureau of Indian Affairs, U.S. Department of the Interior, BIA 50-1 form, part 1 (1974).

66. Senate hearing before the Select Committee on Indian Affairs, 101st Cong., 2d sess., "Oversight Hearing on BIA Management and Operation of Indian Irrigation Projects," July 12, 1990, 6.

67. This language is from a proposed, but unpublished, dissenting opinion by Justice Brennan in the Big Horn case, *Wyoming v. United States*, 492 U.S. 406 (1989).

68. This estimate is from the Corps of Engineers' Area Manager's Workshop no. 15: Native American Issues (April 28–29, 1998), minutes reprinted on the Mni-Sose website: www.mnisose. org/update/acoeltr.html

69. *U.S. v. New Mexico*, 438 U.S. 718 (1978).

70. See *Arizona v. California*, 460 U.S. 605 (1983); *State Ex rel. Martinez v. Lewis*, 861 P.2d 235 (N.M. App., 1993).

71. Bureau of Reclamation projects are required by law to have a positive benefit-cost ratio. However, the bureau, not an independent entity, calculates the ratio, and the bureau has proven extremely adept at creative statistics. See McCool, *Command of the Waters*, 96–97; Richard W. Wahl, *Markets for Federal Water: Subsidies, Property Rights, and the Bureau of Reclamation* (Baltimore: Resources for the Future and the Johns Hopkins University Press, 1989).

72. *Congressional Record*, 100th Cong. 2d sess., 1988, 9348.

73. *U.S. v. Superior Court*, 144 Ariz. 270; 697 P.2d. 663.

Chapter 2. A Vision of Good Faith

1. Quoted in William Rowley, *Reclaiming the Arid West: The Career of Francis G. Newlands* (Bloomington: Indiana University Press, 1996), 3.

2. Ibid., p. 6.

3. See Brigham Madsen, *The Shoshoni Frontier and the Bear River Massacre* (Salt Lake City: University of Utah Press, 1985), 119-20.

4. Ralph Tarr and Frank McMurry, *New Complete Geography* (New York: Macmillan, 1916), 12, 215, 1220–21.

5. National Irrigation Congress, proceedings (1907), 119.

6. National Irrigation Congress, proceedings (1911), 58.

7. There is extensive literature on western water development. The conflict between the BIA irrigation program and the non-Indian projects built by the bureau and the corps was the focus of my previous book, *Command of the Waters: Iron Triangles, Federal Water Development, and Indian Water* (Berkeley: University of California Press, 1987: reprint, Tucson: University of Arizona Press, 1994).

8. National Irrigation Congress, proceedings (1905), 28.

9. Another popular saying at the time was, " 'Tis a crime to let our rivers reach the sea." Quoted in Donald C. Jackson, *Building the Ultimate Dam: John S. Eastwood and the Control of Water in the West* (Lawrence: University Press of Kansas, 1995), 1.

10. Remarks of Congressman Hepburn of Ohio; *Congressional Record*, 57 Cong. 1 sess., 1902, 35, 6742.

11. See William E. Smythe, *The Conquest of Arid America* (New York: Macmillan, 1911); Rich Johnson, *The Central Arizona Project, 1918–1968* (Tucson: University of Arizona Press, 1977); Michael Robinson, *Water for the West: The Bureau of Reclamation* (Chicago: Public Works Historical Society, 1979); William E. Warne, *The Bureau of Reclamation* (New York: Praeger, 1973); Lawrence B. Lee, *Reclaiming the American West: An Historiography and Guide* (Santa Barbara, Calif.: ABC-Clio Press, 1980).

12. Daniel Halacy, *The Water Crisis* (New York: E. P. Dutton, 1966); Frank Moss, *The Water Crisis* (New York: Praeger, 1967); George Nikolaieff, *The Water Crisis* (New York: Bronx, 1967); Terry Anderson, *Water Crisis: Ending the Policy Drought* (Baltimore: Johns Hopkins University Press, 1983).

13. For the conflict between the two programs, see H. Burness, R. Cummings, W. Gorman, and R. Lansford, "United States Reclamation Policy and Indian Water Rights," *Natural Resources Journal* 20 (Oct. 1980): 808-26; McCool, *Command of the Waters*; Michael Moore, "Native American Water Rights: Efficiency and Fairness," *Natural Resources Journal* 29 (1989): 763–91; Lloyd Burton, *American Indian Water Rights and the Limits of Law* (Lawrence: University Press of Kansas, 1991); Monique Shay, "Promises of a Viable Homeland, Reality of Selective Reclamation: A Study of the Relationship between the Winters Doctrine and Federal Water Development in the Western United States," *Ecology Law Quarterly* 19 (1992): 547–91.

14. Public Law 87-483 (1962).

15. John Leeper, "Avoiding a Train Wreck in the San Juan Basin," *Water Resources Update* 107 (Spring 1997): 34. In late 1999 the project was still only 60 percent complete, with seven of the eleven blocks under irrigation, according to *The Spillway* (Oct. 1999), published by the Upper Colorado Region of the Bureau of Reclamation.

16. Judith Eve Jacobsen, *A Promise Made: The Navajo Indian Irrigation Project and Water Politics in the American West* (cooperative thesis 119, University of Colorado and National Center for

Atmospheric Research, 1989), 212. See also Judith Jacobsen, "The Navajo Indian Irrigation Project and Quantification of Navajo Winters Rights," *Natural Resources Journal* 32 (Fall 1992): 825–53; Robert Young and Roger Mann, "Cheap Water in Indian Country: A Cost-Effective Rural Development Tool?" in *Indian Water in the New West*, ed. Thomas McGuire, William Lord, and Mary Wallace (Tucson: University of Arizona Press, 1993): 185–94.

17. Today there are 557 federally recognized Indian tribes on 314 reservations. Indian Country now totals 55,379,399 acres of trust lands. Another 44 million acres are held by Alaska Natives. Source: BIA website, www.doi.gov/bia/realty/area.html, and Office of American Indian Trust website, www.doi.gov/oait/natives/htm (June 1999).

18. Forced imitation was not abandoned completely, however. The IRA model government was based on Anglo concepts of organization, and made no provision for recognizing traditional forms of indigenous government.

19. There are many fine histories of American Indian policy. See, for example, Robert Bee, *The Politics of American Indian Policy* (Cambridge, Mass.: Schenkman, 1982); Francis Paul Prucha, *The Great Father: The United States Government and the American Indian* (Lincoln: University of Nebraska Press, 1984); Vine Deloria Jr. and Clifford Lytle, *The Nations Within: The Past and Future of American Indian Sovereignty* (New York: Pantheon Books, 1984); Stephen Cornell, *Return of the Native: American Indian Political Resurgence* (New York: Oxford University Press, 1988); Donald Parma, *Indians and the American West in the Twentieth Century* (Bloomington: Indiana University Press, 1994).

20. *U.S. v. Kagama*, 118 U.S. 375 (1886).

21. Richard Lamm and Michael McCarthy, *The Angry West* (Boston: Houghton Mifflin, 1982), 189.

22. There have been numerous land settlements, but they are beyond the purview of this book.

23. Steven Shupe, "Water in Indian Country: From Paper Rights to a Managed Resource," *University of Colorado Law Review* 57 (Spring 1986): 561.

24. Lois Witte, "Averting a Water Rights War," *State Government News*, Nov. 24–25, 1990, 24.

25. For background see Daniel McCool, "Intergovernmental Conflict and Indian Water Rights: An Assessment of Negotiated Settlements," *Publius* 23 (Winter 1993): 85–101; Daniel McCool, "Indian Water Settlements: The Prerequisites of Successful Negotiation," *Policy Studies Journal* 21, no. 2 (1993): 227–42.

26. Roger Fisher and William Ury, *Getting to Yes: Negotiating without Giving In* (New York: Penguin, 1981).

27. See, for example, Howard Raiffa, *The Art and Science of Negotiation* (Cambridge, Mass.: Harvard University Press, 1982); Christine B. Harrington, *Shadow Justice: The Ideology and Institutionalization of Alternatives to Court* (Westport, Conn.: Greenwood Press, 1985); Lawrence Susskind and Jeffrey L. Cruickshank, *Breaking the Impasse: Consensual Approaches to Resolving Public Disputes* (New York: Basic Books, 1987); William Ury, Jeanne Brett, and Stephen Goldberg, *Getting Disputes Resolved* (San Francisco: Jossey-Bass, 1988); Deborah Kolb and Jeffrey Rubin, "Research into Mediation," *Dispute Resolution Forum* (Oct. 1989): 3–8; Kaleen Cottingham, "Restoring Faith in Natural Resource Policy-Making: Incorporating Direct Participation through Alternative Dispute Resolution Processes" (Natural Resource Law Center, occasional paper, Sept. 1992).

28. See Dennis Sandole and Ingrid Sandole-Staroste, eds., *Conflict Management and Problem Solving: Interpersonal to International Applications* (New York: New York University Press, 1987).

29. David Getches, foreword to the *Tribal Water Management Handbook* (Oakland, Calif.: American Indian Resources Institute and the American Indian Lawyer Training Program, 1988), xv.

30. Christopher Kenney, "The Legacy and the Promise of the Settlement of Indian Reserved Right Water Claims," *Water Resources Update* 107 (Spring 1997): 22.

31. Benjamin Simon and Harvey Doerksen, "Conflicting Federal Roles in Indian Water Claims Negotiations," in *Indian Water in the New West*, ed. Thomas McGuire, William Lord, and Mary Wallace (Tucson: University of Arizona Press, 1993), 28–29.

32. Lawrence Bacow and Michael Wheeler, *Environmental Dispute Resolution* (New York: Plenum Press, 1984), 38–39.

33. Peterson Zah, "Water: Key to Tribal Economic Development," in *Indian Water 1985: Collected Essays*, ed. Christine Miklas and Steven Shupe (Oakland, Calf.: AILTP/American Indian Resources Institute, 1986), 77–78.

34. Walter Rusinek, "A Preview of Coming Attractions? *Wyoming v. United States* and the Reserved Rights Doctrine," *Ecology Law Quarterly* 17 (1990): 398.

35. Susskind and Cruikshank, *Breaking the Impasse*, 31; John Folk-Williams, "The Use of Negotiated Agreements to Resolve Water Disputes Involving Indian Rights," *Natural Resources Journal* 28 (1988): 73–75.

36. Claudia Marseille, "Conflict Management: Negotiating Indian Water Rights" (joint publication of the Lincoln Institute of Land Policy and the Western Legislative Conference, no. 102, Cambridge, Mass., 1983), 5–6; Bacow and Wheeler, *Environmental Dispute Resolution*, 360.

37. Stanley Pollock, an attorney with many years' experience with negotiated settlements, made this observation in regard to including all stakeholders: "The amount of work you get done at the negotiation table is in inverse proportion to the number of people at the table."

38. John Folk-Williams, "Parties and Permanence: Alternative Dispute Resolution Principles," in *Indian Water in the New West*, ed. Thomas McGuire, William Lord, and Mary Wallace (Tucson: University of Arizona Press, 1993), 150.

39. See Susskind and Cruikshank, *Breaking the Impasse*, 21–22; Max Stephenson and Gerald Pops, "Conflict Resolution Methods and the Policy Process," *Public Administration Review* (Sept.–Oct. 1989): 463; M. Cormick, "Strategic Issues in Structuring Multi-Party Public Policy Negotiations," *Negotiation Journal* 125 (April 1989).

40. Stephenson and Pops, "Conflict Resolution Methods," 67.

41. There are an estimated 75,000 dams higher than six feet in the United States. Some are federally funded, some are state dams, and some are private. Very few are Indian owned. Michael Collier, Robert Webb, and John Schmidt, *Dams and Rivers*, U.S. Geological Survey circular 1126 (June 1996), 2.

42. This estimate is from a 1991 report by the Federal Emergency Management Administration, quoted in Sarah Bates, David Getches, Lawrence McDonnell, and Charles Wilkinson, *Searching Out the Headwaters: Change and Rediscovery in Western Water Policy* (Washington, D.C.: Island Press, 1993), 80.

43. "Investing in the Future," Bureau of Reclamation annual report, FY 1998.

44. Data supplied by Robert Bank, U.S. Army Corps of Engineers, HQ02, Nov. 5, 1999.

45. *Congressional Record*, 101 Cong. 2d sess., 1990, 136, H 11497.

46. Remarks by Marlene Walters, member of the Blackfeet Tribal Council, Symposium on the Settlement of Indian Reserved Water Rights Claims, Western States Water Council and the Native American Rights Fund, Bismarck, N.D., Sept. 1993.

47. Reid Peyton Chambers and John Echohawk, "Implementing the Winters Doctrine of Indian Reserved Water Rights: Producing Indian Water and Economic Development without Injuring Non-Indian Water Users?" *Gonzaga Law Review* 27, no. 3 (1991–92): 469.

48. Remarks by Ray Frost, member of the Southern Ute Tribal Council, Symposium on the

Settlement of Indian Reserved Water Rights Claims, Western States Water Council and the Native American Rights Fund, Bismark, N.D., Sept. 1993.

49. Remarks by Mike Jackson, staff counsel, Committee on Indian Affairs, U.S. Senate, Symposium on the Settlement of Indian Reserved Water Rights Claims, Western States Water Council and the Native American Rights Fund, Bismark, N.D., Sept. 1993.

50. Remarks by Robert Salgado Sr., Chairman, Soboba Band of Mission Indians, Symposium on the Settlement of Indian Reserved Water Rights Claims, Native American Rights Fund and the Western States Water Council, Portland, Ore., Sept. 1995.

51. Jeanne Whiting, "Whither Settlements: Current Policy and Issues, Emerging Trends and Future Needs" (paper prepared for the Symposium on Indian Water Rights, Native American Rights Fund, Stanford School of Law, Sept. 1994), 2.

52. Patricia Zell, staff attorney, Committee on Indian Affairs, U.S. Senate, interview by author, Washington, D.C., June 12, 1996.

53. Remarks by Ronnie Lupe, chairman of the White Mountain Apache Tribal Council, Western Water Policy Review Advisory Commission, "Indian Water—1997: Trends and Directions in Federal Water Policy," Oct. 1997.

54. From an account written by Sgt. William L. Beach quoted in Harold Schindler, "The Bear River Massacre," *Utah Historical Quarterly* 67 (Fall 1999): 307.

55. Brigham Madsen, *The Shoshoni Frontier and the Bear River Massacre* (Salt Lake City: University of Utah Press, 1985), 190–192. Conner was promoted to general as a result of the Bear River massacre. The local Mormons called Conner's attack an "intervention of the almighty, as the Indians had been a source of great annoyance to us"; quoted in Captain Melvin J. Littig, *The Battle of Bear River* (Fort Douglas, Utah: Fort Douglas Museum of Military History, 1977), 12. The conflict at Bear River was the largest massacre of Indian people in the western Indian wars. See Brigham Madsen, *Glory Hunter: A Biography of Patrick Edward Connor* (Salt Lake City: University of Utah Press, 1990), 86.

56. "Treaty of Fort Bridger," 1878, Article 6.

57. Mr. Edmo passed away in 1997.

Chapter 3. Decades and Dollars

1. Charles Supplee, Douglas Anderson, and Barbara Anderson, *Canyon De Chelly: The Story Behind the Scenery*, ed. Mary L. Van Camp (Phoenix: KC Publications, 1993), 26. The site of the massacre is known as Massacre Cave.

2. Captain Adna A. Chaffee, U.S. Army, report, 1878, quoted in Senate report S. 2153, 100th Cong., 2d sess., report 100-495, p. 2.

3. General Irvin McDowell to General Willam Sherman, 1878, quoted in Senate report S. 2153, 100th Cong., 2d sess., report 100-495, p. 2.

4. Report by Indian Superintendent M. Steck, quoted in Senate report to accompany S. 291, 102d Cong., 1st sess., 1991, report 102-133, p. 2.

5. For example, in his war against the Sioux, Sherman wrote, "We must act with vindictive earnestness against the Sioux, even to their extermination, men, women, and children." Quoted in Alvin M. Josephy Jr., *500 Nations: An Illustrated History of North American Indians* (New York: Alfred A. Knopf, 1994), 391.

6. Ibid., 3.

7. Ibid., 4.

8. PL 95-328, preamble.

9. Herbert Yates, interview by Floyd O'Neil, Albuquerque, Aug. 1, 1994.

10. A BIA memo from about 1913 identified twelve reservations that were experiencing serious water rights problems; six of them are among those that have now signed settlement acts, three are currently in negotiation, and two have been the focus of recent litigation. See John Shurts, "The Winters Doctrine: Origin and Development of the Indian Reserved Water Rights Doctrine in Its Social and Legal Context, 1880s–1930s" (Ph.D. diss., University of Oregon, 1997), 348–49.

11. U.S. Department of the Interior, "Watt Seeks Negotiated Settlement for Indian Water Claims Suits," press release, July 14, 1982.

12. U.S. Department of the Interior, "Secretary Watt to Meet with Indian Leaders, Governors, and Industry Spokesmen to Continue Process of Resolving Indian Water Claims," press release, Dec. 8, 1982.

13. William Broadbent, Assistant Secretary for Water and Science, U.S. Department of the Interior, to the Secretary of the Interior (memorandum: federal reserved water rights, May 1984).

14. Peter Sly, *Reserved Water Rights Settlement Manual* (Washington, D.C.: Island Press, 1988), 38.

15. Director of the Office of Water Policy to David Houston, Deputy Assistant Secretary for Land and Water Resources, memorandum: report on BIA technical support of water rights negotiations, 1982.

16. The Uintah and Ouray Ute Water Compact has yet to be ratified, and the Southern Ute settlement was essentially renegotiated, so the settlement of water rights on these reservations will require additional time.

17. Miller, "Taming the Rapids: Negotiation of Federal Reserved Water Rights in Montana," *Public Land Law Review* 6 (1985): 175.

18. For a critique of the state's agreement with the Crow, which was signed in June 1999, see George Ochenski, "The River Comes Last," *High Country News*, Aug. 2, 1999, 4.

19. John Folk-Williams, "The Use of Negotiated Agreements to Resolve Water Disputes Involving Indian Rights," *Natural Resources Journal* 28 (1988): 101.

20. John Thorsen, "Resolving Conflicts through Intergovernmental Agreements: The Pros and Cons of Negotiated Settlements," in *Indian Water 1985: Collected Essays*, ed. Christine Miklas and Steve Shupe (Oakland, Calif.: AILTP/American Indian Resources Institute, 1986), 25–42.

21. Remarks by Patricia Zell, Democratic Staff Director and Chief Counsel, Indian Affairs Committee, U.S. Senate, "Indian Water — 1997. Trends and Directions in Federal Water Policy" (report to the Western Water Policy Review Advisory Commission), 81 (final report on compact disc).

22. Library of Congress, Congressional Research Service, "Study of Indian-Related Federal Spending Trends, FY 1975–98" (Feb. 1997).

23. U.S. Department of the Interior, "Babbitt, Gover to Discuss BIA Management Report," press release, Sept. 8, 1999.

24. I did not include funding for "Indian" irrigation projects in this table because so many of these projects serve primarily non-Indians. Thus it would be unfair to characterize such expenditures as spending for Indian water needs.

25. Lloyd Burton, *American Indian Water Rights and the Limits of Law* (Lawrence: University Press of Kansas, 1991), 81.

26. U.S. Department of the Interior, "Explanation of the Ten Year Plan of Water Inventories and Water Resources Development Planning" (internal departmental document, mimeographed, November 1981).

27. The chairman of the Nez Perce Tribe recently estimated that the federal government and his tribe have spent $10 million preparing their water case for trial and will spend an additional $2

million per year in the years ahead. See Samuel Penney, Chairman of the Nez Perce Tribal Executive Committee, summary of remarks made to the Western Water Policy Advisory Council, "Indian Water—1997: Trends and Directions in Federal Water Policy," 79.

28. Western States Water Council, "Indian Water Rights in the West" (study prepared for the Western Governors' Association, mimeographed, 1984).

29. U.S. Department of the Interior, "Criteria and Procedures for Indian Water Rights Settlements" *Federal Register* 55, no. 48 (March 12, 1990): 9223.

30. Christopher Kinney, Director, Native American Affairs Office, Bureau of Reclamation, interview by author, Washington, D.C., June 10, 1996.

31. Thomas Colosi, "A Core Model of Negotiation," *American Behavioral Scientist* 27 (1983): 246.

32. John Folk-Williams, "The Use of Negotiated Agreements to Resolve Water Disputes Involving Indian Rights," *Natural Resources Journal* 28 (Fall 1985): 71.

33. U.S. Department of the Interior, "Explanation of the Ten Year Plan of Water Inventories and Water Resources Development Planning" (internal department document, November 1981).

34. David Getches, "Management and Marketing of Indian Water: From Conflict to Pragmatism," *University of Colorado Law Review* 58 (1988): 523; Peterson Zah, "Water: Key to Tribal Economic Development," in *Indian Water 1985: Collected Essays*, ed. Miklas and Shupe, 78.

35. House Appropriations Committee, Subcommittee on Interior and Related Agencies, "Testimony of Antone Minthorn, Chairman of the board of trustees of the Confederated Tribes of Umatilla Indian Reservation," 105th Congress, 1st sess. March 5, 1998, p. 80.

36. A water supply for the San Luis Rey settlement was included in the "4.4" agreement regarding Colorado River water use. See Bruce Babbitt, speech before the Colorado River Water Users Association, Las Vegas, Nev., Dec. 17, 1999; U.S. Department of the Interior website, www.doi.gov/news.archives/speeches&articles,nevada.htm

37. John Duffy, chairman of the Interior Department Working Group on Indian Water Settlements, interview by author, Washington, D.C., June 10, 1996.

38. Christopher Kenney, Native American Affairs Office, Bureau of Reclamation, U.S. Department of the Interior, interview by author, Washington, D.C., June 10, 1996.

39. Herb Becker, former director of the Office of Tribal Justice in the Justice Department, interview by author, Washington, D.C., June 13, 1996.

40. House Report 98-1026 to accompany HR 6206, Sept. 1984, p. 15.

41. House Report 100-868 to accompany HR 4102, Aug. 1988, p. 28.

42. House Report 101-496 to accompany HR 4148, May 1990, p. 5.

43. "Central Arizona Project: Costs and Benefits of Acquiring the Harquahala Water Entitlement," GAO/RCED-95-102, May 1995.

44. Nearly everyone I interviewed in regard to this matter wanted to remain anonymous.

45. Remarks by Eddie Brown, former Assistant Secretary for Indian Affairs, U.S. Department of the Interior, "Settlement of Indian Water Rights Claims," sponsored by Western States Water Council and the Native American Rights Fund, Albuquerque, Sept. 1, 1992.

46. Remarks by John Echohawk, Director of the Native American Rights Fund, "Reserved Water Rights and Water Related Issues," sponsored by the Mni-Sose Intertribal Water Rights Coalition, Albuquerque, Jan. 1994.

47. Senate Report 102-347 to accompany S. 1607, July 1992, 13.

48. *Congressional Record*, 101st Cong., 1st sess., May 4, 1989, S4856.

49. *Budget of the United States for Fiscal Year 1994—Appendix*. Indian Affairs, Federal Funds, p. 734.

50. House Committee on Appropriations, Subcommittee on Interior and Related Agencies, *BIA Justification for FY 1998* (BIA-282), 105th Cong, 2d. sess., 1997.

51. Remarks in "Indian Water—1997. Trends and Directions in Federal Water Policy" (report to the Western Water Policy Review Advisory Commission), 69 (final report on compact disc).

52. Ibid., p. 71.

53. Francis Schwindt, Chair, Western States Water Council, to the Honorable Trent Lott, U.S. Senate, Sept. 8, 1999.

54. Remarks made at the Sixth Symposium on the Settlement of Indian Reserved Water Rights Claims, Missoula, Mont., Sept. 8–10, 1999.

55. Reuben Briggs Davenport, "Report on the Battle of Rosebud Creek, June 17, 1876," in *Battles and Skirmishes of the Great Sioux War*, comp. and ed. Jerome A. Greene (Norman: University of Oklahoma Press, 1993), 27.

56. Ernie Robinson, Coordinator, Tongue River Dam Project, interview by author, Sept. 6, 1996.

57. *Congressional Record*, 102d Cong., 1st sess., March 21, 1991, S4032.

58. Final Environmental Impact Statement, Tongue River Basin Project, Bureau of Reclamation, U.S. Department of the Interior, March 1996 (summary).

59. The famous Crow chief Yellowtail vigorously opposed this dam, but the federal government named it after him anyway, against his wishes.

60. Resolution No. 92-14, "A Resolution of the Crow Tribal Council Pertaining to Settlement of the 107th Meridian and Water Rights Compact Disputes with the Northern Cheyenne Tribe," January 11, 1992.

61. Statement by Llevando Fisher, Tribal President, published in the *Tongue River Update* 1 (Winter 1995): 1.

62. Black Kettle was one the "peace chiefs" who tried to live in harmony with the encroaching whites. It was his unarmed village that was massacred by Colonel Chivington's troops at Sand Creek. Miraculously, Black Kettle survived that slaughter, only to be killed by Custer's men when they attacked the Cheyenne on the Washita in 1868.

63. Ms. Little Bird and Ms. Cano, interview by author, elder's center in Lame Deer, Mont., Sept. 6, 1996.

64. *In the Matter of the Adjudication of Existing and Reserved Rights to the use of Water, Both Surface and Underground, of the Northern Cheyenne Tribe of the Northern Cheyenne Indian Reservation Within the State of Montana in Basins 42A, 42B, 42C, & 43P.* Cause No. WC-93-1, Water Court for the State of Montana, Aug. 3, 1995, C. Bruce Loble, Chief Water Judge.

Chapter 4. Eternity on the Block

1. Charles F. Wilkinson, *American Indians, Time, and the Law: Native Societies in a Modern Constitutional Democracy* (New Haven, Conn.: Yale University Press, 1987), 13.

2. Article the Third, Northwest Ordinance, 1 Stat. 51.

3. Donald Jackson, ed., *Letters of the Lewis and Clark Expedition, with Related Documents, 1783–1854*, 2d ed. (Urbana: University of Illinois Press, 1978), 1:202.

4. "An Act to Regulate Trade and Intercourse with the Indian Tribes and to Preserve Peace on the Frontiers" 25 U.S. C. 117, June 30, 1834.

5. Treaty with the Cherokee (July 2, 1791) 7 Stat. 359.

6. John S. Gray, *Custer's Last Campaign: Mitch Boyer and the Little Bighorn Reconstructed* (Lincoln: University of Nebraska, 1991), 38.

7. Treaty between the United States of America and the Navajo Tribe of Indians (ratified July 25, 1868), Art. XIII.

8. Art. 1. Reprinted in "Shoshone-Bannock Tribes, Fort Hall, Idaho" (publication of the tribes published in conjunction with the Idaho Centennial Celebration, no date).

9. See *Nevada v. United States*, 463 U.S. 110 (1983); *Arizona v. California*, 460 U.S. 605 (1983).

10. David Getches, *Water Law in a Nutshell* (St. Paul: West Publishing, 1990), 334.

11. This is called *res judicata* in legal terms, meaning that existing legal precedent must be sustained.

12. John Weldon, "Non-Indian Water Users' Goals: More Is Better, All Is Best." In *Indian Water in the New West*, ed. Thomas McGuire, William Lord, and Mary Wallace (Tucson: University of Arizona Press, 1993), 81.

13. "Interlocutory Review of September 30, 1988 Order, Superior Court in Maricopa County," *In Re the General Adjudication of All Rights to Use Water in the Gila River System and Source*, Judge Noel A. Fidel, on behalf of the Arizona Supreme Court (1999).

14. Remarks by Dan Decker, co-counsel, Chippewa-Cree Tribe, Symposium on Reserved Water Rights and Water Related Issues, sponsored by the Mni-Sose Intertribal Water Rights Coalition, Albuquerque, Jan. 26–28, 1994.

15. *In Re the Rights to use Water in Big Horn River*, 753 P. 2d 76 (Wyo. 1988); *Wyoming v. U.S.*, 492 U.S. 406 (1989); *State v. Lewis*, 116 N.M. 194, 861 P. 2d 235 (N.M. Ct. App. 1993).

16. Remarks by Jeanne Whiting, Conference on Indian Water Rights, Stanford University School of Law, Sept. 9–10, 1994.

17. William Ury, Jeanne Brett, and Stephen Goldberg, *Getting Disputes Resolved* (San Francisco: Jossey-Bass, 1988), 12; Claudia Marseille, *Conflict Management: Negotiating Indian Water Rights* (Cambridge, Mass.: Lincoln Institute of Land Policy and the Western Legislative Conference, 1983), 6.

18. Cathy Wilson, BIA attorney, telephone interview by author, Phoenix, June 25, 1999; Debby Saint, Bureau of Reclamation, telephone interview by author, Phoenix, Sept. 30, 1999.

19. S. 1903 (Feb. 22, 1994).

20. *Congressional Record*, 103rd Cong., 2d sess., March 8, 1994, 2502.

21. Robert Snow, Office of the Solicitor, U.S. Department of the Interior, telephone interview by author, Riverside, Calif., Oct. 12, 1999; Rick Gundry, BIA, telephone interview by author, Riverside, Calif. Oct. 13, 1999. I interviewed others as well.

22. Bruce Babbitt, secretary of the interior, speech before the Colorado River Water Users Association (Dec. 18, 1997); www.usbr.gov/main/infozone/speeches/97-12-18.html

23. HR 4392 (Aug. 4, 1998).

24. PL 105-256 (Oct. 14, 1998), sec.11.

25. HR 100-868, p. 28; Acting Assistant Attorney General Thomas Boyd to Congressman Morris Udall, May 10, 1988.

26. Debby Saint, Bureau of Reclamation, telephone interview by author, Phoenix, Sept. 30, 1999; Lawrence Marquez, BIA, telephone interview by author, Phoenix area, Sept. 30, 1999; Joe Kanovich, Fort McDowell farm project employee, telephone interview by author, Oct. 15, 1999; Harold Payne, Fort McDowell farm manager, telephone interview by author, Oct. 15, 1999.

27. *Statement of Goals and Objectives for Implementation of Public Law 101-618 and Related Truckee-Carson Issues*, U.S. Department of the Interior internal memorandum, June 4, 1999, p. 1.

28. PL 105-256, sec. 10 (Oct. 14, 1998).

29. Animas–La Plata Project, "Summary of the Draft Supplemental Environmental Impact Statement," prepared by the Bureau of Reclamation, Upper Colorado Region, Jan. 2000, s-73.

30. Les Taylor, attorney, telephone interview by author, Albuquerque, Oct. 26, 1999.

31. Jason Whiteman, director, Northern Cheyenne Water Resources Department, telephone interview by author, Lame Deer, Mont., Oct. 4, 1999.

32. Honorable Susan Bolton, Superior Court of Arizona, Maricopa County. contested case no. w1-204 (Dec. 7, 1999), p. 5.

33. Office of the Secretary, U.S. Department of the Interior, press release, May 21, 1999, 1.

34. John Thorson, special master, "Partial Report of the Special Master on the Proposed San Carlos Apache Tribe Water Rights Settlement," *In Re the General Adjudication of All Water Rights to Use Water in the Gila River System and Source*, Sept. 10, 1999.

35. SR 102-133 to accompany S. 291, 16.

36. Thorson, partial report, 54.

37. Pamela Williams, delivering remarks by John Duffy, Counselor to the Interior Secretary and Chair of the Interior Working Group, Symposium on Negotiated Water Settlements, sponsored by the Native American Rights Fund and the Western States Water Council, Portland, Ore., Sept. 6–8, 1995.

38. Remarks by John Duffy, Counselor to the Interior Secretary and Chair of the interior working group, Symposium on Indian Water Settlements, sponsored by the Native American Rights Fund, Stanford School of Law, Sept. 9–19, 1994.

39. See Carla Bennett, "Quantification of Indian Water Rights: Foresight or Folly?" *Journal of Environmental Law* 8 (1989): 267–85; Michael Moore, "Native American Water Rights: Efficiency and Fairness," *Natural Resources Journal* 29 (1989): 779.

40. Dan Tarlock, "One River, Three Sovereigns: Indian and Interstate Water Rights," *Land and Water Law Review* 22 (1988): 271.

41. Peter Sly, *Reserved Water Rights Settlement Manual* (Washington, D.C.: Island Press, 1988), 85.

42. The laws were HB 2193 and HB 2276. See FY 1995 report, Phoenix Area Office, Division of Trust Resources Development (Nov. 1995), 14.

43. Remarks made by Judy Knight-Frank, chair, Ute Mountain Ute Tribe, Symposium on Negotiated Water Settlements, sponsored by the Native American Rights Fund and the Western States Water Council, Portland, Ore., Sept. 6–8, 1995.

44. Remarks made by Dan Decker, co-counsel, Chippewa-Cree tribe, Symposium on Reserved Water Rights and Water Related Issues, sponsored by the Mni-Sose Intertribal Water Rights Coalition, Albuquerque, Jan. 26–28, 1994.

45. John Folk-Williams, "Parties and Permanence: Alternative Dispute Resolution Principles," in *Indian Water in the New West*, ed. Thomas McGuire, William Lord, and Mary Wallace (Tucson: University of Arizona Press, 1993), 157.

46. A. Dan Tarlock, "The Illusion of Finality in General Water Rights Adjudications," *Idaho Law Review* 25 (1988–89): 271–89.

47. Carla Bennett, "Quantification of Indian Water Rights," 267–85.

48. The Northern Ute settlement was accompanied by a separate water compact that has yet to be ratified. It states: "The purpose of this Compact is to remove the causes of present and future controversy over the quantification, distribution, and use of all water claimed by or through the Ute Indian Tribe."

49. Remarks by Pamela Williams, Office of the Solicitor, U.S. Department of the Interior, Conference on Indian Water Rights, Stanford University School of Law. Sept. 9–10, 1994.

50. See Lawrence Bacow and Michael Wheeler, *Environmental Dispute Resolution* (New York: Plenum Press, 1984), 32; Roger Fisher and William Ury, *Getting to Yes: Negotiating without Giving*

In (New York: Penguin Books, 1981), 104; Lawrence Susskind and Jeffrey Cruikshank, *Breaking the Impasse: Consensual Approaches to Resolving Public Disputes* (New York: Basic Books, 1987), 81–85.

51. Presentation by Susan Williams, attorney, Mni-Sose Intertribal Water Rights Coalition Symposium on Reserved Water Rights and Water Related Issues, Albuquerque, Jan. 1994.

52. Remarks by John Leshy, solicitor general, U.S. Department of the Interior, Conference on Indian Water Rights, sponsored by the Stanford School of Law and the Native American Rights Fund, Stanford University, Sept. 10, 1994.

53. The American Indian/Eskimo/Aleut population grew from 1.4 million in 1980 to an estimated 4.3 million in 1994 (1 percent of the total population of the United States). http://www.census.gov/population/estimates/state/stts/st809ts.txt

54. Quoted in Charles S. Marsh, *People of the Shining Mountains: The Utes of Colorado* (Boulder, Colo.: Pruett Publishing, 1982), 79–80.

55. Portions of the Ute Mountain Ute Reservation are in New Mexico and southeastern Utah. Another reservation for Utes was created in Utah and is the focus of a case study in chapter 8.

56. I traveled to the Colorado Ute reservations in May 1997. In November 1999, Clement Frost was defeated in his re-election bid; he lost to John Baker by forty-one votes.

57. Bureau of Reclamation, U.S. Department of the Interior, "Executive Summary of the Final Supplement to the Final Environmental Statement, Animas–La Plata Project," April 1996, S-8.

58. See *United States v. Akin*, 504 F. 2D 115 (10th. Cir., 1974); *Colorado River Water Conservation District v. United States*, 424 U.S. 800 (1976); *Arizona v. San Carlos Apache Tribe*, 103 S. Ct. 3201 (1983).

59. *Congressional Record*, 100th Cong., 2d sess., Oct. 3, 1988, H 9345.

60. In 1990 the Fish and Wildlife Service identified only the Colorado Squawfish (pike-minnow), but were later forced to identify additional species due to a lawsuit filed by the Sierra Club Legal Defense Fund.

61. "Animas–La Plata: Water to Share," mimeographed handout produced by project supporters, no date.

62. Hydrosphere Resource Consultants, "Animas–La Plata: Alternatives Study" (report prepared for the Four Corners Action Coalition, Taxpayers for the Animas River, Sierra Club, and Sierra Club Legal Defense Fund, Oct. 8, 1995), 11.

63. Acting Assistant Inspector General for Audits to Assistant Secretary for Water and Science (memorandum), reprinted in U.S. Department of the Interior, Office of Inspector General, "Development Status of the Dolores and the Animas–La Plata Projects, Bureau of Reclamation" audit report no. 94-1-884, July 1994. This was not the first time that the Interior Department conceded that ALP was not economically feasible; in letters to relevant congressional committees in 1987, the department admitted that the project was not economically justifiable. See General Accounting Office, "Animas–La Plata Project: Status and Legislative Framework," GAO/RCED-96-1 (Nov. 1995), 11.

64. Southern Ute Tribal Council to the membership, memorandum, January 17, 1986.

65. "Ute Legacy Land and Water Fund (An Alternative to the Animas La Plata Project)," photocopy distributed by the Southern Utes Grassroots Organization, no date.

66. See "Animas–La Plata Alternative Study" (report prepared by Hydrosphere for Four Corners Action Coalition, Taxpayers for the Animas River, the Sierra Club, and the Sierra Club Legal Defense Fund, Oct. 1995).

67. *Congressional Record*, Oct. 3, 1988, H9346.

68. Quoted in the *Los Angeles Times*, Dec. 27, 1994, sec. A, p. 5.

69. *CQ Weekly Report*, Jan. 17, 1998, 122.

70. Quoted in the *National Journal*, March 28, 1998, 713.

71. PL 106-554.

72. ALP, draft supplemental EIS, S-7.

73. S. 1771 (Oct. 13, 1998)/H. R. 3478 (March 17, 1998). Congressmen McInnis re-introduced this legislation October 20, 1999, as H. R. 3112.

74. HR 745.

75. Remarks by Clement Frost, Chairman, Southern Ute Tribe, written transcript provided for the Indian Water Rights Settlement Conference, sponsored by the Native American Rights Fund and the Western States Water Council, Missoula, Mont., Sept. 8, 1999.

Chapter 5. The Cup of Living Water

1. John G. Neihardt, *Black Elk Speaks* (New York: William Morrow, 1932), 232–33.

2. Daniel McCool, *Command of the Waters: Iron Triangles, Federal Water Development, and Indian Water* (Tucson: University of Arizona Press, 1994), 58–59.

3. David Getches, "Indian Water Conflicts in Perspective," in *Indian Water in the New West*, ed. Thomas McGuire, William Lord, and Mary Wallace (Tucson: University of Arizona Press, 1993), 19.

4. Remarks by Dan Decker, Mni-Sose Intertribal Water Rights Coalition Symposium, Albuquerque, Jan. 1994.

5. Thomas McGuire, introduction to "Notes on Context and Finality," in *Indian Water in the New West*, ed. Thomas McGuire, William Lord, and Mary Wallace (Tucson: University of Arizona Press, 1993), 2.

6. Southern Ute Tribal Council to the Southern Ute Membership, memorandum, Jan. 17, 1986, p. 3.

7. John Folk-Williams, "Parties and Permanence: Alternative Dispute Resolution Principles," in *Indian Water in the New West*, ed. Thomas McGuire, William Lord, and Mary Wallace (Tucson: University of Arizona Press, 1993), 156.

8. Austin Nunez and Mary Wallace, "Solutions or Symbols? An Indian Perspective on Water Settlements," in *Indian Water in the New West*, ed. Thomas McGuire, William Lord, and Mary Wallace (Tucson: University of Arizona Press, 1993), 39.

9. Sam Burns and Michael Preston, "Indian Participation in Water Resource Development: A Policy Issue Inventory" (paper prepared for the 26th annual conference of the Western Social Science Association, San Diego, Calif., April 25, 1984).

10. Robert Young and Roger Mann, "Cheap Water in Indian Country: A Cost-Effective Rural Development Tool?" in *Indian Water in the New West*, ed. Thomas McGuire, William Lord, and Mary Wallace (Tucson: University of Arizona Press, 1993), 182.

11. Jon Hare, "Indian Water Rights: An Analysis of Current and Pending Indian Water Rights Settlements" (report prepared by the Chehalis Reservation and the Office of Trust Responsibility, BIA, 1996), 4.

12. Christopher Kenney, Native American Affairs Office, Bureau of Reclamation, U.S. Department of the Interior, interview by author, Washington, D.C., June 10, 1996.

13. Debby Saint, Bureau of Reclamation, telephone interview by author, Phoenix, Sept. 30, 1999, and Dec. 23. 1999; Harold Payne, former Ak-Chin employee, telephone interview by author, Phoenix, Oct. 15, 1999.

14. "Water Projects Office Purged after CAP Delivery Problem Unravels at Schuk Toak Farms," *The Runner* 8, no. 3 (March 9, 2000), 1.

15. Debby Saint, Bureau of Reclamation, telephone interview by author, Phoenix, Sept. 30, 1999; Joe Antonio, Schuk Toak project manager, telephone interview by author, Tucson, Arizona, Nov. 15, 1999; Dennis Rule, Tucson Water, telephone interview by author, Tucson, Ariz., Feb. 3, 2000.

16. Robert Snow, Office of the Solicitor, U.S. Department of the Interior, telephone interview by author, Oct. 12, 1999; Rick Gundry, BIA, telephone interview by author, Riverside, Calif., Oct. 12, 1999; and material from www.burec/lowercolorado river region/facilities/tolinks

17. Paul Evans, farm manager, Ute Mountain Farms, telephone interview by author, Towaoc, Colo., Feb. 9, 2000.

18. Scott Loveless, Office of the Solicitor, U.S. Department of the Interior, telephone interview by author, Salt Lake City, Oct. 13, 1999; Mike Conner, Indian Water Rights Office, U.S. Department of the Interior, telephone interview by author, Washington, D.C., Oct. 13, 1999; Mike Black, Tax-payers for the Animas River, telephone interview by author, Durango, Colo., Oct. 25, 1999; Patrick Schumacher, Bureau of Reclamation, telephone interview by author, Durango, Colo., Dec. 16, 1999; Paul Evans, General Manager of Farm Enterprises, Ute Mountain Ute Tribe, telephone interview by author, Towaoc, Colo., Dec. 16, 1999; Sage Douglas, Southern Ute Grass Roots, telephone interview by author, Ignacio, Colo., Dec. 16, 1999; Scott McElroy, water attorney for the Southern Ute Tribe, telephone interview by author, Durango, Colo., Dec. 21, 1999.

19. This amount may sound generous, but it is considerably less than the tribe's claim of 202,000 af plus damages in the Gila adjudication.

20. For example, the BIA placed measuring devices in the water delivery system upside down, so they just gave everyone about the same amount of water regardless of their need. This information came from a farm employee.

21. HR 2820 (July 1999).

22. Debby Saint, Bureau of Reclamation, telephone interview by author, Phoenix, Sept. 30, 1999; Lawrence Marquez, BIA, telephone interview by author, Phoenix, Sept. 30, 1999; Mike Roche, Division Manager of Water Resources, Salt River Pima-Maricopa Community, interview by author at reservation headquarters, Oct. 1, 1999; Ed Sampson, Economic Development Department, Salt River Pima-Maricopa Community, telephone interview by author, reservation headquarters, Nov. 1, 1999; Richard Wilks, attorney, telephone interview by author, Phoenix, Nov. 10, 1999; anonymous sources.

23. Candy Jackson, attorney for the Shoshone-Bannock Tribes, telephone interview by author, Fort Hall, Idaho, Dec. 23, 1999.

24. Debby Saint, Bureau of Reclamation, telephone interview by author, Phoenix, Sept. 30, 1999; Lawrence Marquez, BIA, telephone interview by author, Phoenix, Sept. 30, 1999; Joe Kano-vich, interview by author, Fort McDowell farm, Oct. 15, 1999; Harold Payne, Farm Manager, interview by author, Fort McDowell Farm, Oct. 15, 1999.

25. The settlement merely states that the 1988 OCAP shall remain in effect through 1997 unless the secretary decides that "changes are necessary to comply with his obligations, including those under the Endangered Species Act, as amended" (Sec. 209 [j] [2]). The OCAP adjustment that had the greatest impact on lake level (10 feet) went into effect in 1967.

26. Tom Strekel, BIA, telephone interview by author, Carson City, Nev., Oct. 26, 1999; Elisa-beth Rieke, Bureau of Reclamation, telephone interview by author, Carson City, Nev., Oct. 28, 1999; Cathy Wilson, BIA, telephone interview by author, Phoenix, Nov. 5, 1999; Bill Bettenburg, Office of Policy Analysis, U.S. Department of the Interior, telephone interview by author, Washington, D.C., Nov. 2, 1999; anonymous sources.

27. HR 102-955 (Sept. 29, 1992), 6–7.

28. Allowable depletions are 25,500 af from Navajo Reservoir and 6,500 af for San Juan Chama.

29. Les Taylor, attorney, telephone interview by author, Albuquerque, Aug. 30, 1994, Oct. 15, 1999.

30. Jason Whiteman, Director of Water Resources, Northern Cheyenne Tribe, telephone interview by author, Lame Deer, Mont., Oct. 4, 1999.

31. PL 103-434, 108 Stat. 4527, Sec. 102 (a) (9).

32. Western States Water Council, "Indian Water Rights in the West" (study prepared for the Western Governors' Association, May 1984).

33. Remarks by Richard Bad Moccasin, "Indian Water — 1997: Trends and Directions in Federal Water Policy," sponsored by Western Water Policy Review Advisory Commission, Oct. 1997, p. 57 (proceedings on compact disc).

34. Daniel McCool, *Command of the Waters*, 184.

35. Elizabeth Checchio and Bonnie Colby, *Indian Water Rights: Negotiating the Future* (Tucson, Ariz.: Water Resources Research Center, University of Arizona, June 1993), 45.

36. Robert Faber, staff director, Subcommittee on Water and Power, and Steve Lanich, minority staff, House Resources Committee, telephone conference, Sixth Symposium on the Settlement of Indian Reserved Water Rights Claims, sponsored by the Native American Rights Fund and the Western States Water Council, Missoula, Mont., Sept. 8–10, 1999.

37. Reid Peyton Chambers and John Echohawk, "Implementing the Winters Doctrine of Indian Reserved Water Rights: Producing Indian Water and Economic Development without Injuring Non-Indian Water Users?" *Gonzaga Law Review* 27 (1991–92): 449.

38. U.S. National Water Commission, Final Report (1977), 474–75.

39. Peter Sly, *Reserved Water Rights Settlement Manual* (Washington, D.C.: Island Press, 1988).

40. Fort McDowell Indian Community, 1994 Annual Report, inside front cover.

41. Sigrid Khera, "The Yavapai: Who They Are and from Where They Come," in *The Yavapai of Fort McDowell: An Outline of the History and Culture of a Community*, Fort McDowell Yavapai Tribe (Fountain Hills, Ariz.: Fort McDowell Yavapai Tribe, n.d.), 25.

42. George Schneider, "Historical Documents of the Fort McDowell Reservation," in *The Yavapai of Fort McDowell*, 29.

43. House Committee on Interior and Insular Affairs, Subcommittee on Irrigation and Reclamation, "Colorado River Basin Project," Part 2, 90th Cong, 2d sess., Jan. 30, 1968, p. 833.

44. This story is eloquently told in Wendy Nelson Espeland, *The Struggle for Water: Politics, Rationality, and Identity in the American Southwest* (Chicago: University of Chicago Press, 1998). See also "Fact Book: Public Forums" (Nov.–Dec. 1980), Central Arizona Water Control Study, Central Arizona Project Office, Phoenix, Ariz.; Jeanne Nienaber Clarke and Daniel McCool, *Staking Out the Terrain: Power and Performance Among Natural Resource Agencies*, 2d ed. (Albany: SUNY Press, 1996), 143.

45. In the 1910 Kent Decree the tribe was allocated 390 miner's inches per year, which is about 7,000 af.

46. I visited Fort McDowell in 1996. The farm is now complete.

47. Fort McDowell Indian Community, 1994 Annual Report, p. 6.

48. Farrer Consulting Services, "Environmental Assessment and Biological Assessment for the Fort McDowell Indian Community," prepared for the U.S. Bureau of Reclamation, May 1991, s-5.

Chapter 6. In the Shadow of the Eagle

1. This story is actually an amalgam of several individuals' experiences. The people who related these stories to me will remain anonymous.

2. Remarks by Rita Pearson, director, Arizona Department of Water Resources, Sixth Symposium on the Settlement of Indian Reserved Water Rights Claims, co-sponsored by the Native American Rights Fund and the Western States Water Council, Missoula, Mont., Sept. 8–10, 1999.

3. Herbert Becker, director, Office of Tribal Justice, U.S. Department of Justice, interview by author, Washington, D.C., June 13, 1996.

4. Bill Sinclair, Assistant Secretary's Office for Policy, Management, and Budget, U.S. Department of the Interior, interview by author, Washington, D.C., Aug. 27, 1990.

5. *Congressional Record—House*, 101st Cong., 2d sess. Oct. 22, 1990, H11498.

6. *Congressional Record*, 100th Cong., 2d sess., March 8, 1988, H726.

7. Select Committee on Indian Affairs and Committee on Energy and Natural Resources, "Colorado Ute Settlement" (report on S 1415), 100th Cong., 1st sess. Dec. 3, 1987, 246.

8. Christopher Kenney, "The Legacy and the Promise of the Settlement of Indian Reserved Right Water Claims," *Water Resources Update* 107 (Spring 1997): 22.

9. James Watt, Secretary of the Interior, press release, Dec. 8, 1982. At about the same time, Watt called Indian reservations examples of failed socialism.

10. See John Folk-Williams, "The Use of Negotiated Agreements to Resolve Water Disputes Involving Indian Rights," *Natural Resource Journal* 28 (1988): 73–74; Max Stephenson and Gerald Pops, "Conflict Resolution Methods and the Policy Process," *Public Administration Review* 49 (Sept.–Oct 1989): 467.

11. Phil Corke, former BIA employee, telephone interview by author, Washington, D.C., June 28, 1990.

12. U.S. Department of the Interior, internal memorandum, no date (ca. 1982).

13. Leona Kakar, quoted in *Arizona Republic*, Jan. 2, 1983, 1; quote from Leona Kakar.

14. Joe Ely, symposium wrap-up handout, "Settlement of Indian Reserved Water Rights Claims," sponsored by the Western States Water Council and the Native American Rights Fund, Bismarck, N.D., Sept. 7–9, 1993. Mr. Ely is the former chairman of the Pyramid Lake Tribe and negotiated their settlement.

15. "States and Tribes: Building New Traditions" (report prepared for the National Conference of State Legislatures' Task Force on State-Tribal Relations, Washington, D.C., Nov. 1995), 55.

16. Lois Witte, "Averting a Water Rights War," *State Government News*, Nov. 1990, 24–25.

17. *U.S. Water News*, May 1991, 15.

18. *High Country News*, Aug. 27, 1990, 11.

19. The authors of the southern Arizona settlement, aware of the possible precedential impact of this early settlement, made the point that the settlement was "not intended to be applied to any other Indian water rights claims in other areas." HR 97-855, accompanying HR 5118 (1982), 37.

20. In a statement fraught with irony and error, presidential candidate George Bush Sr. issued a letter to all "Indian leaders" with the following paragraph: "It is important to me that you know my basic beliefs. First of all, I believe strongly in the continuance of the legacy of President Abraham Lincoln, who fully recognized the importance of Indian sovereignty in a nation of sovereign states" (Oct. 30, 1988, paid for by Bush-Quayle '88). Lincoln never recognized Indian sovereignty, and he fought America's bloodiest war to prove we were a sovereign nation and not a "nation of sovereign states."

21. *Federal Register* 55, no. 48 (March 12, 1990): 9223–25.

22. Ibid.

23. Ibid.

24. Remarks at a conference on water rights sponsored by the Western Water Policy Project of the Ford Foundation and the University of Colorado School of Law. Boulder, Colo., Sept. 21, 1990.

25. Remarks at a conference on water rights sponsored by the Western Water Policy Project of the Ford Foundation and the University of Colorado School of Law. Boulder, Colo., Sept. 21, 1990.

26. Herbert Becker, director, Office of Tribal Justice, Department of Justice, interview by author, Washington, D.C., June 13, 1996.

27. William Clinton to heads of the executive departments and agencies, "Government to Government Relations with Native American Tribal Governments" (memorandum), April 29, 1994.

28. Daniel Beard, commissioner, Bureau of Reclamation, "Blueprint for Reform: The Commissioner's Plan for Reinventing Reclamation" (Nov. 1, 1993), 2.

29. Bureau of Reclamation, Indian Trust Asset Policy, "Indian Trust Chapter: Assessment of Impacts on Indian Trust Assets" (photocopy, n.d., circa 1994), 1.

30. Remarks by Joe Miller, director, Native American Affairs Office, Bureau of Reclamation, Mni-Sose Intertribal Water Rights Coalition Symposium on Reserved Water Rights and Water Related Issues, Albuquerque, Jan. 1994.

31. Mni-Sose Coalition and Great Plains Region of the Bureau of Reclamation, *Federal Resources Guidebook on Water Resources and Environmental Programs* (1998).

32. Deborah Saint, program manager, Native American Affairs Office, lower Colorado River region, Bureau of Reclamation, interview by author, Phoenix, March 26, 1996.

33. Remarks prepared by Commissioner Martinez, Federal Indian Program, BIA, Bureau of Reclamation, Albuquerque, March 13, 1997, U.S. Department of the Interior press release.

34. See Jeanne Nienaber Clarke and Daniel McCool, *Staking Out the Terrain: Power and Performance among Natural Resource Management Agencies*, 2d ed. (Albany, N.Y.: SUNY Press, 1996), chap. 2.

35. Sarah Bates, David Getches, Lawrence MacDonnel, and Charles Wilkinson, *Searching Out the Headwaters: Change and Rediscovery in Western Water Policy* (Washington, D.C.: Island Press, 1993), 121. See also Michael L. Lawson, *Dammed Indians: The Pick-Sloan Plan and the Missouri River Sioux, 1944–1980* (Norman: University of Oklahoma Press, 1982).

36. General Accounting Office, "Indian Issues: Cheyenne River Sioux Tribe's Additional Compensation Claim for the Oahe Dam," GAO/RCED-98-39 (Jan. 1998), appendix 3.

37. Charles F. Wilkinson, *Crossing the Next Meridian: Land, Water, and the Future of the West* (Washington, D.C.: Island Press, 1992), 179. See also Columbia River Intertribal Fish Commission, "The Spirit of the Salmon" (report).

38. Martin Reuss, Senior Historian, to Director, Civil Works, "Corps Contact with BIA in Late 1970s," memorandum, n.d., 2–3.

39. Task Force on Native American Intergovernmental Relations, preface to preliminary report to Institute for Water Resources, U.S. Army Corps of Engineers. A final report is yet to be released.

40. Task Force on Native American Intergovernmental Relations, executive summary of preliminary report to Institute for Water Resources, U.S. Army Corps of Engineers.

41. Army Corps of Engineers Tribal Policy Principles, Feb. 10, 1998; reprinted at: www.mnisose.org/update/acoeltr.html (accessed March 15, 1999).

42. *Mni Sose News*, Nov. 30, 1995, 4.

43. Bruce Babbitt, Office of the Secretary, U.S. Department of the Interior, order 3175, no. 8, 1993.

44. Task Force on Native American Intergovernmental Relations, preliminary report to the Institute for Water Resources, U.S. Army Corps of Engineers.

45. HR 255, 104th Cong., 1st sess., Oct. 30, 1995.

46. S. 446/H.R.1156, 107th Congress, 1st. sess. March 1, 2001.

47. *In Re Salt River Basin Adjudication*, case no. 39576, Fifth Judicial District of Idaho, Barry Wood, Presiding Judge, Nov. 11, 1999, 19.

48. *Congressional Record*, Oct. 14, 1988, s16248.

49. Fred Rippy, "A Ray of Light on the Gadsden Purchase," *Southwestern Historical Quarterly* 24 (Jan. 1921): 238.

50. For an excellent history of the Tohono O'odham, see Winston Erickson, *Sharing the Desert* (Tucson: University of Arizona Press, 1994).

51. Daniel McCool, "Federal Indian Policy and the Sacred Mountain of the Papago Indians," *Journal of Ethnic Studies* 9 (Fall 1981): 57–69.

52. Quoted in Bernard Fontana, *Of Earth and Little Rain: The Papago Indians* (Tucson: University of Arizona Press, 1989), 74.

53. In an interview, two tribal elders described the Santa Cruz riparian zone as so lush that mosquitoes were a problem. See *Arizona Daily Star*, April 8, 1990, 1B.

54. Fontana, *Of Earth and Little Rain*, 134.

55. Erickson, *Sharing the Desert*, 163–64.

56. Testimony of Austin G. Nunez, chairman, San Xavier District of the Tohono O'odham Nation, before the joint hearing of the House Interior and Insular Affairs Committee and the Senate Select Committee on Indian Affairs, Aug. 6, 1992.

57. Papago Tribe, *Tohono O'odham: History of the Desert People* (Salt Lake City: University of Utah Printing Services, 1985), 47–49.

58. John Leshy, Solicitor of the Department of the Interior, to the Honorable John McCain, United States Senator from Arizona, Dec. 22, 1994, p. 3. The San Xavier allottees estimate their losses and damages due to the dewatering of their farms to total $92 million; see testimony of Austin G. Nunez, chairman, San Xavier District of the Tohono O'odham Nation, before the joint hearing before the House Interior and Insular Affairs Committee and the Senate Select Committee on Indian Affairs, Aug. 6, 1992.

59. Testimony of Austin G. Nunez, 3.

60. Thomas Luebben, Counsel for the Allottees, to the Honorable John McCain, United States Senate, Jan. 31, 1995, p. 11.

61. *Arizona Daily Star*, Jan. 26, 1993, 1B.

62. John Leshy, Solicitor, U.S. Department of the Interior, to the Secretary of the Interior, "Entitlements to Water under the Southern Arizona Water Rights Settlement Act (SAWRSA)," memorandum, March 30, 1995, p. 1.

Chapter 7. Last Refuge

1. Quoted in Stephen E. Ambrose, *Undaunted Courage: Meriwether Lewis, Thomas Jefferson, and the Opening of the American West* (New York: Simon and Schuster, 1996), 216.

2. Quoted in William H. Goetzmann and William N. Goetzmann, *The West of the Imagination* (New York: W. W. Norton, 1986), 19.

3. See Michael Lawson, *Damned Indians* (Norman: University of Oklahoma Press, 1982).

4. Ibid., 217.

5. Warren Angus Ferris, *Life in the Rocky Mountains*, rev. ed., ed. Leroy R. Hafen (Denver, Colo.: Old West Publishing, 1983), 100.

6. Quoted in Francis Haines, *The Buffalo* (Norman: University of Oklahoma Press, 1995), 33.

7. Ibid., 306. Isenberg estimates that there were 30 million bison. See Andrew C. Isenberg, *The Destruction of the Bison: An Environmental History, 1750–1920* (Cambridge, Mass.: Cambridge University Press, 2000), ii.

8. Zenas Leonard, *Adventures of Zenas Leonard, Fur Trader and Trapper, 1831–1836*, ed. W. F. Wagner (Cleveland: Burrows Brothers Company, 1904), 69.

9. George Bird Grinnell, *The Passing of the Great West: Selected Papers of George Bird Grinnell*, ed. John F. Reiger (New York: Winchester Press, 1972), 136.

10. Richard White, *The Organic Machine: The Remaking of the Columbia River* (New York: Hill and Wang, 1995), 21.

11. Frederick Young, ed. *The Correspondence and Journals of Captain Nathaniel J. Wyeth, 1831–1836* (New York: Arno Press, 1973), 169.

12. Washington Irving, *The Adventures of Captain Bonneville, U.S.A., in the Rocky Mountains and the Far West*, ed. Edgeley W. Todd (Norman: University of Oklahoma Press, 1961), 221.

13. See the three-part series published in *The Idaho Statesman* (July 20, 21, 22, 1997), which advocates breaching the four dams on the lower Snake River.

14. General Accounting Office, "Water Resources: Corps of Engineers' Actions to Assist Salmon in the Columbia River Basin" (April 1998) GAO/RCED-98-100, p. 12.

15. Osbourne Russel, *Journal of a Trapper*, ed. Aubrey L. Haines (Lincoln: University of Nebraska Press, 1965), 13.

16. Grinnell, *The Passing of the Great West*, 46–47.

17. J. W. Powell. *The Exploration of the Colorado River and Its Canyons* (1895; reprint, New York: Dover Publications, 1961), 232–233.

18. Ibid., 227.

19. Russel, *Journal of a Trapper*, 4.

20. Captain J. H. Simpson, *Report of Explorations across the Great Basin of the Territory of Utah* (Reno, Nev.: University of Nevada Press, 1983), 47.

21. Proceedings of the National Irrigation Congress (1893), 106–7. At the time of that speech, Powell was the director of the U.S. Geological Survey; he retired the following year.

22. Grinnell, *The Passing of the Great West*, 149.

23. Alvin Alm, Deputy Administrator, Environmental Protection Agency, to assistant administrators, regional administrators, and general counsel, memorandum, Nov. 8, 1984.

24. See Annie Booth, "Ties that Bind: Native American Beliefs as a Foundation for Environmental Consciousness," *Environmental Ethics* 12 (1990): 27–38.

25. "Have Minorities Benefited? A Forum," *EPA Journal* (March–April 1992): 33. See also James Huffman, "An Exploratory Essay on Native Americans and Environmentalism," *University of Colorado Law Review* 63 (1992): 901–20.

26. U.S. Environmental Protection Agency, Office of External Affairs, "Indian Policy" (Nov. 8, 1984), signed by William Ruckelshaus.

27. "The Native American Policy of the U.S. Fish and Wildlife Service," signed by the director, Mollie Beattie, June 28, 1994.

28. Department of the Army, Corps of Engineers, "Native American Policy," April 15, 1994.

29. U.S. Department of the Interior, Bureau of Reclamation, "Reclamation's Strategic Plan," June 1992.

30. See Daniel McCool, *Command of the Waters: Iron Triangles, Federal Water Development, and Indian Water* (Tucson: University of Arizona Press, 1994), generally, chapters 2, 4, and 7.

31. Hearings before the House Subcommittee on Energy and Water Development, Committee on Appropriations, "Energy and Water Development for FY 1995; Testimony of Animas–La Plata Water Conservancy District," 103rd Cong., 2d sess., April 12, 1994.

32. Uintah Unit Replacement Project, Central Utah Water Conservancy District, draft of environmental impact statement (Feb. 1997), s-2.

33. Upalco Unit Replacement Project, Central Utah Water Conservancy District, draft environmental impact statement (Feb. 1997), s-2, s-4.

34. Utah Rivers Council, *Water Lines* 6 (Spring 1998).

35. Quoted in the *Salt Lake Tribune*, July 6, 1998, sec. B, p. 1.

36. Ronald Wopsock, Chairman, Ute Indian Tribe Business Committee, to Ronald Johnson, Program Director, Central Utah Project Completion Act, April 29, 1999.

37. Ute Business Committee, tribal council, interview by author, Fort Duchesne, Utah, Oct. 5, 1999. Roland McCook Sr. is now the chair of the business committee.

38. The economics of the proposed Ute Indian unit were indeed dubious, but no more so than the irrigation component of the CUP that was designed to take water off the reservation and pipe it across the state for use by Anglo farmers. In October 1988, this component of the project—the Spanish Fork–Nephi irrigation project—was abandoned due to high costs, extremely limited benefits, and political opposition. See U.S. Department of the Interior, Office of the Assistant Secretary-Water and Science, "Notice of Intent to Discontinue Planning on the Spanish Fork Canyon-Nephi Irrigation System as presented in the Draft Environmental Impact Statement DES 98-13," Billing Code 4310-RK, Oct. 7, 1998.

39. Uintah and Ouray Agency, resolution 88-19, Fort Duchesne, Utah, Feb. 10, 1988.

40. BIA, Division of Trust Resources Development, FY 1995 report, Phoenix, Nov. 1995, 49.

41. Tongue River Basin Project, Final Environmental Impact Statement, March 1996, 9–11.

42. Ibid., 9–47.

43. The same approach was used in the settlement for the Chippewa-Cree of the Rocky Boys Reservation.

44. I gratefully acknowledge the assistance of Laura Kirwan in the preparation of material in this section of the book.

45. *TVA v. Hill*, 437 U.S. 153 (1978), 174.

46. Northern Ute Business Committee, interview by author, Fort Duchesne, Utah, Oct. 5, 1999. Comment by committee member Smiley Arrowchis.

47. "Judge Rules Interior Must Divulge Documents on Colorado Irrigation Project," *BNA Environmental Law Update* (Dec. 10, 1992).

48. Lori Potter, attorney for the Sierra Club Legal Defense Fund, which has led the fight against ALP in the courts, believes that failure to include environmental group participation was a major flaw in the settlement process. According to Potter, if environmental groups in the San Juan basin had been included in the negotiations, it is possible that they could have "flagged" the issues that later stopped construction on ALP and hampered the implementation of the settlement.

49. John Lancaster, "Endangered Squawfish Halts Colorado Project: $589 Million Reservoir May Be Blocked," *BNA Environmental Law Update*, Dec. 21, 1992.

50. In addition to SCLDF, plaintiff groups were the Four Corners Action Coalition, the Colo-

rado Wildlife Federation, Tax Payers for the Animas River, and the Southern Utah Wilderness Alliance.

51. "Judge Rules Interior Must Divulge Documents on Colorado Irrigation Project," *BNA Environmental Law Update*, Dec. 10, 1992.

52. *Four Corners Coalition v. Underwood*, U.S. District Court of Colorado, Docket Number 92-Z-341 (1992).

53. *Four Corners Coalition v. Department of the Interior*, U.S. District Court of Colorado, Docket Number 92-Z-2106 (1992).

54. "EPA Lists Environmental Objections to Animas–La Plata Water Project," *BNA Environmental Law Update*, Dec. 21, 1992.

55. Judy Knight-Frank, chairperson, Ute Mountain Utes, "The Settlement of Indian Reserved Water Rights Claims," sponsored by the Native American Rights Fund and the Western States Water Council, Portland, Ore., Sept. 6–8, 1995.

56. Bureau of Reclamation, final environmental impact statement for the Animas–La Plata Project (1996), S-4.

57. *Southern Ute Drum*, Aug. 18, 1995, 2.

58. The draft was issued on January 14, 2000.

59. PL 106-554 (Dec. 21, 2000), 114 stat. 2763A-259.

60. In the Rio Grande basin, the endangered species is the silvery minnow. See *Federal Register* 64, no. 128 (July 6, 1999): 36274–290. An agreement to resolve some of these problems was signed in June 2001 by the U.S. Department of the Interior, the State of New Mexico, and the Corps of Engineers. See U.S. Department of the Interior, "Landmark State-Federal Water Agreement Protects Endangered Fish and Water Users in New Mexico," news release, June 29, 2001.

61. PL 102-441 (1992).

62. It was not a settlement in the sense that it did not quantify all rights to the San Juan Basin and result in a final decree of Navajo Nation water rights.

63. Stanley Pollack, Navajo Nation water attorney, telephone interview by author, Window Rock, Ariz., Nov. 2, 1994.

64. Leslie Fitzpatrick, U.S. Fish and Wildlife Service, telephone interview by author, Albuquerque, Nov. 16, 1994.

65. Stanley Pollack, interview by author, Window Rock, Ariz., March 21, 1996.

66. Stanley Pollack, telephone interview by author, Window Rock, Ariz., Aug. 22, 1994.

67. "Proposed Endangered Status for the Plant Puccinellia Parishii," *Federal Register* 59 (1994): 14,378–80.

68. Speaker from the floor, "The Settlement of Indian Reserved Water Rights Claims," sponsored by the Native American Rights Fund and the Western States Water Council. Portland, Ore., Sept. 6–8, 1995.

69. See Tribal Recovery Plan: Columbia River Inter-Tribal Fish Commission. "Wy-Kan-Ush-Mi, Wa-Kish-Wit: Spirit of the Salmon: The Columbia River Anadromous Fish Restoration Plan of the Nez Perce, Umatilla, Warm Springs, and Yakima Tribes" (1995). This does not mean there has been no conflict between the tribes and the ESA; see the "Legal and Institutional" segment of plan, pp. 17–22. See also Don Miller, "Of Dams and Salmon in the Columbia/Snake Basin: Did You Ever Have to Make Up Your Mind?" *Rivers* 6, no. 2 (April 1997): 69–79.

70. Website of the Columbia Inter-Tribal Fish Commission, http://www.critfc.org/text/trp.htm (Jan. 27, 1999).

71. See Michael Blumm, "Unconventional Waters: The Quiet Revolution in Federal and Tribal Minimum Streamflows," *Ecology Law Quarterly* 19, no. 3 (1992): 445–80; Ann Wechsler, "The Poli-

tics of Instream Flow," in *Waters of Zion: The Law, Policy and Politics of Water in Utah*, ed. Daniel McCool (Salt Lake City: University of Utah Press, 1995).

72. Instream flow played a minor role in the Fort McDowell settlement.

73. Washington Irving, *The Adventures of Captain Bonneville, U.S.A., in the Rocky Mountains and the Far West*, ed. Edgeley Todd (Norman: University of Oklahoma Press, 1961), 332–33.

74. HR 101-831, "Approving the Fort Hall Indian Water Rights Settlement, and for Other Purposes," 101st Cong., 2d sess., Oct. 10, 1990, p. 7.

75. Candy Jackson, attorney for the Shoshone-Bannock tribes, telephone interview by author, Ft. Hall, Idaho, Nov. 22, 1994.

76. The purpose of the other dam—the one not built—was to provide benefits to the Ute tribe and others in the Uinta basin.

77. *Salt Lake Tribune*, July 2, 1988, sec. B, p. 1.

78. "Instream Flow Agreement," Feb. 27, 1980, signed by the secretary of the interior, the governor of Utah, and the Central Utah Water Conservancy District.

79. PL 102-575, sec. 505 (b) and (d).

80. See David Getches," Management and Marketing of Indian Water: From Conflict to Pragmatism," *University of Colorado Law Review* 63, no. 4 (1988): 515–49; Gover, Stetson, and Williams, preparers for National Indian Policy Center, foreword to "Survey of Tribal Activity to Protect Water Quality and the Implementation of the Clean Water Act." Sept. 1994.

81. Secretary of the Interior Bruce Babbitt, interior order 3175, Nov. 9, 1993.

82. See William Weeks, *Beyond the Ark: Tools for an Ecosystem Approach to Conservation* (Washington, D.C.: Island Press, 1996); Hanna Cortner and Margaret Moote, *The Politics of Ecosystem Management* (Washington, D.C.: Island Press, 1999).

83. Remarks made to the Western Water Policy Review Advisory Commission, "Indian Water—1997: Trends and Directions in Federal Water Policy" (summary of conference proceedings) Oct. 1997, p. 33, on compact disc.

84. Gerald Peabody, interview by author, Towoac, Colo., May 15, 1997.

85. For a discussion of a new water ethic, see Sarah F. Bates, David Getches, Lawrence Macdonnell, and Charles Wilkinson, eds, *Searching Out the Headwaters: Change and Rediscovery in Western Water Policy* (Washington, D.C.: Island Press, 1993).

86. Joe Ely, "More than Romance," *Nevada Public Affairs Review* 1 (1992): 60–63.

87. See Martha Knack and Omer Stewart, *As Long as the River Shall Run: An Ethnohistory of the Pyramid Lake Indian Reservation* (Berkeley: University of California Press, 1984; reprint, Reno: University of Nevada Press, 1999); Kate Berry, "Of Blood and Water," *Journal of the Southwest* 39 (Spring 1997): 79–111.

88. *U.S. v. Orr Water Ditch Company et al.*, equity no. A3, final decree, Sept. 4, 1944.

89. See, generally, SR 101-555, "Providing for the Settlement of Water Rights Claims of the Fallon Paiute Shoshone Indian Tribes and For Other Purposes," 101st Cong., 2d sess., 1023, Oct. 25, 1990, pp. 10–12.

90. Found under general provisions, no page number, in *U.S. v. Orr Water Ditch Company et al.*

91. The initial case was *Pyramid Lake Paiute Tribe v. Morton*, 354 F. Supp. 778 (1979). The Supreme Court case was *Nevada v. U.S.*, 103 S. ct. 2906 (1983).

92. Arthur Darling, *The Public Papers of Francis G. Newlands* (Boston: Houghton Mifflin, 1932), 69.

93. Joe Ely, former tribal chairman of the Pyramid Lake Paiutes, interview by author, Phoenix, March 26, 1996.

94. PL 101-618, 104 Stat. 3294, sec. 202 (d).

95. Mervin Wright was defeated in his 1998 reelection bid by Norm Harry.

96. Paul Wagner, director, Fisheries Program, Pyramid Lake Paiute tribe, interview by author, Sutcliffe, Nev., June 9, 1997. See also U.S. Department of the Interior, "Babbitt, Tribe, Public Restore Monster Trout Near Reno," press release, April 16, 1998.

97. State engineer's ruling 4863, Nov. 24, 1998; Melvin Wright, telephone interview by author, Nixon, Nev., Dec. 9, 1999.

98. John Jackson, director, Water Resources Department, Pyramid Lake tribe, interview by author, Nixon, Nev., June 10, 1997.

99. PL 101-618, sec. 205 (a)(9).

Chapter 8. Another Kind of Green

1. The flow of the river since the signing of the compact has been "considerably less" than the period just prior to the compact, which was used to arrive at the 15 million af figure. See "Forty-Ninth Annual Report of the Upper Colorado River Commission," Salt Lake City, Utah, Sept. 30, 1997, 25–26.

2. This brief description was culled from Norris Hundley Jr., *Water and the West: The Colorado River Compact and the Politics of Water in the American West* (Berkeley: University of California Press, 1975).

3. Governor Bruce Babbitt, foreword to "The Future of the Colorado River," in *New Courses for the Colorado River*, ed. Gary Weatherford and F. Lee Brown (Albuquerque: University of New Mexico Press, 1986), xi.

4. Quoted in Hundley, *Water and the West*, 212.

5. Article 7, Colorado River Compact.

6. "The Hoover Dam Documents," House doc. 717, no. 11229, 81st. Cong., 1st sess. (1948), A42.

7. This meeting was held at the Doubletree Hotel on Sept. 1, 1992. Most of the participants were attendees at the symposium "Settlement of Indian Reserved Water Rights Claims," sponsored by the Native American Rights Fund and the Western States Water Council, Hyatt Regency Hotel, Albuquerque, Sept. 1–3.

8. The ten member tribes are Chemehuevi, Cocopah, Colorado River, Fort Mohave, Fort Yuma, Jicarilla Apache, Navajo, Southern Ute, Ute Mountain, and Northern Ute.

9. Bureau of Reclamation, U.S. Department of the Interior, *Westwide Study Report on Critical Water Problems Facing the Eleven Western States* (Washington, D.C.: Government Printing Office, April 1975), 154.

10. *Transaction Update* 12 (Spring 1998): 17.

11. Ibid., p. 11; *Transaction Update* 8 (Jan. 1995), 11.

12. *Transaction Update* 1 (Jan. 1995), 11; *Transaction Update* 8 (Jan. 1995), 20.

13. B. Delworth Gardner, "The Untried Market Approach to Water Allocation," in *New Courses for the Colorado River*, ed. Gary Weatherford and F. Lee Brown (Albuquerque: University of New Mexico Press, 1986), 157.

14. Frank Waters, *The Colorado* (New York: Holt, Rinehart and Winston, 1946), 336.

15. 373 U.S. 546.

16. The recent "4.4" agreement is an attempt to negotiate an end to California's overconsumption of Colorado River water. See H.R. 2764, "Colorado River Quantification Settlement Facilitation Act."

17. See Richard Wahl, *Markets for Federal Water: Subsidies, Property Rights, and the Bureau of Reclamation* (Washington, D.C.: Resources for the Future, 1989), 272–73.

18. For a discussion of this claim, see John Weldon Jr., "Non-Indian Water User's Goals: More Is Better, All Is Best," in *Indian Water in the New West*, ed. Thomas McGuire, William Lord, and Mary Wallace (Tucson: University of Arizona Press, 1993), 82–83.

19. UCRC, Resolution of the Upper Colorado River Commission Concerning a Proposal by the Galloway Group, Ltd., to Lease Water Apportioned to the Upper Basin States to the San Diego County Water Authority, Dec. 17, 1984, Salt Lake City.

20. Governor Michael Leavitt has broken this long tradition and has dared to suggest that water marketing might actually be lucrative for the state. See Brent Israelsen, "Political Leaders See Cash Cow in Milking the River," *Salt Lake Tribune*, Dec. 30, 1998, sec. B, p. 7.

21. Gardner, "The Untried Market Approach," 167.

22. House Committee on Interior and Insular Affairs, dissenting report, HR 2642, Sept. 16, 1988, 25–28.

23. *Congressional Record*, 100th Cong., 2d sess., Oct. 14, 1988, 16251.

24. Senate Select Committee on Indian Affairs and Senate Committee on Energy and Natural Resources, "Colorado Ute Settlement Bill: Report on S. 1415," 100th Cong., 1st sess., Dec. 3, 1987, 384.

25. The court held that any water in excess of 7.5 million af (8.5 million af with the Mexican treaty obligation) delivered to the lower basin would be split 50–50 between Arizona and California. *Arizona. v. California*, 376 U.S. 342 (1963).

26. For an excellent discussion of this issue, see Richard Wahl, *Markets for Federal Water: Subsidies, Property Rights, and the Bureau of Reclamation* (Washington, D.C.: Resources for the Future, 1989), 276–82.

27. Article XIX (a), Upper Colorado River Basin Compact, signed Oct. 11, 1948, Santa Fe, New Mexico.

28. See Reid Peyton Chambers and John Echohawk, "Implementing the Winters Doctrine of Indian Reserved Water Rights: Producing Indian Water and Economic Development without Injuring Non-Indian Water Users?" *Gonzaga Law Review* 27 (1991–92): 464; Lee Herold Storey, "Leasing Indian Water off the Reservation: A Use Consistent with the Reservation's Purpose," *California Law Review* 76 (Jan. 1988): 182–83.

29. Office of the Solicitor, U.S. Department of the Interior, to Water Policy Advisory Group, memorandum, Oct. 22, 1984; William Coldiron, Solicitor, U.S. Department of the Interior, to Evan Griffith, General Manager, Metropolitan Water District of Southern California, March 29, 1983.

30. See Tod. J. Smith, "Legal and Institutional Issues in Marketing Indian Water Rights: A Colorado River Perspective" (paper presented at the Fourth Symposium on the Settlement of Indian Reserved Water Rights Claims, Portland, Ore., Sept. 7, 1995), 8.

31. Senator Jon Kyl of Arizona has declared his opposition to any form of Indian marketing. According to one tribal spokesman, Kyl "has taken it upon himself to throw a stick in the spokes of all tribal water marketing."

32. Sue Cottingham, Program Manager, Montana Federal Reserved Water Rights Commission, presentation before the Sixth Symposium on the Settlement of Indian Reserved Water Rights Claims, co-sponsored by the Native American Rights Fund and the Western States Water Council, Missoula, Mont., Sept. 9, 1999. See S. 1903, a bill introduced, but not passed, that would have authorized the "delivery, use or transfer" of tribal water rights for a 50-year contract period "within or outside the Reservation." 103rd. Cong., 2d sess., Feb. 22, 1994.

33. Ricky Shepherd, Mark Tilden, and Dwayne Fowles, "Tribal Water Marketing" (report prepared in conjunction with the 1995 Symposium of the Settlement of Indian Water Rights Claims, Portland, Ore., Sept. 5–7, 1995), 25–26.

34. See Andrew Graham, "Marketing of Indian Water in the Colorado River Basin: A Framework for Analyzing Tribes' Choices" (paper submitted for Master of Public Policy, Harvard University, April 8, 1997), on file.

35. *Christian Science Monitor*, Oct. 26, 1999, 1.

36. Brief of Petitioner on Writ of Certiorari, p. 35, *Wyoming v. U.S.*, 109 S. Ct. 3265 (1989).

37. Remarks from the floor at a symposium on the "Settlement of Indian Reserved Water Rights Claims," sponsored by the Native American Rights Fund and the Western States Water Council, Portland, Ore., Sept. 6–8, 1995. See also the statement by Daniel Preston quoted above in the vignette for chapter 6.

38. Quoted in the *Salt Lake Tribune*, May 12, 1989, sec. B, p. 1.

39. Vine Deloria Jr., *The Metaphysics of Modern Existence* (New York: Harper and Row, 1979), 135.

40. Dennis Rule, planner for Tucson Water, interview by author, Tucson, Ariz., April 1, 1996.

41. Article 3 (G) of the Fort Peck–Montana Compact.

42. Final report of the Tribal Negotiating Team to Fort Peck Tribal Executive Board on Fort Peck–Montana Water Compact, April 19, 1985, 18–22.

43. Sec. 5 (c) of PL 100-585.

44. Sec. 5 (a) of PL 100-585.

45. Sec. 103 (E) of PL 101-618.

46. Article 3 (B), Water Rights Compact, State of Montana, Northern Cheyenne Tribe, SB 0472/03, June 11, 1991, 52d Legislature.

47. Calvin Wilson, tribal attorney, interview by author, Lame Deer, Mont., Sept. 5, 1996; Jason Whiteman, director of water resources for the Northern Cheyenne tribe, telephone interview by author, Oct. 4, 1999.

48. Sec. 503 (c) of PL 102-575.

49. Sec. 503 (a) of PL 102-575. The 1990 compact was authorized by the settlement act contingent upon its approval by the state of Utah and the Ute Tribe; neither has occurred, thus the compact is not yet valid.

50. Article 3 of the 1990 Ute Indian Water Compact.

51. Dee Hansen, interview by author, Salt Lake City, April 10, 1991.

52. Shepherd, Tilden, and Fowles, "Tribal Water Marketing."

53. Office of the Secretary, U.S. Department of the Interior, "California's Colorado River Water Talks Successful," press release, Aug. 4, 1999. These talks involve an agreement to transfer 200,000 af of agricultural water from the Imperial Valley to San Diego. In regard to water banking, see "Final Programmatic Environmental Assessment for Rulemaking for Offstream Storage of Colorado River Water and Development and Release of Intentionally Created Unused Apportionment in the Lower Division States," 43 CFR part 414, prepared by the U.S. Bureau of Reclamation (October 1999).

54. Order of Oct. 3, 1861. His order was in response to a letter from Caleb B. Smith, Secretary of the Interior, dated the same day.

55. This nickname was recently used in a headline in the Tribe's newspaper: "Tribute to the Blue Sky People," *Ute Bulletin*, Oct. 14, 1998, 1. See also Charles Marsh, *People of the Shining Mountains: The Utes of Colorado* (Boulder, Colo.: Pruett, 1982), 3.

56. Originally known as the Uncompahgre and Uintah Reservations, today this reservation is

known as the Uintah and Ouray Reservation. The Northern Ute tribe consists of three Ute bands: the Uintahs, the Uncompahgres, and the White River Utes.

57. Cyrus Cates Babb, "The Water Supply of the Uinta Indian Reservation, Utah," *Surveys and Examination of the Uinta Indian Reservation*, 57th Cong., 1st sess., HR 671, June 19, 1902.

58. Those first tentative efforts by Heber Valley farmers provided the seed that eventually grew into the giant CUP.

59. Craig Woods Fuller, "Land Rush in Zion: Opening of the Uncompahgre and Uintah Indian Reservations" (Ph.D. diss., Brigham Young University, Aug. 1990), 112–14. The farmers in the Heber Valley discontinued using the water because the new CUP Daniel's Canyon Replacement Project provided another source of water. This was not the last time the federal government took basin water without tribal approval. The Provo River project takes water from the Duchesne River through a tunnel to the Provo River and hence to the city of Salt Lake. This project has been diverting water from the reservation since the mid-1950s. This diversion equals about 35,000 af per year. I could find no record that the tribe gave its approval for this diversion.

60. Floyd A. O'Neil, "The Reluctant Suzerainty: The Uintah and Ouray Reservation," *Utah Historical Quarterly* 39 (Spring 1971): 140. See also Floyd A. O'Neil and Kathryn L. MacKay, "A History of the Uintah-Ouray Ute Lands," occasional paper, American West Center, University of Utah, n.d.

61. U.S. Department of the Interior, Office of Indian Affairs. file no. 36349, 6-1-1939, Uintah and Ouray, on file at the American West Center, University of Utah. A recent agreement, if ratified by Congress, would return 84,000 acres to the Utes. See *Deseret News*, Jan. 22, 2000, sec. B, p. 3.

62. Quoted in Floyd O'Neil, "An Anguished Odyssey: The Flight of the Utes, 1906–1908," *Utah Historical Quarterly* 36 (Fall 1968): 318 (originally appeared in *Vernal Express*, June 9, 1906).

63. According to the BIA, 60 percent of Utah's surface water originates in the Uinta basin. "The Uintah and Ouray Indian Reservation," prepared for the Ute Indian Tribe by the Planning Support Group of the BIA, report 214, 1974, p. 37.

64. Bureau of Reclamation, "Duchesne River Land and Water Resource Review" April 1962, 5, on file in the Bureau of Reclamation, Bennett Federal Office Building, Salt Lake City.

65. Ute Deferral Agreement, contract 14-06-W-194, Sept. 2, 1965.

66. *Deseret News*, May 7, 1965, sec. B, p. 8. For an astounding account of John Boyden's habits, see Charles Wilkinson, *Fire on the Plateau* (Washington, D.C.: Island Press, 1999), ch. 8.

67. A. C. Tonner, Acting Commissioner, to the Secretary of the Interior, June 12, 1902, accompanying the Babb report to the 57th Cong., 1st sess., HR 671, June 19, 1902.

68. The Ute Indian Unit was never even authorized by Congress. The Bureau of Reclamation claimed it did not have sufficient funding for the Ute unit. It did, however, have enough money to build a bowling alley for the Anglo enclave of Duchesne, Utah. For more details, see Daniel McCool, ed., *Waters of Zion: The Politics of Water in Utah* (Salt Lake City: University of Utah Press, 1995), chaps. 1, 2, and 9.

69. *Salt Lake Tribune*, April 20, 1989, sec. A, p. 14, and May 4, 1989, sec. B, p. 1. The official name of the tribal council is the Ute Business Committee.

70. Tribal Resolution 89-176, Sept. 20, 1989.

71. House Committee on Interior and Insular Affairs, "Ute Indian Water Rights Settlement," 100th Cong., 2d sess., HR 5307, serial no. 100-77, Oct. 4, 1988.

72. Interview by author, tribal headquarters Fort Duchesne, Utah, June 21, 1990; also see Daniel McCool, "The Northern Utes Long Water Ordeal," *High Country News*, July 15, 1991, 8–9.

73. This is a sum of the funds authorized in sections 504, 505, and 506, and does not include the payments for the water diverted into the Bonneville unit.

74. Sec. 501 (b) (3) of PL 102-575.

75. Sec. 503 (a) of PL 102-575.

76. This meeting was held at Whiterocks, Utah, on Feb. 3, 1993.

77. *Hagen v. Utah*, 92-6281 Sup. Ct. (Feb. 23, 1994). See Daniel McCool, "Utah and Ute Tribe Are at War," *High Country News*, June 27, 1994, 12.

78. Ute Business Committee, interview by author, Fort Duchesne, Utah, Oct. 5, 1999.

79. The federal government has fallen behind schedule in its payments to the tribe due to Republican efforts to cut the budget for Indian programs, but eventually the entire settlement fund will be paid—with a considerable amount of interest accruing to the tribe due to the late payments.

80. Sec. 502 of PL 102-575.

81. The failure of this program is described clearly and succinctly in David Rich Lewis, *Neither Wolf nor Dog: American Indians, Environment, and Agrarian Change* (New York: Oxford University Press, 1994), chaps. 2 and 3.

82. See Fred Conetah, *A History of the Northern Ute People*, ed. Kathryn MacKay and Floyd O'Neil (Uintah-Ouray Ute tribe, 1982). See also Marsh, *People of the Shining Mountains*.

83. Quoted in Marshall Sprague, *Massacre: The Tragedy at White River* (Boston: Little Brown, 1957), 92; originally quoted in an 1877 *Denver Tribune* article.

Chapter 9. "Come On, Big Village. Be Quick"

1. *San Francisco Evening Bulletin*, Oct. 8, 1862, as reported in *The Almo Massacre*, Idaho Historical Society Reference Series, no. 232 (Feb. 1971): 10.

2. This report appeared in a Carson City, Nevada, newspaper. See *The Almo Massacre*, 9.

3. *The Alamo Massacre*, 10.

4. This quotation is from an account of the Alamo massacre in Charles Walgamott, *Reminiscences of Early Days: A Series of Historical Sketches and Happenings in the Early Days of the Snake River Valley* (Twin Falls, Idaho: C. S. Walgamott); also quoted in Brigham Madsen, *The Shoshoni Frontier and the Bear River Massacre* (Salt Lake: University of Utah Press, 1985), 101.

5. Merrill D. Beal, *A History of Southeastern Idaho* (Caldwell, Idaho: Caxton Printers, 1942), 237–38.

6. The "Almo Massacre" tale was cleanly dispatched by Brigham Madsen's cogent and perspicacious historical research. See "The 'Almo Massacre' Revisited," *Idaho Yesterdays* (Fall 1993): 54–64. See also Madsen, *The Shoshoni Frontier*, 101–2.

7. William Dodge, "The Emergence of Intercommunity Partnerships in the 1980s," *National Civic Review* 78 (Jan.–Feb. 1989): 5–14.

8. Robert Agranoff, *Intergovermental Management: Human Services Problem-Solving in Six Metropolitan Areas* (Albany, N.Y.: SUNY Press, 1985).

9. Beryl Radin et al., *New Governance for Rural America* (Lawrence: University Press of Kansas, 1996).

10. Barbara Gray and Don Wood, "Collaborative Alliances: Moving from Practice to Theory," *Journal of Applied Behavioral Science* 27 (March 1991): 3–22.

11. See Vine Deloria Jr. and Raymond J. DeMallie, *Documents of American Indian Diplomacy: Treaties, Agreements, and Conventions, 1775–1979* (Austin: University of Texas Press, 1999).

12. See "Southwest Native Tourism Conference Provided a Forum," *News from Indian Country*, June 1994, 11.

13. Doug Goodman, F. Ted Hebert, and Daniel McCool, "Two Cultures, Two Communities,

One County: Devolution and Retrenchment" (paper delivered at the annual meeting of the American Political Science Association, Sept. 3–6, 1998).

14. See Stephen Sachs and LaDonna Harris, "Strategy and Choice: Opting for Cooperation or Competition—Investigation of Tribal and Sub-National Government Relations" (paper presented at the annual meeting of the American Political Science Association, Sept. 3–6, 1998).

15. Title 22, Navajo Tribal Code, chap. 7.

16. *Mni Sose News*, June 1997, Rapid City, S.D.

17. Personal communications with E. Richard Hart, director of the Institute of the North American West, Oct. 14, 1997, and Jan. 12, 2000. Mr. Hart was an expert witness in ethnohistory for the Department of Justice in the water case. The case was dismissed with prejudice.

18. "Corruption Case," *USA Today*, March 4, 1997; "Ex-U.S. Attorney Pleads Guilty," *Albuquerque Journal*, March 8, 1997; "Ex-Indian Affairs Head to Plea," *Washington Post*, internet page, www.washingtonpost.com/wp-srv/front.htm (March 3, 1997).

19. Mark Rogacki, Executive Director, Wisconsin Counties Association, to state association executives and presidents, et al., memorandum, Nov. 17, 1989. The subject was the "National Coalition on Federal Indian Treaties: Informational/Organizational Meeting," Jan. 18–20, 1990, Salt Lake City, Utah. See also Daniel McCool, "Indians Defend Tribes from Attack, *High Country News*, May 21, 1990, 14.

20. See HR 1977, Interior Appropriations Bill for FY 1996. See also "Gorton, Lummis in War of Words," *Bellingham Herald*, Sept. 1, 1995, sec. B, p. 1.

21. See Lesley Linthicum, "Navajo Farm Project Struggles Financially Despite Millions of Dollars in Government Funding," *Albuquerque Journal*, Oct. 3, 1999, sec. B, p. 1.

22. See Daniel McCool, "A River between Two Cultures," *Catalyst* 16 (Aug. 1997): 14–15.

23. See Thomas Michael Power, *Western Landscapes and Lost Economies* (Washington, D.C.: Island Press, 1996).

24. See Michael Blumm, "Unconventional Waters: The Quiet Revolution in Federal and Tribal Minimum Streamflows," *Ecology Law Quarterly* 19 (1992): 445–81.

25. This is only 7 percent of the nation's total hay production. These statistics are from 1986, which was apparently the last time the bureau did a comprehensive analysis. Data were provided by the Bureau of Reclamation.

26. See generally Richard Wahl, *Markets for Federal Water: Subsidies, Property Rights, and the Bureau of Reclamation* (Washington, D.C.: Resources for the Future and the Johns Hopkins University Press, 1989); Jeanne Nienaber Clarke and Daniel McCool, *Staking Out the Terrain: Power and Performance among Natural Resource Agencies*, 2d ed. (Albany, N.Y.: SUNY Press, 1996), 149–51.

27. "Investing in the Future, 1998," Bureau of Reclamation annual report 1998, 2.

28. Perhaps the most sensible legislation proposed in recent years was the "Public Resources Deficit Reduction Act of 1995," which provided that "no Federally owned water, and no hydroelectric energy generated at a Federal facility may be sold, leased, or otherwise disposed of by any department, agency, or instrumentality of the United States for an amount less than fair market value" (HR 721, 104th Cong., 1st. sess., Jan. 27, 1995). This bill was immediately squelched by western legislators.

29. *Bismark Tribune*, June 17, 1874, as quoted in Evan S. Connell, *Son of the Morning Star* (New York: Harper Perennial, 1984), 241.

30. Bills to lift the freeze were introduced in Congress in 1998, 1999, and 2000, but none has become law.

31. My interviews with the Canyons, Mr. Tso, and Mr. Akee took place on May 30 and 31, 1997.

32. Bruce Babbitt, Secretary of the Interior, to Ferrell Secakutu, Chairman of the Hopi tribe; Peterson Zah, Chairman of the Navajo Nation; and Peter Lilly, Executive Vice-President of Peabody Holding Company, Aug. 22, 1994.

33. Stanley Pollack, water attorney for the Navajo nation, telephone interview by author, Window Rock, Ariz., Sept. 30, 1999.

34. Remarks by Rita Pearson, director, Arizona Department of Water Resources Sixth Symposium on the Settlement of Indian Reserved Water Rights Claims, co-sponsored by the Native American Rights Fund and the Western States Water Council, Missoula, Mont., Sept. 9, 1999.

35. An estimated 18,000 Navajo households still haul water. See *The Spillway*, the newsletter of the Upper Colorado River Region, Bureau of Reclamation, Nov.–Dec. 1999, 1.

Index

McInnis, Congressman, 98

Michaud Agreement, 41

Miles City water decree, 67

Milk River: water rights on, 10–14

Miller, George, 93, 121

Missouri River, 103, 107, 122, 135, 162, 168

Mitchell, Venus, 42

Mni-Sose Intertribal Water Rights Coalition, 107, 124, 185

Mohawk irrigation district, 60

Mondell, Congressman, 25

Montana, 10, 60; Fort Peck Compact and, 76–77, 162; negotation in, 47–48; water rights in, 67–68

Montana Department of Fish and Wildlife, 173

Montana Reserved Water Rights Compact Commission, 47–48; compact of, 67–68, 71–72

Montana Riparian and Wetland Association, 144

Montezuma, Carlos (Wassaja), 110–11

Muerto, Canyon del, 44

Nambe Pueblo, 46, 198n. 4

National Congress of American Indians, 30, 50

National Environmental Policy Act (NEPA), 95, 146

National Irrigation Congress, 26–27

National Tribal Chairman's Association, 30

National Water Commission, 109

Native American Rights Fund, 30, 50, 62, 176

Navajo Indian Irrigation Project (NIIP), 29, 58, 125, 147, 202n. 15

Navajo Mountain, 3, 4–5, 6

Navajo Nation/Reservation, 4–6, 44, 74, 108, 125, 185, 187, 189, 198n. 4; Endangered Species Act and, 147–48; and Little Colorado River, 192–96; San Juan Basin and, 28–29, 145

Navajo Reservoir, 106

negotiation, 184–85, 204n. 37; costs of, 50–55, 56; for deliverable water, 100–101; finality and, 80–82; length of, 48–49; Northern Cheyenne water rights, 67–68; participation in, 116–18; procedures for, 33–35, 118–20; tribal governments and, 186–87; water settlements, 46–47, 49–50, 75–76, 77–78

NEPA. *See* National Environmental Policy Act

Nevada, 153, 156

Newlands, Francis, 155–56

Newlands Project, 105, 155–56

New Mexico, 146

New Mexico v. Aamodt, 46

Nielson, Howard, 180

NIIP. *See* Navajo Indian Irrigation Project

Ninth Circuit Court of Appeals, 13, 15

no-harm rule, 108–9

Northern Arapaho, 16

Northern Cheyenne, 66, 139, 173; water rights of, 67–68, 69, 78, 84

Northern Cheyenne Reservation, 65–66, 67, 69

Northern Cheyenne Reserved Water Rights Settlement Act, 7, 47, 48, 49, 57, 60, 62, 78, 125, 144; acceptance of, 69–72

Northern Utes, 28, 178; and Central Utah Project, 60, 142–43, 180, 219n. 38, 226n. 79; instream flow and, 149, 150; intertribal conflict, 124, 187; water marketing by, 173–74, 181–82; water rights for, 84, 85, 106; and water settlement, 49, 51, 57, 210n. 48

Northwestern Shoshone, 39

Northwest Indian Fisheries Commission, 152

Northwest Ordinance, 73

Nunez, Austin, 132

O'Connor, Sandra Day, 18

Office of Management and Budget (OMB), 54, 55, 61, 100–101, 118, 146

Orme Dam, 111

Orr Ditch Decree, 155

Osage, 73

Ouray Indian Reservation, 28, 47, 58, 142, 178, 182

overgrazing, 5, 6

Owens Valley (Calif.), 170

Page (Ariz.), 5, 6

Paiutes, 25. *See also* Fallon Paiutes; Pyramid Lake Paiutes

Palisades Reservoir, 143

Papago. *See* Tohono O'odham Nation, 127

Papago Reservation, 128

Parker Dam, 164

payoffs to non-Indians, 59–61

About the Author

Daniel McCool is professor of political science, director of the American West Center, and director of the Environmental Studies Program at the University of Utah. He received his PhD from the University of Arizona in 1983.

Professor McCool's research focuses on Indian water rights and voting rights, water resource development, and public lands policy. He is the author of *Native Waters: Contemporary Indian Water Settlements and the Second Treaty Era* (2002) and *Command of the Waters: Iron Triangles, Federal Water Development, and Indian Water* (1994). He co-authored *Staking Out the Terrain: Power and Performance Among Natural Resource Agencies* (1996, 2d ed.), *Public Policy Theories, Models, and Concepts* (1994), and *Native Vote: American Indians, the Voting Rights Act, and Indian Voting* (forthcoming 2006). He edited two books with his students, *Waters of Zion: The Politics of Water in Utah* (1995) and *Contested Landscape: The Politics of Wilderness in Utah and the West* (1999). He has served as a consultant for the National Oceanic and Atmospheric Administration, the U.S. Department of Justice, the ACLU's Voting Rights Project, and the Southwest Center for Environmental Research and Policy. He is currently writing a book about the politics of river restoration.